NOT PLAYING
FOR CELTIC

NOT PLAYING FOR
CELTIC

Another Paradise Lost

David Bennie

MAINSTREAM
PUBLISHING
EDINBURGH AND LONDON

First published in Great Britain in 1995 by
MAINSTREAM PUBLISHING COMPANY (EDINBURGH) LTD
7 Albany Street
Edinburgh EH1 3UG

ISBN 1 85158 757 8

A catalogue record for this book is available from the British Library

Typeset in Stempel Garamond by Bibliocraft, Dundee
Printed and bound in Great Britain by Butler & Tanner Ltd, Frome

In memory of my late father, William G. Bennie,
and for my mother, Ellen

CONTENTS

ACKNOWLEDGEMENTS

The author would like to thank and acknowledge the generous assistance given by Eileen Howson and Lynn Murray, for transferring my chaotic copy from floppy discs on to state-of-the-art software, rearranging the page layout, and getting the manuscript pages laser printed.

INTRODUCTION

Real Madrid 7
Eintracht Frankfurt 3

(European Cup final, 18 May 1960)

'Imparadised in one another's arms . . . Hail wedded love, mysterious law, true source / Of human offspring, sole propriety / In Paradise of all things common else.'

(*Paradise Lost*, IV)

'Into a Limbo large and broad, since called / The Paradise of fools, to few unknown.'

(*Ibid*, IV)

'The childhood shows the man, / As morning shows the day.'

(*Ibid*, IV)

'Thence up he flew, and on the Tree of Life, / The middle tree and highest there that grew, / Sat like a cormorant.'

(*Ibid*, IV)

'How soon hath Time, the subtle thief of youth, / Stoln on his wing my three and [thirtieth] year!'

(Sonnet: *On being arrived at the age of twenty-three*)

'For who would lose, / Though full of pain, this intellectual being, / Those thoughts that wander through eternity, / To perish rather, swallowed up and lost / In the wide womb of uncreated night, / Devoid of sense and motion?'

(*Paradise Lost*, II)

'Tears such as angels weep, burst forth.'

(*Ibid*, I)

'Nor love thy life, nor hate; but what thou livs't, / Live well, how long or short permit to heav'n.'

(*Ibid*, XI)

'The first and wisest of them all professed / To know this only, that he knew nothing.'

(*Paradise Regained*, IV)

A trawl through football statistics and match reports can occasionally throw up jarring juxtapositions with personal historical landmarks (as with old records in the *Guinness Book of British Hit Singles* aiding recall of memorable moments in life and adding to their nostalgic poignancy), but I'm afraid I cannot suspend the weight of reader disbelief by claiming that I was conceived at the very moment 34-year-old Alfredo di Stefano scored Real's seventh and his own hat-trick-conjuring third goal at Hampden Park, Glasgow. I cannot, either, pretend that I am able to relate my life from the moment of conception, even with 20–20 hindsight and imaginative ultra-sounding, à la Tristram Shandy coming into being in the womb as Mrs Shandy asks her ejaculating husband, 'Pray, my dear . . . have you not forgot to wind up the clock' (or in Mrs Bennie's fictional case, asking my father, 'Oh, Bill . . . have you not missed di Stefano's lethal finish after three unbelievable one–twos on the telly?').

However, I can confidently claim that I was conceived a few hours after this classic football match ended, my father having spectated as part of the 127,621[1] crowd and having sailed the next day from Liverpool as third engineering officer on board a Merchant Navy freighter bound for various ports in the Southern Hemisphere. And like Laurence Sterne's hero-narrator in *Tristram Shandy* I firmly believe that my 'life and opinions' were to a large degree determined by the unusual circumstance and irregular timing of my foetal creation, since the sperm which won that night's particular egg-and-womb race was a tadpole jackboy pumped up on testosterone, adrenaline, endorphin-simulated morphine, nicotine tar, a pint of heavy and a protoplasmic poison chaser, caffeine, and fish-supper carbohydrates, proteins and vitamins. The successful sperm must have hit the ovulating egg at the spermicidal speed of light, necessitating a sudden stop like a steroid-fuelled Ben Johnson running straight into the crash-pad at the end of an indoor 60-metre sprint.

Sterne's 'homonculus' is obviously the fertilising sperm, and I can relate to his description of its journey into the unknown:

> . . . my little gentleman had got to his journey's end miserably spent;
> – his muscular strength and virility worn down to a thread; – his
> own animal spirits ruffled beyond description, – and that in this sad

disorder'd state of nerves, he had laid down a prey to sudden starts, or a series of melancholy dreams and fancies for nine long, long months together. – I tremble to think what a foundation had been laid for a thousand weaknesses both of body and mind, which no skill of the physician or philosopher could ever afterwards have set thoroughly to rights.

According to my father – 34 years old at the time like the similarly balding di Stefano – he was still 'buzzing' from the excitement of the game when he arrived home, inspired by the revelation that to be in one's mid-30s was not necessarily to be over-the-hill and on the verge of middle age. Otherwise he would never have diverted from the traditional once-a-week exercise of his conjugal missionary-position marital duties. Allegedly, he made passionate 'Continental-style' love to my mother standing up in the landing cludgie, the Dennistoun room-and-kitchen not being equipped with an inside toilet of its own. I am more than slightly sceptical about this amorous boast, not because the tenement in Walter Street was posh with a tiled wally-dug close (it wasn't), but because genteel working-class morality would have precluded doing 'it' within sight or hearing of the upper-working-class neighbours waiting impatiently to relieve themselves outside the locked WC (our communal close was most certainly not the kind of run-down passageway where 'hairies' – hatless slum girls – lifted up their skirts and opened their legs for male razor-gang members they'd just picked up at the Dennistoun Palais or Barrowland Ballroom). More credible is the still quite shocking scenario of their coupling in the mad choreography of sexual intercourse on *top* of the pink candlewick bedspread, rather than doing it chastely underneath with the lights out. I'm even prepared to accept that they dispensed with their Paisley-patterned pyjamas and high-necked goonie, respectively, and that the dentures were not removed and placed in tumblers of fizzing pink Steradent prior to the procreative act (an explosion of anti-Calvinistic, spontaneous lust that they would have been shocked to read about in the vote-Tory-and-cure-your-varicose-veins *Sunday Post*, which for all I know still refers to sex as 'carnal knowledge' and 'coital commerce').

If my parents had waited until the national anthem was played at the close-down of BBC1, before making love, a different sperm would almost undoubtedly have won the Buchan Firkin trophy for successfully reaching its gynaecological objective first (or to paraphrase this real trophy in the Spooneristic *Sportsound* style of the day, the 'Fuchan Birthin' cup). Even if my mother and father had decided to clean their teeth before going to bed, chances are a different sperm would still have crossed the finishing line first, since each male orgasm starts a stampede of competitors that makes the London marathon seem positively low on head-count numbers. I would therefore have been a fundamentally – or at least significantly – different person (possibly not even male, without my current extra Y chromosome).

Differences in genetic structure and pregnatorial environment may well have prevented 'me' from being born three weeks early on 27 January 1961[2]. And not being born prematurely, in and of itself, could have resulted in incalculable differences in the nature-nurture equation which determines individual personality, intellect, health, etcetera.

A butterfly flaps its wings in China and through a complicated schema of cause-and-effect a 6.8 earthquake on the Richter scale hits southern California. Di Stefano scores a hat-trick in a European Cup final and the first offspring of William and Ellen Bennie is genetically and environmentally different to an unquantifiable degree.

All this raises vaguely worrying questions about the nature of individual identity (especially mine). For example, could it be that my predilection for football as a recreation, as a source of significance and as a paradigm for interpreting the world began eight months and one week before I was even born?

England 9
Scotland 3

(Home Championship, 15 April 1961)

Even although I do not have any conscious memory of this embarrassing thrashing by the Auld Enemy at Wembley, it may well have caused my pram-bound person some serious mirror-phase, pre-linguistic, pre-Oedipal trauma.

My father did not make the weekend trip to London, but at the time he still followed the footballing fortunes of Rangers and Scotland with some interest and enthusiasm. Having just resigned from the Merchant Navy and taken a hefty cut in wages to become a Glasgow

Corporation bus driver[3] (so that he could be with his young wife and baby on a permanent basis), I can only conject as to the atmosphere in the front room as England's score continued to mount (if it was followed live on TV, the neighbours would have been in; otherwise wireless commentary would have relayed the nightmare game over the ether to the disbelieving ears of a solitary, self-absorbed figure sitting hunched forward in an armchair, chain-smoking Capstan cigarettes). My father soon gave up all interest in football – in fact, he became highly antagonistic towards all professional footballers – and this massacre of the national team on a foreign field was undoubtedly one of the triggers. Propped up on my pillows in my blue Ladybird baby-suit, the sight of my father on his knees dunting his head against the iron fireplace grating must have left some kind of psychological lesion or scar on my psyche, even if my self-conscious ego had not yet properly formed.

From a personal point of view, even today I experience a *frisson* of horror when I realise that I was *alive* when Celtic's Frank Haffey let in nine goals against England. Haffey must have been a broken man after this brutal blow to his masculine self-image (and even if he wasn't, I hate to speculate on the mental state and physical stature of any red-haired Haffey offspring conceived after 15 April 1961). Celtic got rid of him within three years of the Wembley fiasco, and during his time with the club (1957–1964) he won absolutely nothing, losing in cup finals to Dunfermline in '61 and Rangers in '63. And reputedly he was so badly paid that prior to the Wembley game he was forced to try his slippery hand at selling encyclopedias door-to-door, little knowing that he would end up as an entry in many of them (see Villians, Notorious; Clowns, Sad; Headed Clearances, Inept).

In one of Celtic's unusually advantageous transfer deals he was sold for £8,000 to a criminally gullible Swindon Town, where he was such a success that he emigrated to Australia soon after (Swindon fans clubbing together to raise the steerage-class boat fare). He played in goal for Sydney for a short time, until replaced by a glove-wearing kangaroo when the directors discovered his true identity. In *A Celtic A-Z* (Greenfield Press, 1992), Tom Campbell and Pat Woods describe Haffey as 'prone to lapses of concentration', a generous football euphemism for narcoleptic ball-blindness and hand-eye-ball dyslexia.

The above diatribe against Frank Haffey may seem to be an overreaction, and intellectually I know it to be so, but in my emotional heart I really do have a burning hatred of Haffey. My father needed the 9–3 result like he needed testicular cancer, because at the time his sense of identity and self-worth was tied up inextricably with the fortunes of the national team. Giving up an exciting *career* on the high seas for a boring *occupation* on the bus routes of Glasgow was a genuine sacrifice, and not many men of that era would have been New Manish enough to put the emotional welfare of their family before job satisfaction and pecuniary advantage. My father had been the dux of his secondary school, but was forced to leave at the earliest legal opportunity in order to find work and financially support his widowed mother and younger sister (all his older brothers died in either the RAF or Royal Navy during WWII). The 9–3 scoreline came at a time when his self-esteem was at a low ebb, living in a room-and-kitchen not much more salubrious or well appointed than the one he grew up in in Kinning Park – what with the bed-recess in the kitchen, linoleum flooring and a shared outside lavatory with shiny toilet paper. Without the necessity of supporting a wife and child my father would have been able to afford the one capitalist consumer good he always craved – a brand new motor car. Thereafter he was the unhappy owner of a series of second-hand rust-buckets, and his perming of pools numbers each week was intended to win him the money for a 'braw, brand-new jalopy', the possession of which would have made him deliriously happy (his one-third dividend pools win was spent on buying *me* a brand new car – a James Bond E-type Jaguar manufactured by Dinky Motors and costing one pound six shillings).

Again from a self-centred perspective, the 9–3 humiliation must have affected my development, even if it didn't quite arrest it. In *A Dream of Perfection* Alan Sharp writes brilliantly about what he calls the 'geegs', or the terrors of infancy 'stemming as they do from birth and its abattoir, from that whole swaddling process of being a helpless, mucus-filled organism . . .' To this universal trauma of being a baby must be added the uniqueness of personal environment, which in my case has resulted in the full spectrum of neurotic possibilities: loneliness, self-doubt, hypersensitivity, catastrophising imagination, wilful perversity, social estrangement and pessimistic paranoia. If as Freud believed most writers are neurotic, at the very least, and are padded-cell mad at the extreme end of the writing spectrum, then the writing of this book is a manifestation of the warp in my mind resulting from unresolved childhood conflicts – and possibly, too, a cathartic attempt to hammer out the inner dent in my psyche. Whatever the underlying cause/hoped for effect, it is undeniable that the combining of neurotic experience and a nominally objective or plausible view of the world that this book represents is a characteristic trademark of much modern literature.

Much of this book existed previously in the fevered daydreams and imaginings of my mind, and as Freud[4] correctly pointed out both writers and children rearrange worldly things in order to please themselves. However, to please a paying readership, imagination must be channelled and shaped on the page by the tool of technique. I have no doubt that my overactive imagination is a potentially rich seam of entertainment, (mis)understanding and (dis)information, and I just hope that I have been self-disciplined enough to mine my mind with ruthless technical efficiency.

My hatred, then, of Mr Frank Haffey arises from the fact that he destroyed the illusion of my rational self-determination, which however much I may protest, does *not* totally transcend my social and biological background.

Portugal 5
North Korea 3

(World Cup, 23 July 1966)

This is the first televised game I remember seeing, if only flickeringly in black and white, during which my father constantly referred to the North Korean underdogs as 'the Diddymen' in, for him, an uncharacteristically disparaging tone of voice (the Yellow Peril Eleven averaging out at just over five feet five inches in height). His antagonism stemmed from the only occasion he was fired at in anger during his seafaring days towards the end of the Korean War, when a shell whistled past the funnel he was descaling (a projectile which got closer to its target with each subsequent retelling of the tale, until it actually scraped red paint off the outside of the funnel at the exact level where his sweaty brow was resting on a sooty metal ledge on the inside). He closed the sliding mahogany-and-louvred doors with a flourish at the final whistle, and stood back to admire the new TV disguised to look like a drinks cabinet when not in use (in fact, when the Rediffusion innards of valves and miles of soldered wiring went on the blink for the last time, they were ripped out and the wooden shell *was* converted into an embarrassingly hideous drinks cabinet).

England 4
West Germany 2

(World Cup final, 30 July 1966)

During most of this match between the Anglo-Saxon and Teutonic master races, I was playing tanner-ba' football with my wee, bare-footed urchin pals on one of Alexandra Park's red-baize pitches, and when I returned home for my jelly piece the TV commentator was yelling, 'There are people on the pitch. They think it's all over . . . It is now!' Most of the male neighbours were in, having brought their own chairs and liquid refreshments, both of which were lobbed at the TV when the final whistle was blown.

Kenneth Wolstenholme is a fine commentator, but his current voice-over contributions to Channel 4's *Football Italia* still make me cringe in recognition at the plummy tones which recorded the English victory for posterity in 1966 (despite the fact that he was behind the microphone for BBC Television's live coverage of the Celtic-Inter Milan European Cup final almost a year later). If Wolstenholme gets a repeat fee each time England's fourth goal is rebroadcast – approximately once a week (in slow motion!) – he must be a multi-millionaire by now. Each repeat showing of Geoff Hurst's final goal, however, tears at the cholesterol-clogged heartstrings of every patriotic Scotsman (Scottish patriotism being defined in negative terms of not being, and hating, the English; English patriotism of course does not even include a passing acknowledgment of Scottish existence, such a combination of indifference, ignorance and ingenuousness towards their northern neighbours inciting even more hostility towards them amongst Scotsmen who resent not having even a walk-on, never mind starring, role in the picture of what makes up the English sense of identity).

That night I drifted off to sleep in the kitchen's bed recess with a laconic lullaby emanating from my father's sneering lips: 'The ball didnae cross the line in its *entirety* . . .'; a mantra repeated for days afterwards up and down the close by the disbelieving menfolk. But in a curious sort of way, the 'controversial' nature of England's win salves the open wounds of grief north of Gretna Green, where the Russian linesman could probably now visit without being strung up from a home-made noose slung from the crossbar of the nearest municipal playing-field goalposts.

Scots try hard to convince themselves that England only won the World Cup because they 'cheated' and because they hosted the tournament. No 'cheating' was involved, obviously, even if the ball didn't cross the line in its *entirety*, but Sir Alf Ramsey's 'Wingless Wonders' probably did *only* succeed because all their matches were home fixtures, including, and especially, the final. However, the concomitant claim that Scotland would win the World Cup if it were held in Scotland is palpable nonsense, because like other mediocre minnows who have been the hosts – Sweden, Mexico and Spain, for example – Scotland would do well to get past the first round of the competition (although the 1989 Under-16 World Cup was held in Scotland, and the host nation lost honourably in the final to a bunch of six foot six inch Arabs with iron thighs and blue-tinged five o'clock shadows).

England in 1966 did have the odds tilted in their favour, but being English they lacked the self-doubt which would have caused a Scottish host team to self-destruct, and being English they had the dour determination to make good use of every and any advantage that came their way. For Scotland to win the Jules Rimet Trophy, the odds would have to be so heavily weighed against them that bookmakers would refuse to accept any more Scottish punters' money out of sheer altruistic sympathy, and the only suitably hostile venues would be those of Goodison Park, Anfield, Highbury, Old Trafford, etcetera, and finally the Twin Towers of Wembley. In other words, Scotland would need to qualify when England play hosts for the second time, and be so seeded that they are scheduled to meet the Auld Enemy in the final (during which England would need to go ahead early in the match through a highly dubious penalty, with at least one Scottish player sent off in the first half because of a perfidiously dramatic English dive).

England 2
Scotland 3

(Home International, 15 April 1967)

This is the last international game my father ever watched from start to finish (on TV), and, paradoxically, although it was one of Scotland's greatest ever results – the poor provincial peasants overrunning the recently-crowned kings of world football – it capped his growing disenchantment with Scottish football and Scottish footballers.

Goals from Law (Manchester United), Lennox (Celtic) and McCalliog (Sheffield Wednesday) secured victory against an English team intent on carrying out the tedious blackboard tactics devised by head dominie Sir Alf Ramsey, a style of play that its proponents probably thought of as a methodology of play (based on surrendering the midfield by withdrawing wingers, packing the defence with 'stoppers' and attacking sneakily on the break).

Even at 3–2 up, my father was almost speechless with frustration, as Scotland toyed with their opponents. If the circumstances had been reversed England would undoubtedly have dispensed with the cross-park shenanigans and gone for the maximum score tally achievable, the footballing equivalent of shooting all prisoners. Instead, Scotland, and in particular Baxter, preferred to show off like cheekily chivalrous schoolboys, teasing the at-their-mercy opposition with unhurried possession and ball-juggling skills. My father was convinced that by failing to go in for the kill Scotland were leaving themselves dangerously exposed to a late English counter-charge, especially when McCreadie walked away from the ball in his own half, leaving it for Slim Jim to saunter over with his socks crumpled round his ankles. When he *finally* reached the ball he proceeded to play keepie-up with it!

But in the end Scotland did win! And as long as your team actually does win, no matter how slender the margin, then the criterion for judging their overall performance is not just by *how much* they won by, but in *what manner* they won (a statistical victory is like the compulsory component in ice-skating routines; winning with aesthetic style and emotional panache is the artistic expression element). Scotland won this match in a uniquely flamboyant way, as only Scotland could, but my father was incapable of appreciating the artistic arrogance involved (either that or his shattered nerves couldn't stand the strain). Whatever the reason for his disapproval, it was at this point that our footballing and life philosophies began to diverge (although I must admit that if this match had been a World Cup final and Baxter's overconfidence had led to a late equaliser, I would have been running on to the pitch towards Slim Jim with hatred in my heart and a loaded six-pack in my hand).

The main title of this book is derived from the annuals published by Stanley Paul & Co, cut-and-paste books of rehashed journalistic clippings and pages of photographic padding which help 'Old Firm' fans to relive the highlights of the previous season, but which as I have got older have supplied less and less reading pleasure (to the point where I have not *bought* one since *Playing for Celtic No. 6*).

The subtitle of *Another Paradise Lost* is a reference to both Milton's epic poem and Celtic Park, which is known colloquially as 'Paradise' by Celtic fans (or the 'Piggery' if being referred to by proletarian Protestant Hunnery).

The epigraphs at the start of this Introduction I've quarried from Milton's vast text and have rearranged to encapsulate my 34 years of existence, during most of which as a Celtic fan I've spent a quite inordinate and rationally unjustifiable amount of time just thinking about football – daydreaming and intellectualising – with even more synaptic brain-cell connections being devoted to the sport than to sex, although they do occasionally overlap (and I don't just mean when reciting obscure team formations from 1982 in my head in order to postpone premature ejaculation).

The formal structure of the book was also inspired by Milton's magnum opus, in which the first three books reflect the triumph of the divinely good (Nine in a Row: 1966–1974), with the last three books redolent of despair because God's kingdom will never again be of this world (Embarrassing the Hoops: 1974–1989). *Paradise Regained* is the basis for the last section (Trophyless, Rudderless and Absolutely Bloody Hopeless: 1989–1994). In the *Paradise Regained* of 1671, good-humoured reason finally triumphs over pointless passion.

The following pages, then, constitute an anatomy of an obsession and a not totally unreliable memoir of a life. An unremarkable life it may be, but as those well-known 20th-century obsessives Walter Benjamin and Nick Hornby have proved, the recounting of an unremarkable life in print is not *necessarily* a literary endeavour devoid of any interest to a general readership. If the micro-detailed analyses of 19th-century shopping malls and Arsenal Football Club by Messrs Benjamin and Hornby, respectively, are compelling reads – which they are – then there is no good reason why the recent history of Glasgow Celtic should not be a subject of equal 'associative richness'. Benjamin himself rejected the idea that revolutionary art can be achieved by attending to the 'correct' subject matter. For him writers create something new by revolutionising the artistic forces of production – in other words through technique. Therefore *Playing for Celtic No. 1* was not a ground-breaking example of *avant-garde* publishing. On the other hand, Hornby's *Fever Pitch* was a piece of football criticism as art, which had never really been done before (in fact, in his case the criticism as art – *Fever Pitch* – was a damn sight more interesting than the 'art' it was describing – namely Arsenal FC). Luckily for me, Celtic are *inherently* more interesting than Arsenal, and thankfully I have not been commissioned to write an all-encompassing *Official History Of Glasgow Celtic Football Club*, à la Brian Wilson. One does not have to be a Benjaminian deconstructionist to see the futility of such a dryly grandiose scheme,[5] because there is no totality or ultimate point of view that can be successfully or truthfully expressed (although the Celtic board of directors would probably disagree; and hence the commissioning of the celebratory and propagandistic stage show *The Celtic Story*). As a critic of, or writer about, Celtic all I can hope to do is provide glimpses of how things connect together, by highlighting some personal fragments, which I am able to do because, paraphrasing, the trivia of Celtic's results are intimately bound up with the details of my personal growth[6] (physically, emotionally and intellectually).

Benjamin's most famous quote was almost used as the epigraph for this book, and even if one substitutes 'Celtic Football Fan' for 'Angel of History' the meaning and power of the phrase is in no way confused or diminished. Indeed, it would make a good club motto, printed on all club stationery and replacing the tawdry 'Hail! Hail!' painted above the players' tunnel:

> The Angel of History flying backwards sees only rubble, blown by the wind from Paradise.

FOOTNOTES

1 & 2 Seekers of profound meaning in the arbitrary coincidences of statistical analysis should note that the crowd of 127,621 can be interpreted as a numerical omen as to my predestined date of arrival in the world: 27/01/61. This is quite a tempting inference to draw, except for the annoying fact that for the attendance figure to be exactly rearrangeable into my date of birth, 20 less Glaswegians would have had to be at the game. Your average conspiracy theorist/lay-line perceiver/corn-circle collector would *not* at this point – confronted by hard facts that do not neatly fit his theory – change his theory to accommodate the new data; instead he would assume the 'facts' were incorrectly reported in the first place, changing them by trial-and-error until they fitted the fallacious hypothesis, whereupon the new 'facts' would be excitedly cited as conclusive evidence of the proposition! (This is a good example of deductive rather than reductive reasoning, and a way of making up one's mind by reaching a strongly held and prejudiced conclusion first, and then searching selectively for supportive evidence to back it up, that Scottish intellectuals are worryingly prone to indulge in, especially in the areas of social science, literary criticism and revisionist history.) And even if the crowd was 127,601 it would be one of those coincidences which mean absolutely nothing in the grand order of

things. Also, it would be lessened in Nostradamusian precognitive impact because dates other than 27/01/61 can be created by rearranging the number 127,601 – *viz* 27/10/61, 07/12/61 and 17/02/61, the latter being my exact (well, almost) ETA as diagnosed by the Robroyston Hospital obstetrician responsible for overseeing my gestation and delivery (one Dr Oonagh Anderson, or as first-year medical students acronymed her 'DoA'!).

3 Celtic conspiracy theorists often claim that the Red Hand of Ulster pulls behavioural strings within the City Chambers of Glasgow, most council sub-committees commonly believed to be chaired by bowler-hatted, militant Masons. One unexplained phenomenon of the middle/late '70s is grist to the conspiracy-theory mill, when almost overnight the livery of Glasgow Corporation double-decker buses changed from Fenian green, yellow and white to bright, King Billy orange. This may be good old deductive reasoning again, but occasionally the correct conclusion can be drawn in spite of flawed logic in the reasoning process. The transport sub-committee which initiated this change may have done so because they had access to a job-lot of cheap industrial orange paint, but I personally believe the change in colour-coding owed more to the committee voting on the proposal by a show of hands, while under the conference table right trouser legs were rolled up as far as they would go.

4 My citing of Freud in this one instance should not be interpreted as uncritical authorial approval of the man, his theories or his modern-day disciples. Indeed, in my deductive opinion the orifice-fixated old buffer did not *discover* the subconscious as much as he *invented* it.

5 One honourable exception is *The Glory and the Dream* by Tom Campbell and Pat Woods, an *unofficial* history of Celtic F.C. 1887–1986, the reading pleasure to be derived from it *not* being in inverse proportion to the staggering amount of research which must have gone into its production, a footballing equivalent of *Gibbon's Rise and Fall of the Roman Empire*.

6 Matt ffytche, 'Benjamania', *The Modern Review* (February–March 1994).

NINE IN A ROW
1966–1974

Glasgow Celtic 2
Inter Milan 1

(European Cup final, 25 May 1967)

This victory in Lisbon's Estadio Nacional becomes ever more incredible as time passes, and from a quotidian distance of just 28 years its significance has become almost mystical. 2,000 years from now it could conceivably evolve into a powerful religious folk myth amongst Celtic peoples, eclipsing the belief-system of Anglo-Saxon Christianity (especially if the development of technological civilisation is interrupted by some kind of catastrophic discontinuity like genetic plague or nuclear war, à la *The Planet of the Apes*). After all, Jesus Christ and the Disciples probably never even dreamed of the bureaucratic, totalitarian organisations that would be founded and grow like Topsy in their names. The Celtic team sheet of 25 May 1967 could become a sacred relic for the faithful, with the eleven players raised to demi-god status, and the manager Jock Stein elevated to the position of supramundane personal deity (with a healthy black-market trade in locks of Jimmy Johnstone's red curls, bones from the skeleton of Tommy Gemmell, and original remnants from the goalkeeper's jersey of Ronnie Simpson – some of which might even be authentic).

How future generations interpret the events of that mild day in May remains to be seen, but the fact that 90 minutes of football played on a Portuguese soccer pitch in 1967 can still send the spirits of thousands of souls in Scotland soaring in 1995 is testimony to the importance of the match (at least in the psyches of Celtic supporters, not all of whom even remember the day or were alive at the time). In *The Varieties of Religious Experience*, William James outlined various religious psychologies, and followers of Glasgow Celtic Football and Athletic Club can also be analysed in such Jamesian terms.

Celtic's victory in the European Cup final was patently not due to the influence of supernatural intervention, despite the invasion of the pitch at the end by supplicating pilgrims who dropped to their knees in gratitude and mouthed prayers of thanks to as many Catholic saints as their alcohol-befuddled brains could recall (probably no more than three – namely, St Andrew, St Mungo and St Christopher).

However, if William James himself had witnessed the post-match sacraments/shenanigans he would most definitely not have dismissed them out of hand, preferring I'm sure to class them as a legitimate variety of religious experience. For James the important point was not whether a religious concept – be it the actual existence of God or the historical fact of miracles – was objectively true, but whether belief in it by the individual or the masses led to some action or behaviour being performed that would not otherwise have been the case. In other words, *truth* is merely a *function* of *belief*. 'What is it to be "real"?' he asked. 'The best definition is . . . "anything is real of which we find ourselves obliged to take account in any way".' Therefore it is no exaggeration to claim that contemplation of this match – whether based on personal experience or aided by newspaper clippings or video clips – brings thousands of people with a God-shaped hole in their life closer to the transcendental awe and ecstasy of traditional religious faith than any number of contemporary masses, contrite confessionals or pulpit sermons.

I actually started to support Celtic because of this game, but I hasten to add that my pledge of lifelong allegiance was made *during* the worrying first half, when Celtic found themselves trailing cruelly by 1–0, and not *after* the final whistle when they had reversed the one-goal deficit to become glorious and unexpected victors.

By May of 1967 our family had moved upmarket from the cramped and damp Dennistoun tenement to a relatively modern estate in Carntyne, a nearby council house scheme of some popularity because of its big gardens and spacious, well-appointed interiors. Admittedly it was South Carntyne, and not the even more enviable North Carntyne[1] (which required the housing-point equivalent of 180! in darts to get transferred to, like Knightswood or Riddrie), but it was a definite step up in social cachet. My parents had been lucky enough to arrange a private transfer with the previous tenant – some old woman who wanted to die in the Dennistoun milieu where she was born – and the socialist Housing Corporation of Glasgow reluctantly permitted such private enterprise arrangements (I think my father must have slipped the old battleaxe a few quid in a brown envelope to grease the wheels of the transaction; at the very least he paid for her removal expenses). I remember standing in the back garden and being overwhelmed by the greenness of the grass. It all seemed vaguely unreal compared to the communal back court of Walter Street, what with the lack of uncollected rubbish overflowing from the middens, small rats and/or big mice scampering underfoot, and white walls of bed linen flapping in the sooty wind. Our new street was pleasant but dull, the four-in-a-block houses built by the Corporation in the 1920s being stolid but bland (only now, however, having acquired middle-class moral values and aesthetic tastes, do I find myself being offended by the two rows of almost identical buildings with about as much 'character' as a Legoland development).

No one famous has ever come out of Carntyne – whereas Dennistoun has produced world famous superstars like Lulu and Cliff Hanley – and its one claim to artistic fame is to be found in the ribald lyrics of a Billy Connolly song: 'Ten Woodbine/ A Bottle of wine/ and three wee men from Carn-tyne.' This characterisation is only strictly true of South South Carntyne, which had within its boundaries the greyhound stadium and the notorious Inverleith Street (which any Sheriff Court defendants from Carntyne, as reported in the pages of the *Evening Times*, almost invariably give as their home address). Carntyne proper had no public houses within its environs and to get to a drink-dispensing hostelry the above three wee men would have had to walk to one of the surrounding districts, the names of which are more evocative of Glasgow's rich working-class history: for example, Dennistoun, Riddrie, Shettleston, Ruchazie and Cranhill. When first built – circa 1926 – Carntyne would have been a literal and geographical suburb, but Glasgow thereafter soon sprawled further eastwards in the form of Cranhill, Easterhouse, Springboig and Garrowhill.

As a quasi-suburb, Carntyne had of course its own finely tuned social gradations. South of Carntyne Road lived the degenerate underclass of the *News of the World* readership, none of whom possessed anything as bourgeois as 'Sunday best' clothing (and if they did were constantly hocking it to and redeeming it from pawnbrokers). North of Carntyne Road but south of Edinburgh Road, where we found ourselves, lived the *Sunday Mail* brigade, who attended either South Carntyne Church of Scotland or Carntyne Road Chapel. North of Edinburgh Road dual carriageway but south of Cumbernauld Road, *Sunday Post* readers were in the majority – and a few radical free-thinkers even had the *Observer* on order at the Gartcraig Road newsagent, from where it was delivered to addresses in Morningside Street, Warriston Street, Loretto Street and Fettes Street (their counterparts in Edinburgh housing the capital's *haute bourgeoisie*). The *crème-de-la-crème* of this area either attended North Carntyne Church of Scotland (which got capacity crowds whenever *Songs of Praise* cameras were covering the service) or St Thomas's Chapel.

We lived in the upstairs apartments, and during the live television broadcast of the European Cup final the Dolans underneath were making enough noise to waken the dead in Lisbon. An Irish-Catholic family of five, Mr Dolan was a postal worker with numerous relatives in the 'notorious East End of Glasgow', most of whom seemed to be in front of the TV for the game. Surprisingly, none of the Dolan clan had set off from Alexandra Parade (in Dennistoun) in the Lisbon Motorcade, which had been led off by the official *Evening Times* Hillman Imp on the previous Sunday (the final was held on the following Thursday, kicking off at 5.30 p.m. Lisbon time). Alexandra Parade was the main thoroughfare into the city centre for traffic coming off Edinburgh Road, and our old flat in Walter Street was the next parallel street to the south. If we hadn't moved house, I would certainly have seen the colourful procession set off, and to this day I deeply regret not having witnessed the closest thing to a Roman Catholic Orange Walk winding its way through the streets of Glasgow, or a modern-day equivalent of a medieval pilgrimage (since thousands of devout worshippers from industrial Glasgow followed an overland route similar to that taken by their 11th-century forefathers bound for Santiago de Compostela in north-west Spain, and in both cases the pilgrimages were undertaken by individuals *and* large groups consisting of the devout, the curious and the penitent.)

And so to the game itself (with a little bit of historical background to set the remarkable outcome in context) . . . Prior to new manager Jock Stein's arrival in March 1965 Celtic were a once-great club going nowhere – at top speed – with the last league championship flag to fly over Parkhead a tattered and faded memory, occasionally stirred by puffs of nostalgic wind blown from 1954. In the first full season under Stein's management, 1965–66, Celtic won the League and the League Cup, were runners-up in the Scottish Cup, and reached the semi-final of the Cup Winners' Cup. In season 1966–67, Celtic had won every domestic trophy available to them, winning the Treble with the fast and exciting style of attacking play for which the club had always been renowned.

Internazionale, on the other hand, were the uncrowned kings of European football – having lost their title to Real Madrid the previous year, after having won the European Cup in both 1964 and 1965 – and the Milanese aristocrats confidently expected to regain their throne. Apart from Inter and Real, the only other clubs to win the European Cup for Champions had been Benfica and AC Milan. Real Madrid were the most successful in terms of titles won, and with their Latin panache and flair were worthy of the description 'Popes of European Soccer'; Inter Milan, however, can fairly be characterised as the Anti-Popes of European Club Football, playing as they did an ultra-defensive style of game which won more games than plaudits.

Upon Jock Stein's broad shoulders lay the responsibility for devising a game-plan which would unlock the *Catenaccio Bolt* system, as perfected by Moroccan coach Helenio Herrera. The Inter coach was the highest paid manager in world football, and although Stein's salary did not bear any comparison to Herrera's both men shared similar working-class roots – Herrera growing up in the slums of Casablanca and Stein coming from the Lanarkshire mining town of Burnbank.

Nevertheless, surviving in these equally harsh environments probably required different social skills, and like the town of Casablanca, where no one is quite as they appear to be, Herrera cultivated an air of magical mystique, enabling him to make tactical alterations during a game which supposedly had the stamp of genius – and all communicated to his players by a snap of the fingers or through complicated hand signals. Such slyness and sleight-of-hand allowed him to escape the souks of Casablanca, where the main source of employment for the poor was begging, after which Herrera plied his coaching trade in Spain.

Stein, like the products of most Lanarkshire mining communities, was superficially blunt and uncultured, preferring to make an impression with a few well-chosen and ripe phrases. An undistinguished player with Albion Rovers, non-league Llanelly and Celtic, Stein made the transition from the miner's lift-cage to the manager's front office by dint of a powerful personality, keen footballing intelligence and a highly developed capacity to recognize bullshit when he heard it (Stein's brutal honesty and Herrera's conniving duplicity, if transposed from Burnbank to Casablanca, and vice versa, would probably have led to the same tragic consequences: being stabbed to death in some rat-infested back alley).

In essence, then, the final pitted Herrera's 'Anti-Popes of Defence' against Stein's 'Apostles of Attack', a cosmopolitan squad of sophisticated stars versus a provincial team of indigenous Scotsmen. Even a cursory glance at the team sheets makes a Scottish inferiority complex explode in involuntary nervous tics and uncontrollable cold sweats:

CELTIC: Simpson; Craig, Gemmell; Murdoch, McNeill, Clark; Johnstone, Wallace, Chalmers, Auld, Lennox.

INTER: Sarti; Burgnich, Facchetti; Bedin, Guarneri, Picchi; Domenghini, Cappellini, Mazzola, Bicicili, Corso.

In terms of moral superiority, however, Celtic held the high ground, having scored 16 goals on the way to the final, with the loss of only four, as they eliminated in successive rounds FC Zurich, Nantes, Vojvodina and Dukla Prague. Inter reached the final with a record of tight 1-0 wins and sterile 0-0 draws. Celtic could also feel self-righteously proud of their charitable beginnings, the club having been formed in 1888[2] by Marist Brother Walfrid in order to raise funds for the poor of the East End of Glasgow, such good works including the provision of a Poor Children's Dinner Table. Inter, presumably, were formed by rich Milanese merchants as they stuffed themselves in front of Leonardo da Vinci's *Last Supper*.

The view of historical revisionists, who delight in deconstructing commonly believed histories written by prejudiced victors, is probably worth acknowledging in passing. Deconstructionists with season tickets to the Ibrox Glee Club would stress the following: (a) in the semi-final second leg against Dukla in Czechoslovakia, Celtic defended a 3-1 first-leg lead with everyone behind the ball except Stevie Chalmers, who was left up front simply to hold the ball whenever the increasingly desperate defenders managed to blooter it upfield in his general direction, a what-we-have-we-bloody-well-hold performance that earned a stupefyingly dull 0-0 draw and rave reviews from Herrera; (b) although Celtic were originally created to subsidise poor Catholic parishes, within ten years of its inception the club had incorporated itself into a *private* limited liability company, dispensing with all donations to charity by 1898, when a dividend of 20 per cent was awarded to the share-holding directors; and (c) from its formation Celtic specialised in poaching from other clubs big-name star players, professionals in all but name whom the club rewarded with 'bungs' or unofficial under-the-table payments siphoned off from the gate-money receipts by declaring artificially low attendance figures, much to the disgust of genuinely amateur clubs like Queen's Park, although Herrera would have approved of Celtic's ruthlessly professional and businesslike attitude in its early years.

Having watched extended highlights of the final on video numerous times, I never cease to be amazed at the artistically satisfying nature of the unfolding drama, a plotted structure that Hollywood scriptwriter Alan Sharp would have eschewed in any fictional treatment on the basis of sentimental serendipity and lack of creative credibility. For example, any movie script along the following lines would have been consigned to the bottom of the sock drawer:

THE LISBON LIONS AND THE HOLY GRAIL
by Alan Sharp
1966

1.   Int. Bed recess. Glasgow circa 1890.
BROTHER WALFRID *giving last rights to six-year-old boy dying of consumption.*
BOY: Father, will the Celtic ever win the Scottish Cup?
BROTHER WALFRID *(hesitating):* Of course, my son. (*Then, not quite convincingly.*) And after that, one day our team of fine young men will win the cup for the best team in all Christendom.
Close shot of young boy dying in BROTHER WALFRID's *arms with a satisfied smile on his angelic face.* BROTHER WALFRID *holds the limp young body tight.* Close up of BROTHER WALFRID's *haggard face, down which a single tear is falling.*
BROTHER WALFRID *(with conviction):* Begorra, yes, my son. One day. One day – for sure!

DISSOLVE TO:

2.   Ext. Establishing shot – aerial view of Estadio Nacional.
CAPTION: Lisbon, 25 May 1967: 80 years later.

CUT TO:

3.   Ext. Day.
Crane shot pans down and moves in and along tunnel.
The two lines of players are waiting nervously side by side.
Zoom in on square face of Bertie Auld.
AULD *starts to lead a chorus of* The Celtic Story.
(*This is a deliberate homage and reference to the scene in* Casablanca *where the Free French customers and band drown out* Deutschland über Alles *with a rousing rendition of* La Marseillaise).

CUT TO:

4.   Reaction shot of Inter's Captain Picchi.
His features are momentarily confused and concerned.

5.   Crane camera gradually pans back.

Players walk towards the end of the tunnel. A deafening roar greets the Celtic team.
Cheers amplified to maximum by sound engineer.

CUT TO:

6. Long shot of pitch just before kick-off.

CUT TO:

7. Slow panning shot of Celtic's 7,000 supporters.
VOICE OVER (WILLIAM McILVANNEY or ORSON WELLES or BRITISH PATHE NEWS COMMENTATOR): **Written off by the cynical European media pundits, Celtic prepare themselves for the most important 90 minutes in their long and honourable history, upon which rests the entire future of football as a spectator sport – one more unpopular win for the ruthlessly effective but tedious Italians being enough to send the game into terminal world decline.**

CUT TO:

8. Close up of Celtic supporter in vest, braces and bunnet crossing himself as kick-off whistle blows.
Portuguese peasant beside man smiles and gives thumbs-up sign.

CUT TO:

9. Seventh-minute penalty award.
CRAIG *tackles* CAPPELLINI, *who goes down like a dying swan.*

CUT TO:

10. West German referee Kurt Tschenscher.
He is pointing to the penalty spot.

CUT TO:

11. Slow-motion replay of penalty incident. Freeze-frame as Cappellini hits the ground. Superimpose flashing red question mark on screen.

CUT TO:

12. Close-up of man with bunnet.
FAN: AwaeyegoTschenscheryaLutheranproddydogye – thatwiznever apenaltyyabigfuckinNaziye.

SUBTITLES: I say, ref – that seems like a highly dubious award, to put it mildly. Let's have some objectivity, sir.

CUT TO:

13.   Mazzola taking penalty (shot from behind goal).
He calmly sends SIMPSON *the wrong way.*

CUT TO:

14.   Split screen close-ups of Jock Stein and bunnet man.
STEIN *is as impassive as granite.*
Bunnet man is pointing a loaded finger at referee and mouthing obscenities.

CUT TO:

15.   Medium shot of Inter players strolling back for kick-off.
VOICE OVER: Having scored the early goal that the Celtic fans dreaded, Inter decide to kill the game as a spectacle by drawing the *Catenaccio Bolt* tight shut. For the rest of the match PICCHI will 'sweep' behind his back-four defenders in order to close out any Celtic attacks that manage to break through – or so the crack Italians confidently believe.

CUT TO:

16.   Edited montage of great saves from Sarti.
From Murdoch, Johnstone, Auld (off the face of the crossbar) and Gemmell.

CUT TO:

17.   Medium shot of Celtic goalie Simpson.
A long ball out of Inter's defence finds SIMPSON *ten yards out of his area, with no Celtic defenders in their own half.* SIMPSON *has the ball at his 'tongue-tied' feet and the winger* DOMENGHINI *is bearing down on him.* SIMPSON *appears rooted to his exposed spot.*

CUT TO:

18.   Close-up of bunnet man.
MAN: Simpsonyaoldeejitye-getridathebafirchrissake!

35

CUT TO:

19. Medium shot from Simpson's point of view. Slightly out of focus to represent lack of 20–20 vision.

DOMENGHINI *is charging in ever closer.*

CUT TO:

20. Medium shot from spectator's point of view. Red spots appearing and disappearing.

Just before DOMENGHINI *is on top of him,* SIMPSON *oh-so-casually back-heels the ball to a frantically retreating and red-faced* JOHN CLARK.

CUT TO:

21. Close-up of bunnet man.

MAN (*wiping his brow with a hankie*): Welldoneronniethatwizchust gallusweeman . . . Butdinnaetryonithinlikethataginyaauldbaldbaistard ye!

CUT TO:

22. Referee blowing for half-time. Pan back to reveal picture on television screen. Continue to pan back, until eventually showing a six-year-old boy with short-back-and-sides haircut lying on living-room floor with chin cupped in hands.

BOY: Come on, Celtic. You can do it.

DISSOLVE TO:

23. Int. 'Home' dressing room.

Close-up of Stein.

STEIN: Yer doing fine, lads. Just remember that tae beat a packed defence like Inter's ye've got to *turn* it. Don't go as far as the goal-line before puttin in yer crosses. Just take the ball as far as the 18-yard line and then jist *roll* it back across intae the middle. Do that and ye'll win . . . Right, out ye go.

CUT TO:

24. Ext. The second half is underway.

In 55 minutes BEDIN's *attempted bicycle hitch-kick clearance nearly knocks* WALLACE *unconscious.* TSCHENSCHER *sprints into the penalty box pointing decisively.* Enhanced sound effect of crowd's 'sighing' *as the supporters realise that only an indirect free kick has been awarded.*

From the ensuing rebound GEMMELL*'s shot is deflected off* FACCHETTI, *wrong-footing* SARTI.

CUT TO:

25. Camera shot aligned with the goal line. Slow motion.
SARTI *twists as if double-jointed and claws back the diverted ball.*
Freeze-frame.
Superimposed computer graphic/animation of broken line rising vertically from goal line.
The ball has gone over the line in its entirety.

CUT TO:

26. Int. Saracen Head pub, Barrowland, Glasgow.
The massed patrons rise as one to applaud the 'goal'.

CUT TO:

27. Ext. Close-up of referee Tschenscher.
He waves play on, blindly oblivious.

CUT TO:

28. Int. 'Sarry Heid' pub.
Shot from point of view of TV screen above the gantry.
The patrons sink slowly back down into their seats (despondently).

CUT TO:

29. Ext. 62 minutes have elapsed.
Right-back CRAIG, *who gave away the 'penalty', is wide on the right, apparently intent on reaching the goal line before crossing.*
VOICE OVER (STEIN): Roll it along the 18-yard line, son.
(CRAIG, *the future professional dentist and the nearest thing to a Camusesque intellectual in the Celtic squad – he attended Glasgow University's Dental School – squares the ball inside to his fellow full-back* GEMMELL *– a Danny Kay lookalike – and* GEMMELL *hits a shot from 25 yards out, one of his famous 'specials', unleashed by a knobbly right peg. The ball zooms past* SARTI *into the net, which bulges as if set to burst.)*

CUT TO:

30. Reaction shot of terracing supporters erupting in joy.

CUT TO:

31. SARTI, *all in black, points accusingly at* LENNOX *and* WALLACE, *but no offside decision is given.*

CUT TO:

32. A second montage of great saves and close things.
    (a) SARTI *miraculously turns a* MURDOCH *piledriver over bar.*
    (b) GEMMELL's *cross-cum-shot rebounds off the stanchion of post and bar.*
    (c) WALLACE, *about to tap ball into gaping goal, is pulled down desperately by beaten* SARTI. TSCHENSCHER *waves play on to the surprise of everyone, including and especially the Inter goalkeeper.*

CUT TO:

33. CAPTION: Time is running out, with less than 5 minutes to go . . .

34. Long shot from top of grandstand.
GEMMELL *lays the ball off to* MURDOCH.

CUT TO:

35. Camera shot from behind goal.
MURDOCH's *shot is obviously going wide of the post.*
CHALMERS *sticks out a foot and deflects the ball into the net.*

CUT TO:

36. Rapid series of jump cuts.
STEIN *rising in triumph from the dug-out. The players congratulating the scorer. Terracing exploding with green-and-white. Man with bunnet throwing it in the air. Sarry Heid pub clientele with arms raised in jubilation.*

CUT TO:

37. Close-up of referee blowing for time up.

CUT TO:

38. Medium shot.
Thousands of fans vaulting the security moat and running on to the pitch. Many of them fall to their knees.

CUT TO:

39. STEIN *embracing goalkeeper* SIMPSON *and team captain* McNEILL, *along with one of the first fans – kilted – to scale the moat.*
Freeze-frame on this famous-to-be newspaper photo tableau.

DISSOLVE TO:

40. Int. Carntyne living-room.
Close-up.
Six-year-old boy smiling and crying simultaneously.
FATHER'S VOICE *(out of shot and disgruntled):* Would you listen to that racket the Dolans are making downstairs . . . take it Celtic won, then?
BOY: Yes, dad. They won . . . I mean, *we* won.

CUT TO:

41. Ext. Back garden.
The young boy is kicking a tennis ball around, raising his arms in triumph as another imaginary goal goes past SARTI. Soundtrack of 'It's A Grand Old Team To Play For' builds and builds.
Zoom back and up with crane shot – *revealing a grid system of square back gardens. In each one a young boy is kicking a ball around with wild enthusiasm.*

42. Roll credits . . .

43. **A Walt Disney Production**
No resemblance in this motion picture to any persons living or dead is intended or should be inferred.

THE END

As a six-year-old kicking a tennis ball around in the back garden, emulating my new heroes, I felt as if I was on the threshold of grown-up sophistication. After all, to support a football team required abstract, lateral and symbolic thinking (whereas infant psychology is restricted to responding to directly experienced, physically substantial objects and bodies). It was time to put aside childish things – like teddy bears, blanket comforters and Heinz baby food – and step bravely into the adult world of emotional attachment to arbitrary abstractions. Santa Claus had been demystified the previous Christmas in a flood of childish tears – when my father broke the bad news to me on *Christmas* morning while in his cups over a bottle of Drambuie – but now I had discovered the irrational joys of investing deep reserves of emotion in an ever-changing team of eleven ordinary men. Harvey, my invisible six-foot white rabbit, also disappeared from my daydreams on that May afternoon, because I had eleven new friends, or substitute big brothers, to tag along after. Having been enrolled at Carntyne state primary for a year I knew that being a Celtic-supporting 'Tim' would earn me even more bullying, but I didn't care – because now I had a cause, not to die for, but to have my head battered against hard playground concrete for.

The post-match celebrations downstairs in the Dolans soon spilled out of the back door into the garden, and instead of running away in my normal petrified fashion I let the extended family of rough Irishmen tousle my hair, swing me around in dizzying circles from the end of their muscular arms and carry me on their broad shoulders. And on an adult's shoulders I could see the floodlight pylons of Celtic Park, about a mile distant, where next season I would 'get a lift' over the turnstiles . . . To think that the team I had just watched live on TV win the European Cup had their home ground within sightseeing distance of my new home filled me with rapturous wonder.

The Lisbon Lions – a journalistic alliteration in the style of the Wembley Wizards – had made living history, the ripples of which still ebb and flow in the streams-of-consciousness of tens of thousands, especially in the form of the urban folk myths which are told and retold, and which may not even be totally apocryphal. For example, the Celtic supporter who awoke with a Stella-and-Pernod hangover in the arrivals lounge of Lisbon Airport, whereupon he rushed outside and instructed a bemused taxi-driver to take him home to Rutherglen. Or the miraculous quartet who arrived back at Abbotsinch Airport by charter flight, only to realise upon landing that they had made the outward journey by car, which was presumably still parked slightly closer to one kerb than the other in some Lisbon back street. Or, finally, the solitary hitchhiker just outside Estoril who waved on in dismissive fashion a Mini Cooper bound for Glasgow, since his destination was 'well oot a' yir way in Embra'. And in the words of fellow-Scot Bill Shankly, manager of Liverpool and the only manager of an English club to attend the final: 'Jock, you're immortal.'

40

(A conventional chapter on this game would probably end with Shankly's famous quote, but I think there is another incident which better encapsulates the difference between Stein and Herrera, or more specifically between Celtic's colourful characters and Inter's robotic superstars . . . According to Billy McNeill in his book *Back to Paradise* (Mainstream, 1988) – ghostwritten by Alex Cameron and one of the better cut-and-paste publications – many of the Celtic team almost appeared at the celebratory UEFA banquet, and more importantly on the bus cavalcade along London Road travelling towards Celtic Park and the homecoming Gala Night to be held there, without their false teeth. Apparently, goalkeeper Ronnie Simpson nearly forgot to pick his cap out of the back of the net after full-time – the bunnet containing for safe-keeping during the action numerous sets of false teeth. He barely retrieved it in time, the bunnet having become an object of intense desire for many of the kilted souvenir-hunters who had invaded the pitch at the end. No doubt if Simpson had been a shade slower off his mark, some lucky supporter would now have a drawerful of false teeth in his possession, or possibly these treasured mementoes would have been passed down to a grateful son or gobsmacked grandchild. As far as Facchetti & Co are concerned I wouldn't be surprised if the cost of their collective root-canal and gold-filling dental work surpassed the market value of at least one Celtic player – Jim Craig, for instance, who was a trained dentist for God sake! Celtic may have hailed from the city with Western Europe's worst dental-decay and gum-disease health record, but even without a set of choppers grown inside their own heads McNeill and his girning men were more than a match for the dazzlingly white smiles and expensive bridgework of the toothy Milanese, who on this memorable occasion had bitten off a lot more than they could chew.)

FOOTNOTES

1 North Carntyne is notorious in the annals of market-research folklore, a fact I can vouch for, having served in the infantry of the advertising world for six months as a market-research/opinion-poll interviewer armed only with a clipboard and a black biro (and a few free-sample sachets of coffee or washing powder if a new product launch was imminent). In the jargon of market research, North Carntyne is an intermediate area where the dreaded C1 and C2 genuses have taken root, ie the working class with disposable income. In demographic terms C1s are white-collar paper shufflers and C2s time-served manual workers (or their dependants in both cases) and they can be found lurking behind MFI mock-Georgian front doors, cocooned in 'little palaces' of working-class vulgarity that make Baroque interiors designed by the likes of Bernini look positively plain and subdued by comparison what with

their crazy-paving fireplaces and massive mottled flues, cocktail bars upholstered in buttony vinyl, wallpaper that could put epileptics in hospital, *George and Mildred* light fittings, knick-knacks from Blackpool and the Costa del Sol, and of course the *pièce de resistance*: painting of *The Crying Boy* (or alternatively a dusky Tahitian maiden) purchased at auction from Ali's Discount Cave.

North Carntyne is a combination of four-in-a-block and semi-detached houses, built by Glasgow Corporation circa 1926 with well-tended (and demarcated) gardens. Districts like North Carntyne are market research graveyards, and would be no-go areas if it were not for the fact that a percentage of C1s and C2s are usually required to meet quotas, and therefore provide statistically significant and reliable results.

A market researcher going door-to-door can quite easily waste a whole Saturday morning, afternoon or evening without getting *one* interview successfully completed in North-fucking-Carntyne. I remember spending a *whole* day from 10 a.m. to 7.30 p.m. tramping its grey streets without getting one willing respondent. The basic attitude of a North Carntynese gook is: 'Have you got any free samples? . . . Well, get away from my mock-Georgian door or I'll set the pug (*dog*) on you.'

North Carntyne is slightly atypical, however, in that every second ground-floor flat seems to have a wheelchair ramp and a cripple car parked outside (in its own specially painted rectangle). It also has an extremely high proportion of retired widows who live behind twitching net curtains on their state pensions *and* late-husbands' work pensions, from employers such as British Gas, British Coal, British Rail, British Telecom, the Post Office and Strathclyde Regional Council. However, it is quite representative in that every third, non-cripple car is brand new with a current registration number (but East European, and therefore depreciating faster than the Monopoly currency of the country that sledge-hammered the obsolete Fiat spare parts together with proletarian craftsmanship in the first place).

Approximately 99.9 per cent of its inhabitants are narrow-minded, boringly bigoted, mean-spirited, quasi-moronic, pathologically parsimonious, coldly impolite hypocrites (and that's just the menfolk). The old wizened crones who peered out from behind security-chain-limited cracks with darting distrustful eyes, only to slam doors shut in my face if there were no freebies on offer, brought out a Raskolnikovian rage in me – and I could cheerfully have struck down dozens of Alyona McIvanovnas with a hatchet.

After only a few hours of North Carntynian hospitality (which has driven double-glazing salesmen to commit oral sex with the belching exhaust pipes of their Vauxhall Astras), my Humeian scepticism re Boswell's assertion that humankind *must* be immortal is greatly strengthened, since it would require that 'the trash of every age must be preserved'. If the residents of North Carntyne really are god-like immortals, I'd really rather not live forever; it would seem like an eternity sharing a cloud formation with these bastards, who'd bitch constantly about their wings not fitting properly and their harps being out of tune . . .

2 1888 is the 'official' and commonly accepted date of Celtic's inception, and it appears on everything from club stationery to the neon sign above the main entrance of Celtic Park. However, there is always one pedantic pub bore who will hold forth at tedious length about the historical inaccuracy of this date of formation, and he will invariably be the kind of nitpicker who refuses to accept 31 December 1999 as the last day of the 20th century (instead booking his *fin-de-siècle* function room for new-century celebrations for the last day in the year 2000 and citing as dubious authority the fact that a child does not merit a first birthday party until it is one year or 365 days old). Historical revisionists of this ilk take great pride in pointing out that Celtic Football and Athletic Club were *formed* in November 1887, 1888 merely being the year when the fledgling club *played* its first match – a friendly against Rangers – and 1888–89 being its first regular season of competition.

And if 1887 is accepted as the 'true' date, Celtic would no longer be in the record books as having won the League and Cup double in their centenary year of 1988 (which they partly achieved on a wave of 100th anniversary emotion!).

Glasgow Rangers 0
Bayern Munich 1

(European Cup Winners' Cup final, 31 May 1967)

In their excellent book *A Season in the Sun* (Lion Books, 1992), John Traynor and Tony Griffin make the laudable but implausible claim that Celtic's victory threatened to '"square the circle" by uniting the highly polarised football factions in Scotland', since the whole nation was supposedly on tenterhooks waiting to see if Rangers could win in Nuremberg seven days after Lisbon, which would have meant Glasgow being the first ever city to provide the winners of both major European cup competitions in the same year. To which assertion I can only respond: *absolute bollocks*!

Even at their most magnanimous, celebrating Celtic fans would have been happily indifferent to the possibility of their arch-rivals winning the European Cup Winners' Cup, since this was indisputably an inferior trophy to the European Cup – the former, at least in theory, being open to non-league and semi-professional teams who'd won their national cup competitions thanks to fortuitous home draws against weak opposition; whereas qualification for the latter depended on proving yourself to be the best and most consistent team in your country by winning the league title.

More realistically, Celtic supporters would have reacted to a Rangers win with barely disguised disappointment and despair. In the event, however, Rangers lost in extra-time and the spontaneous outbursts of joy from Celtic fans at this result must have been positively Lisbonesque in their bacchanalian ferocity – almost on a par with winning the European Cup for a second time only a week later. A Rangers victory would have taken the shine off our achievement, whereas their defeat made our achievement sparkle even more gloriously. And the extent to which Rangers' achievement in actually making the final of the ECWC was eclipsed by Celtic's total success is apparent from the fact that before researching this period I wasn't even aware that Rangers had reached a European final in 1967!

Virulent non-supporting of Rangers is inextricably linked with active supporting of Celtic, and my failure to have any conscious

43

memory of Rangers' disappointment in Nuremberg indicates that I had not yet evolved into a fully rounded Celtic fan by the end of May 1967; merely that I had taken the first tentative steps. For genuine, fully fanatical Celtic supporters, the two Friday mornings in weekly succession back at the office or factory after these two European finals must have been sheer, unadulterated bliss and today a perfect Saturday is only complete when a Celtic victory is followed by a gleeful announcement over the Parkhead tannoy to the effect that the Huns have lost away from home (or when a confirmed Celtic win on the *Grandstand* teleprinter is replaced by a Hun defeat scrolling up from the bottom of the television screen).

Celtic 4
Rangers 0

(Scottish Cup final, 26 April 1969)

I presume I watched this match from Hampden live on television, but to be perfectly honest I don't remember doing so. The reason for including it in my selection concerns Jock Stein's rampant and partly justified paranoia at the time with regard to the Scottish media in general and BBC Scotland Television in particular.

In his vastly entertaining volume of memoirs *Action Replays* (Chapmans, 1991), Archie Macpherson recounts how Stein refused to give the relatively inexperienced commentator either team numbers before kick-off or a post-match interview afterwards. Instead, Stein deigned to talk 'down the line' to David Coleman on *Grandstand*, broadcast live from London. In the television area of the enclosure, a banished and abashed Macpherson sat watching a television monitor replaying McNeill's second-minute headed goal. It then cut to Stein's broadly smiling face, and just before the actual transmission of the interview the Celtic manager commented gleefully to anchorman Coleman that 'Macpherson sounded sick there'. Ironically, Shettleston-born Macpherson was one of the few media or newspaper figures willing to give Celtic the recognition and praise which was their due.

Celtic 1
Feyenoord 2

(European Cup final, 6 May 1970)

1967	1970
Simpson	Williams
Craig	Hay
Gemmell	Gemmell
Murdoch	Murdoch
McNeill	McNeill
Clark	Brogan
Johnstone	Johnstone
Wallace	Wallace
Chalmers	Hughes (Connelly)
Auld	Auld
Lennox	Lennox

For Celtic's second European Cup final the nucleus of the Lisbon Lions' side was still intact, and the replacements for Craig and Chalmers – Davie Hay and John Hughes – were arguably even better players than those they replaced (although such a case could most *definitely* not be made for Brogan instead of Clark). Ronnie Simpson had retired in '69 aged 39, and his departure meant that the goalkeeping position would be a problem one and not properly filled until the arrival of Pat Bonner in the early '80s. (Although Simpson was not a *great* goalkeeper he was 'lucky', making unorthodox saves with various parts of his unathletic anatomy and having the admirable ability to retain concentration for long periods of time when he had nothing to do – unlike the rogues' gallery of flapping fairies and stationary statues that followed in his wake:[1] namely, Williams, Connaghan, Hunter, Baines and Latchford . . .)

Three years after the Lisbon victory, I had yet to see my heroes in the flesh, my father point-blank refusing to take me to Parkhead and my mother point-blank refusing to let me go on my own (which I was secretly grateful for since the prospect of making my own way to Celtic Park as a timid nine-year-old frankly terrified me – although this did not stop me sulking on home match days and hanging out of my back-bedroom window in full supporter's clobber in order to hear the roars which accompanied Celtic's many goals; but for one

45

home game early in season 1969–70 I did manage to pluck up enough courage to sincerely intend to go and see my first match. Empty ginger bottles had been assiduously collected since late August, and when I redeemed the collection of Irn Bru empties on the Saturday morning of 4 October I had the necessary entrance money for the boys' gate to the terracing. Decked out in tammy, scarf, football top and *boots*, I announced unilaterally my intention to go and see my team play Raith Rovers, and was promptly locked in my room to prevent me from so doing. In true Famous Five/Secret Seven style I escaped down the drainpipe, but only after hearing on my transistor radio that Celtic were 4–1 up at halftime. I wandered round to the side of the house, out of sight of the kitchen window, and sat disconsolately on the concrete steps leading up to the locked front door. When the full-time result of 7–1 was announced in the classified round-up I was beside myself in outraged indignation and decided to punish my mother for depriving me of the opportunity of being part of the 32,000 crowd which had enjoyed this high-scoring massacre. I lay down in the cabbage patch belonging to the Dolans, directly under their back-bedroom window and 25 feet or so below mine, face down and completely still, after having smashed my radio on the tarmacadamed path for dramatic effect. I must have lain like this for about half-an-hour – utterly motionless except for an occasional shuddering of the shoulders in suppressed hilarity – until my mother opened the bedroom door to call me for dinner at 5.15 p.m. exactly. The scene that would have presented itself to her widening eyes was an empty room with the window pushed up, wide open. She probably only looked out and down prior to closing it to check on the weather – to see if I would return from the game bedraggled and soaked to the skin. But the sight of my 'lifeless', prostrate body provoked a blood-curdling scream, which made the downy hairs on the back of my slim neck stand up. But I didn't. I lay there without moving a muscle, delighted and appalled in equal measure at the success of my subterfuge. In the elongated moments before my father materialised by my side carrying a blanket hastily whipped from my bed, I felt intensely alive, keenly aware of the blood coarsing through my veins and throbbing in my temples. When my father knelt beside me, crying fitfully, I wanted to stop playing dead so convincingly, but I was too petrified of the consequences which would undoubtedly follow to do so (in fact, I wished I *was* dead!). Even when he gently turned me over on to my back, I remained limp and lifeless. Only when the Dolan clan congregated around me and confirmed that an ambulance was on its way did I finally open my eyes and dryly mouth: 'Wh-where am I? Dad, am I in heaven now?' His relief soon turned to black fury and I was carried up the stairs by the loop of the belt at the back of my trousers. The soundness of my thrashing was even more ferocious than the circumstances may have seemed to merit, because I had pulled a similar stunt the previous year when my two-year-old sister Lynn was moved from my parents' front bedroom into my back bedroom. Displeased at having to share my room with a kid sister, I registered a protest by lying at the bottom of the 16 hall stairs – admittedly carpeted – in a mangled heap, with my neck in a 'snapped' position and my tongue lolling grotesquely from my mouth, which was set in a rictus of *rigor mortis*. At the top of the stairs my mother had fainted at the sight of my terrible tumble and had damn near fallen down them herself.

The 1970 final was played in the San Siro stadium in Milan – home ground of the beaten '67 finalists Inter! – and everything about the 1970 final seemed to be a horribly reversed mirror image of the '67 equivalent. Celtic were not the underrated underdogs but were the red-hot favourites instead, having destroyed Don Revie's dourly defensive English champions Leeds United, home and away, in both legs of the semi-final, as well as having disposed of glamour teams like Benfica and Fiorentina in earlier rounds. After becoming unofficial Champions of Britain by beating Leeds 2–1 at Hampden – and setting a European Cup attendance record of 136,505 in the process – Celtic's name seemed *destined* to be engraved on the Cup for a second time, especially after the second-round second-leg against Benfica in Portugal ended 3–3 on aggregate and Billy 'Caesar' McNeill had put his team through by correctly calling a toss of a coin. In fact, he called correctly twice – first for the right to call first (!) and secondly in the toss that would decide the issue, which according to the late and great sports-writer John MacKenzie saw the coin hit the changing-room floor tiles, roll against the referee's boot, and then go round in a wobbly circle before falling exhaustedly the right way up for the green-and-white legions biting their nicotine-stained nails outside (and if that wasn't a good omen and reliable sign from God it's hard to think of a better one).

But the San Siro was the reverse of the Estadio Nacional coin in almost every way, with Celtic's vast and vocal army of travelling support being outnumbered and drowned out by the claxon-honking Dutch fans (who lived only a few hours' drive from the stadium). Even the weather was in polar opposition to the sunny blue skies of Lisbon, it being strangely similar to a wet, dreich night in Glasgow. In addition, rural-reminiscent Lisbon with its oleander and cypress trees was replaced by an industrial landscape transposed from the notorious East End of Glasgow. Natural 'Mediterranean' light was replaced by harsh artificial floodlighting.

To compound the reversal of fortunes, Celtic scored *first* – through Gemmell in 30 minutes – only for Feyenoord to get a deserved equaliser within two minutes, scored by Israel (God apparently reverting to an Old Testament script for this particular evening). In addition, the Rotterdamers were playing the more attractive and attacking football, with Celtic pinned back on the ropes like Inter had been three years previously. Remarkably, Celtic held out for the first 90 minutes, and if they could have survived extra-time they would surely have rediscovered the confidence and determination of the semi-final in a replay, or rather lost the overconfidence and arrogance that had characterised the build-up to this game.

But the hubristic Stein had offended the gods, and his until-now apparently infallible ability to read games and make inspired substitutions and tactical changes had deserted him. Connelly replaced Auld but without altering the depressing nature of the game, whereas a substitution with Craig replacing Hay at right-back could have freed Hay to bolster the retreating and capitulating midfield – thereby salvaging a 1–1 draw and a chance to fight again. Instead, Feyenoord scored with only a few agonising minutes left, McNeill handling inside the box but only for referee Lo Bello to play advantage and allow Kindvall to lob the ball over keeper Williams (who may have saved the penalty if it had been awarded, or more plausibly a weary Wery may have missed it due to twanging nerves and twitching muscles).

I was in tears at the end, and even as an adult today I feel for the devastated nine-year-old of 25 years ago – especially since the unexpected defeat was completely unnecessary and patently avoidable. Archie Macpherson has observed that 'People have become very clever about this game and have laid the blame largely on Stein for misreading Feyenoord. He certainly underrated them and every player I have talked to from that team would admit it. On the other hand hardly anybody says that Feyenoord were simply the better side.' On the night, Archie, yes; on the night . . . But they could and should have been beaten. Dutch football may have been improving, but only steadily, the dramatic developments involving the national team reaching two World Cup finals and Ajax winning three European Cups in a row being a few years in the future.

If Celtic had been properly motivated there was no insurmountable reason why they could not have repeated the semi-final triumph over the supposedly invincible Leeds, a performance accurately described at the time as 'outrageously skilful yet disciplined'. Defeat by an odd, extra-time goal in a European Cup final may not seem like an absolute disaster, an excruciatingly painful nadir, but paradoxically it bloody well was. Because of it Celtic have remained single, once-only winners of the premier European tournament – like Aston Villa, Manchester United and *Feyenoord* – an impressive but distinctly *one-off* achievement. Great teams win the European Cup more than once, and truly great teams retain it the following year – eg Nottingham Forest, Benfica and Inter – while unbeatably brilliant teams win it three years in succession – like Real Madrid, Bayern Munich and *Ajax* (who won in '71, '72 and '73). If we had overcome Feyenoord, our subsequent record could have been comparable to that of Ajax – indeed, it could conceivably have replaced it! – and even if it wasn't we would surely have achieved more than just reaching European Cup semi-finals in 1972 and 1974 (in none of which four games did Celtic manage to score a goal against either Inter Milan or Atletico Madrid, and which were only reached after having been drawn against mediocre opposition in earlier rounds). Defeat in Milan was a watershed which signalled the end of Celtic as a superpower in European football; victory could have been a springboard which would have catapulted the club into the higher echelons on a permanent basis, up there with AC Milan, Barcelona and Liverpool all through the '70s, '80s and early '90s. Instead we are one amongst many solitary European Champions who are unlikely ever to win the trophy again – eg Red Star, Hamburg and Steua Bucharest.

Since 1980 Celtic have failed to reach the quarter-final stage of *any* European competition, and although the decade of the 1970s provided many entertaining and enthralling European nights (especially at Parkhead), it could all have been so much better . . .

FOOTNOTES

1 After Ronnie Simpson retired in 1969, Celtic's refusal to spend large amounts of money on a capable replacement proved to be a false economy, but like many clubs who willingly spend large fortunes on outfield players and next-to-nothing on goalies, Celtic seemed to believe that all goalkeepers were equally talented/untalented, or competent/incompetent, and that it therefore didn't really matter who was between the sticks, as long as he wasn't crippled and/or blind. The possibility of an individual goalkeeper with a footballing brain, keen reflexes and physical agility seemed to be a *non sequitur*, especially if acquiring such a goalkeeper required any financial premium to be paid.

Ironically, the player regarded as Celtic's best post-war keeper – along with Simpson – is

Paddy Bonner, who was signed for a nominal fee from Keadue Rovers of Donegal in 1978 (and even Simpson was signed from Hibs in the mid-'60s as a 'veteran' for a miserly few thousand quid).

But like anything else, you only get what you pay for with goalkeepers, and buying on the cheap Celtic got saddled with a bizarre collection of sad sacks, with only Simpson and Bonner proving to be anything like real bargains (and they were competent rather than brilliant).

Rangers 1
Celtic 1

(First Division, 2 January 1971)

After a guilty lull, during which I tried to ingratiate my way back into my parents' good books and make them forgive if not forget my mock suicide jump of October '69, I stepped up a stormy campaign of uncivil disobedience – in order to emotionally blackmail them into letting me attend a Celtic game.

I was perfectly prepared to lessen my exaggerated negotiating demands and accept paternal chaperoning, but I now wanted quite desperately to see a real football match in person. With no concessions from the parental management team on the kitchen table, however, I decided to step up the pressure with an intellectual work-to-rule, or more accurately go-slow, thereby hitting them where it would hurt most – namely in my report card grades (my pocket money basic was boosted by a generous system of productivity bonus payments for each gold, silver or bronze star awarded by my fifth-grade primary teacher Miss McDurie).

Every few months all of Primary Five were tested in Maths, Science, History, Art and English, and once the collective scores for every pupil were calculated we all played musical desks in accordance with the new intellectual pecking order. For me this normally meant moving up or down the Zephyrs – 12 desks divided into three groups of four – my median position in which was usually in the middle four, having previously deviated as high as second and as low as tenth. The Comets and Meteors were similarly organised, and the difference in IQ levels between the top Zephyr – top left desk – and bottom Meteor – bottom right desk (directly underneath Miss McDurie's mascaraed, myopic eye) – was probably about sixty Eysenck[1] points (140 as compared to 80, say).

My initial plan had been to ease back on English and History, my best subjects (and the easiest), and then to perform as mediocrely as usual in Maths, my worst subject and normally the last one to be taken. I anticipated a shallow slide into the bottom third of the intellectually professional Zephyrs (I had never been relegated into the mentally mediocre, part-time Comets, while demotion to the cerebrally challenged, amateur Meteors was a worst-case scenario too awful to even contemplate). However, that autumn we had been introduced to the joys of long division – which even today is still totally beyond me – and the Maths paper consisted of nothing but long-division questions, for which I only scored higher than wee Georgie Esslemont, the class gowk, and then only because he contrived to score a Norwegian-Eurovision-Song-Contest-equalling *null points*.[2] I don't remember my exact score but it must have been the equivalent of a typical Eurovision entry from Istanbul. To make matters very much worse, the Maths paper was weighted – no doubt to acquaint us with the concept of variable frequency distributions – and carried twice the amount of marks available in the other exams.

When the marks were being totalled, I had a sinking feeling in the pit of my stomach, despite having steeled myself for the possibility of having slightly miscalculated, and thereby having to drop into the top half of the Comets for the first time (which would have been a painful but bearable sacrifice). Doing some quick mental arithmetic, accurately for once, I was utterly appalled to see that I was indeed likely to be relegated, but all the way down to the Morlockian Meteors – all be it in 25th place to become 'Head Meteor' and milk monitor for the slow streamers. No longer would I be a high-flying Zephyr, most of whom could spell the word, or even a Comet, who spelled Zephyr almost correctly with just an occasional supernumary 'e', but I was to become a moronic Meteor, whose attempts to spell my old group name were along the illiterate lines of 'Zeffir'.

I was close to tears, like a professional footballer bribed to let in one soft goal for the 3–0 down opposition, only to see them fight back to win 4–3, sending the slightly corruptible sportsman's team down via the last relegation spot, which only swallows his team up due to a series of freakish last-minute goals elsewhere.

I did eventually burst into lachrymose emotion, but out of relief rather than despair, when for some inexplicable reason and for the first time ever Miss McDurie decided not to move everyone around. Her only explanation for not changing the seating arrangements was that it was too near Christmas. Bless her cotton socks (or rather her knee-length PVC boots from Chelsea Girl). To this day I still wonder if she simply took pity on a nine-year-old boy on the edge of a nervous breakdown, what with my gobsmacked expression, knitted eyebrows and overbrimming eyes.

Later that afternoon I was still too stunned by my disastrous miscalculation and dramatic reprieve to enjoy wee Georgie's annual party piece, when he stood in front of the blackboard, patted down his fright wig of unruly red curls, adjusted his hopelessly crooked NHS spectacles, and then regaled a near hysterical class with his unique rendition of *When Santa Got Stuck Up the Chimney*.

I blamed my disappointing exam results, with not a gold star to be seen, on the frustration of never getting to see my beloved Celtic play at Parkhead, and under protest my parents agreed in principle that I could go to a game 'sometime in the New Year' (my father's concession) or 'after I was ten years old' (my mother's compromise).

Nevertheless, Christmas Day 1970 provided a cornucopia of what amounted to hush money, as well as a pyramid of extravagant bribes in fancy wrapping paper: an Action Man (with accessorised Deep Sea Diver's Suit and homemade Celtic strip), a Spirograph, Hot Wheels car racing track, and various Celtic baubles and trinkets. All these wonderful presents – painfully paid for by savings withdrawn from the Co-op Christmas Club book – were opened and discarded with Little Lord Fauntleroy apathy, and I remained lying on my stomach slamming diecast model cars into the skirting board with what must have been monotonous and maddening regularity.

My father's nervous glance towards my mother was returned by a look of equivalent suspicion, which deepened when he sheepishly disappeared into their front bedroom. He returned moments later with a small brown envelope, the gummed seal of which had been clumsily stuck back with Sellotape. Upon being presented with it I feigned total and moody ignorance. 'What's this, Dad – more money?'

'Open it and see, son.'

The envelope contained two tickets for the 'Old Firm' derby at Ibrox, scheduled for the day after Ne'er Day. I bounced up and down on the sofa in a spontaneous victory dance, waving the precious briefs above my head like a deranged but diminutive dervish. I beamed at, thanked and hugged *both* parents, correctly surmising that possession of tickets for the Broomloan Road terracing didn't necessarily mean in my mother's eyes, and in maternal law, that I was nine-tenths of the way to my first professional football match.

My father looked pleased, but guilty as hell. My mother looked pissed off, but quietly gainsayable, too.

If not for the tragic nature of this game – or rather its immediate consequences – I would have been tempted to either stretch the truth or to have been economical with it, but thankfully this did *not* turn out to be the first match I ever attended. In reality, my mother had waited until Boxing Day before putting her foot down, when she announced I was banned from going to Ibrox, even if accompanied by my father, and he either returned the tickets to the Celtic offices in Kerrydale Street or sold them on to people at work. My mother agreed instead that I could go to see Celtic at Parkhead later in the season, 'playing against a well-behaved wee team with no hooligan supporters', and on the strict understanding that my father and I watched the proceedings from the comfort of seats in the grandstand and not from behind a terracing barrier in the Celtic End or Jungle. I duly protested and pleaded, in equal measure, but to no avail. But in a curious way I felt somewhat relieved, happy enough with this compromise arrangement and the promise of a less traumatic initiation into the mysteries of spectating as a fan.

Sixty-six people were killed at Ibrox on 2 January, with over a hundred seriously injured. But even if my father had taken me to the game, I would definitely still be alive today, since he had bought tickets for the Celtic part of the ground, well away from Stairway 13 where the Rangers fans were crushed and trampled to death. Indeed, like most of the crowd, we would probably have left the stadium in blissful ignorance, with only the Rangers last-minute equaliser spoiling my mood and preying on my mind.

The consequences of Colin Stein's 90th minute score may have been indirect, but even today they seem incredible to the point of evil fantasy, especially when remembering that the cocktail of death and destruction was brewed to a dangerously volatile level by Jimmy Johnstone's *89th* minute opener for Celtic. The distance between cause-and-effect on this occasion was so wide that even Chaos Theory couldn't have predicted the ensuing slaughter, 'caused' by Stein's equaliser. And even in retrospect there is no comfort to be gained from trying to make sense of the tragic consequences. I mean, putting a leather sphere between two wooden posts and under a timber crossbar results in 66 deaths, whereas missing the target would have saved all those lives. All one can say with any certainty is that the Ibrox Disaster was a *non sequitur* from hell.

Dying at something as life-enhancing but essentially trivial as a football match seems offensively incongruous and insultingly inappropriate at the best of times, but the Ibrox Disaster numbs the senses because of the sheer scale of numbers involved and the dreadful manner in which they died. Ceasing to exist on Stairway 13 was not a pleasant way to go, as dejected early leavers responded to the home crowd's roar of triumphant relief and tried to push their way up the steep steps to get a glimpse of the on-field celebrations, only to be met by an unstoppable tidal wave of human jetsam flowing towards the exit in the opposite direction after the *peremptory* final whistle. Those aware of and experiencing the congestion were, of course, unable to stop moving forward, being pushed on inexorably by the weight and momentum of the ever-increasing numbers from behind – from fellow fans totally unaware of the worsening situation. People died without their feet touching the ground, carried along by the irresistible flow, ribcages shattering, lungs collapsing, skulls compacting, with the breath literally being squeezed out of them. Others who stumbled died face down in red baize and mud, underneath an unbearably heavy weight of writhing human bodies.

After leaving the ground my father would have explained away the convoys of ambulances, fire engines and police cars as normal occurrences, assuming them to be in response to the usual outbreaks of vandalism, violence and villainy. The irony is that even with an all-ticket, capacity crowd of 80,000 there had only been two arrests all afternoon (for drunkenness).

My distraught mother, on the other hand, would have heard all about the disaster on TV or radio, and her anxious wait for our return would have been well-nigh unendurable. And once safely home I would have been banned from attending football matches for life – or at least until I was 18. No question about it.

Nobody we knew was amongst the dead, but the town of Markinch in Fife suffered disproportionately, and we had friends and relatives who lived there. Hence a lot of anxious telephone calls and nervous nail-biting. This was my first real experience of death, and I well remember the gruesome pictures in the tabloid newspapers – of mangled crush barriers, covered corpses in serried rows and numerous floral tributes.

Years later I would watch live on television as the disasters of Hillsborough, Heysel and Bradford played themselves out on screen, getting angrier and angrier because spectators at football matches were still dying *en masse*. I suppose I shouldn't have been surprised, since in the intervening years I had been swept along in dangerously scary surges by out-of-control crowds, on *numerous* occasions.

The tragedy at Ibrox had no profound effect on me in terms of my naive, inchoate and unsophisticated religious belief, although I remember a rainy evening spent discussing the 'theological implications' with the two daughters of the Dolans from downstairs, Kathleen and Elizabeth. Their priest and my minister both used the Ibrox Disaster as the subject for their respective Sunday sermons, and we earnestly debated why God let bad things happen to good people.

The Church of Scotland line was that such tragedies afforded ordinary people the opportunity to be heroic, and because I had just read the *Chronicles of Narnia* I recognised his citing of writer C.S. Lewis.[3] The Church of Rome representative had obviously resisted the temptation to cite Job 14:7 – 'Consider, what innocent ever perished, or where have the righteous been destroyed?' – as authority for interpreting the 66 Protestant deaths as some kind of sectarian divine judgment from above.

Although Elizabeth was eight, while I was nine and Kathleen was in her mid-teens, we were all quite content to believe that such disasters were somehow the inevitable consequence of free will – with God, Jesus and the Virgin Mary/Holy Ghost on 24-hour standby like celestial emergency services ready to provide the spiritual equivalent of bottled oxygen, warm blankets and hot tea. The concept of eternal life for believers, and the paradox of God's omnipotence and divine goodness, had us hopelessly confused, however, but rather than succumb to doubt and uncertainty we looked forward in trusting anticipation and good faith to the moment in the hereafter when God would explain everything to our angelic satisfaction.[4]

My only Ibrox-inspired nightmares were waking ones, in bed, when I'd try to recreate the horror of being crushed to death. I'd snuggle down underneath the covers and then pull the sheets around me as tight as they would go. While imagining a dead weight of human bodies on top of me, I could just about keep the sense of claustrophobic panic at bay. To test myself further I then imagined that I was completely immured in fast-drying cement, which when hardened to a solid mass left just enough breathing space for my chest to rise and fall. But if I fully inflated my lungs, my breast bone met resistance from an inexorable weight. At which point I normally exploded from my bedclothes like a Polaris missile from a nuclear submarine punching its way through the surface of the sea, hyperventilating like an asphyxiating asthmatic because

I couldn't have taken another second of immovable, if imaginary, entrapment.

Victims of the Ibrox Disaster, of course, had no choice but to endure the unendurable, second after second, until the merciful moment when they lost consciousness and their last breath left them . . .

FOOTNOTES

1 Instead of the universally detested eleven-plus exam, which irrevocably branded little kids as either future grammar-school successes *or* secondary-modern failures, I sat an official IQ test at age eleven, when my IQ was recorded in the school files as 120 (ie of above average intelligence but not by a helluva lot). This was achieved despite ignoring all arithmetic and mathematical questions, in favour of the more interesting and enjoyable language-facility sections, and only when informed 'off the record' of my selective approach to sitting IQ tests did my parents agree to leave my primary headmaster's office and desist from demanding a second test administered by an independent child psychologist. (I should point out, however, that even if I had attempted the numerous number puzzles, the result wouldn't have been *dramatically* different.) And although not as incontrovertibly deterministic as the draconian eleven-plus, Education Department IQ tests in the late '60s and early '70s still played a major role in deciding future class streaming at secondary school, which I went through in the second-stream registration classes of 1B, 2B, 3B, 4B and 5B, despite yet another parental delegation aimed at getting their child prodigy bumped up to 1A.

As for the predictive utility of IQ tests, there may be something to them if the actual performances of the two individuals at the extreme ends of the 80–140 spectrum are considered. Wee Georgie Esslemont, the class dunce, didn't even make it into registration class 1E of Smithycroft Secondary, presumably being shunted off to Kennyhill Remedial School for the congenitally thick (or special need school to give it its politically correct description).

Then again he may have moved home to California and gone on to become a computer-programming millionaire (but then again I very much doubt it, because any 12-year-old whose main playground recreation was running around with arms outstretched shouting 'Gigantor!' before smashing into brick walls at Mach 1 is hardly likely to have developed into an intellectual overachiever). Caroline '140' Lappin, on the other hand, did go on to achieve something like her full potential, the only primary school contemporary I've ever seen staring out at me from the Arts pages of the *Herald* and *List* – as Administrator for the Scottish National Youth Theatre.

Nevertheless, Intelligence Quotients basically measure nothing accurately but the ability of individuals to score well in IQ tests, and Hans Jurgen Eysenck himself would probably accept there is some validity in this observation, since Eysenck is about the only psychologist I know who appears to be playing with a full deck of cards in the mental poker game of life (all be it with a few unpredictable jokers in his pack – eg *Race, Intelligence and Education* from 1971). And anyone who was a virulent critic of pseudo-scientific and intellectually pretentious psychotherapy in general, and fraudulent Freudian psychoanalysis in particular, couldn't have been all bad. He common-sensibly opted for behaviour therapy techniques, treating *symptoms* rather than rooting around in the overrated and underverified subconscious at $200 an hour. A disciple of Pavlov, he would have understood my conditioned reaction to any IQ-type tests, because since an early age I have salivated like a Pavlovian dog upon hearing an examination bell ring.

2 If Scottish football is handicapped by Continentalcentric decisions emanating from UEFA headquarters in Geneva, the same objectively verifiable claim of discrimination can be made

on behalf of British competitors in the Eurovision Song Contest. The UK has come second on a record number of occasions, due to perfidious Latins and the Dublin jury conspiring to rob us of deserved and outright victory. Indeed, any joint-honours graduate in Media Studies and Politics struggling to think of a suitable PhD proposal could do worse than the following thesis title: *Tactical Voting and Political Point Scoring in the Eurovision Song Contest – Case Studies in Brutal Brit Bashing (With Special Reference to Scotland's Very Own Lulu and Kenneth McKellar)*.

3 As a child I enjoyed Lewis's *The Lion, The Witch and the Wardrobe*, but as an adult I read *The Problem of Pain* with mounting disappointment, which soon turned to contempt and outrage. As a populariser and proselytiser of Christian ethics and theology a degree of simplification and generalisation was to be expected, but Lewis's apologia for the existence of physical and spiritual pain is an offensively sentimental and facile whitewash. The masochistic old buffer positively welcomed that which was painful, since it permitted cheery Christians to become 'perfect through suffering'. In essence his argument was that pain is an efficient and indispensable indicator of underlying malfunctions – physical and spiritual – and that we would all look aesthetically asinine with a flashing red light bulb on our foreheads instead.

But what else can you expect of an author who dedicated *The Problem of Pain* to 'The Inklings' – a sherry-drinking support group of like-minded, Hobbit-homaging academics at Magdalen College, Oxford – which included that hard-boiled dirty realist JRR Tolkein (to whom the maddeningly middle-brow *Screwtape Letters* was dedicated)? Furthermore, old CS was so moved by God striking down his young wife Joy with cancer that in gratitude he penned the delightfully titled autobiography *Surprised by Joy*, as well as the desperately moving *A Grief Observed* (which like all his books inspired a generation of *Daily Mail* readers, not to mention almost all contemporary British film-makers).

4 As a child my faith was unquestioning and strong, and about the time of the Ibrox Disaster I read a film tie-in paperback borrowed from Dennistoun Public Library, based on *The Planet of the Apes* movie. In it one of the human astronauts, catapulted into the future, comes across the now dominant apes attending a religious service in a subterranean cavern. Hidden behind a stalagmite, the man watches in bewilderment as the hairy primates supplicate themselves before an altar, which supports a relic of late 20th-century civilization: an unexploded nuclear warhead. The monkeys, as well as evolving into the dominant species on earth, have also developed a sense of religious belief, in which the gleaming and polished nuclear missile head plays a pivotal part. By touching the bomb the devout monkeys were convinced that they were securing personal immortality for their souls, and that upon physical death they would join the host of ape angels in hirsute heaven.

The man turns to his female companion and remarks with feeling that he would give his right arm to *believe* as sincerely as the apes. I knew the character was an atheist, but at the time I didn't understand why he hadn't offered to forfeit a limb for *actual* immortality (the *POTA* books were surprisingly sophisticated in their construction and representation of human-like ape society). In later life I would appreciate the subtle distinction, since many intelligent non-believers envy the belief systems of the various religions and wish that they too could *believe* as sincerely – for although the unreverberate blackness of the abyss is not removed from human destiny, it no longer has the same dramatic dread in the day-to-day daydreams of atheistic mortals.

Looking back now as a devout atheist myself, and thinking about the Ibrox Disaster, it is clear that it was no Act of God (as insurance companies would have termed it). Even if 'God' exists, He neither caused the disaster (to punish the wicked Protestants) nor could He have prevented it (to protect the virtuous Protestants). The 66 deaths were, if anything, the result of God playing dice with the cosmos; or more accurately they were caused by the second law of thermodynamics – the law of entropy. Sixty-six people died on that January afternoon simply because events in the material world happen at random. Why did 66 people have to die? It may not be very reassuring but quantum physics provides the only rational answer.

Celtic 6
Clyde 1

(First Division, 1 May 1971)

The first game I ever attended. And it's almost a complete blank. All I really remember is a knot of fear in my stomach, which got tighter and tighter every time Clyde got out of their own half in the second 45 minutes. I dreaded a second score for the 'Bully Wee' in case my father's polite handclapping in acknowledgment got him in trouble with the amazingly foul-mouthed and ferociously drunken Celtic supporters who surrounded us (it would be years later before Celtic lost another goal in our joint presence, never mind a game).

Contradicting maternal orders, we somehow ended up in the Jungle terracing, the sway from the large crowd being so powerful that I was tied to a wooden crush barrier with my father's belt, while he stood directly behind me trying to absorb the swaying pressure from the forwards-and-backwards moving crowd. Mercifully he missed Clyde's solitary goal, scored in the 46th minute while he took advantage of the half-time interval to empty his bursting bladder.

Still scared silly during the 30-minute walk home I readily agreed that we would never go on to the terraces again, and I promised faithfully not to tell my mother that we had ended up in the Jungle; otherwise she would have gone absolutely ape.

Looking back now I can see where my father's carefully laid plans for my first game went awry. After the Ibrox Disaster he had been waiting for Celtic to wrap up their sixth League title in a row, so that any outstanding games would have been academic. However, the flag was not clinched until 30 April, when Celtic beat Ayr United 2–0 at Hampden, the change of home venue to the national stadium being necessitated by ongoing repairs and refurbishment to the Parkhead grandstand. And although Celtic were playing their last League game at Celtic Park just two days later, the stand was either still closed or operating at reduced capacity – or so my father had, possibly incorrectly, assumed. Whatever the reason we ended up in the terracing, which was more congested than might have been expected for a meaningless match because of some astute PR hype by Jock Stein. Billing the 'historic' fixture as the last chance for supporters to see the Lisbon Lions in action (before transfers and retirements altered the legendary line-up for good), a massive crowd of 35,000 turned up to acclaim their heroes and pay their final respects.

Celtic 1
Patrick Thistle 4

(League Cup final, 23 October 1971)

Since 1967 I had become used to Celtic winning trophy after trophy, so much so that listening to this game on the radio I couldn't believe my beetroot-reddening ears. Newly promoted Thistle[1] obviously hadn't read the Radio Scotland script for *Sportsound*, and straight from kick-off they besieged Evan Williams in the Celtic goal – breaching it four times in under 40 minutes of fantasy football. Brought up on a rich diet of solid success, I was close to choking on this new diet of indigestible failure.

At half-time I switched off the transistor radio – Bob Crampsey and Co were having multiple orgasms on air – and hammered five great goals past Alan Rough using a practice golf ball (while at Ibrox Teddy Bears headed for the exits in droves, forgetting the League match in progress in order to make their rabble-rousing way to Hampden, where they set up celebratory picnics in the South Stand car park).

In the second half, Rough had a purple patch of great goalkeeping, and only Kenny Dalglish managed to put the ball past the young 20-year-old keeper (an erratic goalie who nevertheless always played out of his skin against us, but who when signed for short-term cover in 1988 only managed two clean sheets in seven overweight appearances).

Watching the TV highlights that night on *Sportsreel*, through a small gap between two cushions held up to my face, I was too young to feel any magnanimity towards the Thistle players as they collected their winners' medals (the first Jags to do so in 50 years). Centre-half and captain Billy McNeill may have missed the game because of injury, and Jimmy Johnstone may have limped off after 20 minutes, but there was no real excuse. Such unpredictable Cup final shocks were supposed to be restricted to south of the border and the Twin Towers of Wembley, and the greater good of Scottish football was the last thing on my mind.

If McNeill had played, however, Evan Williams's future might have been very different, but in the event he carried the can for this oh-so-humiliating defeat. Unpredictability is part of football's fascination, since results depend on the performances of fallible human beings (especially those of Celtic goalkeepers). Within 24 hours Stein went out and bought a replacement keeper for five-feet-ten-inch Williams, who was at fault for at least two of the goals, in the unco-ordinated shape of six-feet-two-inches Denis Connaghan. Although St Mirren's Connaghan had a four-inch height advantage, he was almost equally inept, with a 39 per cent shut-out rate, as compared to Williams's 40 per cent (Ronnie Simpson's average was a commendable 48 per cent). For the next year-and-a-half Williams and Connaghan attempted to outclown each other between the posts on almost alternate Saturdays, until the arrival of the even more unreliable Ally Hunter from Kilmarnock.

The first Monday back at school was the first time that I'd wished I wasn't the only Celtic-supporting pupil at Carntyne Primary. By 4.15 p.m. I'd been involved in four separate fights (not counting the ambushes that had been laid-in-wait for my walk home). Being bullied was not a major problem as a rule, even although when nervous or scared I seemed to suffer from dermographic skin writing of the forehead, which spelled out HIT ME in fiery red letters. I was picked on by bullies who didn't know any better, but rarely more than once because I always fought back in a frenzied parody of Marquis of Queensberry boxing etiquette combined with open-handed ju-jitsu slashes to exposed windpipes.

During the morning break I'd reduced Wanker Wylie to tears, but during the lunch hour I had to stand up to Joe 90, a bespectacled dwarf whom Wanker Wylie used to beat up on with one hand tied behind his back. On paper Joe 90 should have been a handbag-at-six-paces walkover – like Partick Thistle! – but he always had the whammy over me. A borderline sociopath, my legs just turned to jelly when he said, 'Hold on a minute', took off his NHS glasses and instead of putting them safely in a case or satchel stamped on them, shattering frames and lenses alike.

Bruised and bloodied after losing to a psychopathic dwarf, the afternoon play break brought more physical intimidation. John Dunn, two years older and built like a brick outhouse, slapped me on the back of the head four times – once for every Thistle goal, he said – and seeing things through a red mist I watched him walk away towards the bike shed for a sly smoke. I ran after him and smacked him hard on the head with an open palm, but I was too scared to say that the single slap represented Dalglish's consolation goal. Hard as I was running away, I could sense rather than hear him catching up with me. I stopped, turned and lashed out with my right foot all in one instantaneous movement, after which Dunn went down like a sack of potatoes, holding his crotch and gulping like a beached whale for oxygen. A crowd gathered round and counted him out, from ten down. Then they hoisted me up on their shoulders and carried me round the boys' playground, showing me off to the other bullied ten-year-olds and even younger terrorised tots. Embarrassed but ebullient, I raised my arms, interlinked my fingers and took their acclaim. At four o'clock I tried to escape via the girls' playground, but one of Dunn's weightlifting cronies caught me. It took six of them to get me pinned on my back, but once down it took me a long, long time to get back up.

FOOTNOTES

1 Partick Thistle's following is a strange mixture. Situated as they are in Maryhill, the hard core of local supporters are working class, drawn from the surrounding tenements. Like Chelsea, however, the Jags are a 'fashionable' team to support, the Firhill stand catering for AB professionals from nearby North Kelvin and Woodside, bourgeois supporters who relish the club's reputation for dramatic inconsistency. The third strata of support is that of conscientiously objecting Catholics, from all over Glasgow, who refuse to support Celtic for 'blindly sectarian reasons'. These religious *refuseniks* cut across all social boundaries – from sports editors, through chartered accountants, to train drivers – but they are sceptically regarded by both Thistle and Celtic diehards alike. Equivalent conscientiously objecting Protestant Jags just do not exist. And if non-local Jags are romantics at heart, fans of Clyde and Queens Park, who do not come from Rutherglen or Mount Florida, respectively, are either hopeless optimists (Clyde's Shawfield Stadium incorporated a speedway and greyhound racing track) or masochistic eccentrics (Hampden being home to the anachronistic 'gentlemen amateurs' of the Spiders). In 1993 Clyde moved to Cumbernauld New Town, via Douglas Park, Hamilton, but they have yet to establish a significant local support.

Celtic 2
Airdrie 0

(First Division, 15 January 1972)

This was the second Celtic game that I got to go to – an early birthday present – and my father took me to the re-opened Front Stand (which replaced the old enclosure) where we sat in the new seating. The old roof, with its supporting pillars and numerous restricted-view seats underneath, had been replaced the previous summer by a state-of-architectural-art angular structure, which cost a staggering £250,000 (or if you prefer, the equivalent market value of *seven* Tommy Gemmells, who had been sold to Nottingham Forest for £35,000 in December). Aesthetically, it was an impressive piece of modern architecture, especially with the 100-seat press box suspended from its roof like a static blimp, and in which vertigo-suffering journalists have been known to pass out. But although visually successful, it has to be conceded that the new stand was from the outset a bit of a functional nightmare. With any kind of northerly wind blowing, patrons were cruelly exposed to the elements, and occupants of the cheap seats in the Front Stand got well and truly soaked whenever it rained.

Despite a freezing January gale, I was snugly content with my Bovril, pie, Wagon Wheel, programme and George Connelly rosette. Connelly was my favourite player (along with Jim Craig) and I was looking forward to seeing him in the flesh for the first time (he hadn't played against Clyde). Being taciturn, withdrawn and introspective I felt a natural affinity towards him, whereas voluble, confident and extrovert Gemmell, for example, although admired, could never have been my special hero, my role-playing model. Connelly was also supremely talented, and although somewhat slow his ball skills, tackling and vision merited his tag as 'the Scottish Beckenbauer' (or the Scottish Benniebauer as I thought of myself while trying to emulate his keepie-uppie *average* of 2,000). Early in this game he dispossessed Drew Jarvie, nutmegged him and then dribbled past two opponents – all in his own penalty area.

Goals from Dalglish and Bobby Lennox won the game for Celtic, and the only cloud on my personal horizon that afternoon was the behaviour of my father. To be fair, a Saturday afternoon at a football stadium, especially Celtic's, was not his idea of an enjoyable break – in fact it bored him to distraction – and he did actually agree to take me. But only under sufferance, and he sat there making no effort to disguise his chore-like duty. So much so that *I* felt guilty, and spent half the game asking him sympathetic and solicitous questions in a futile attempt to draw him out of himself.

Towards the end of the game, when Airdrie were hitting long hopeful balls at Connaghan in search of a consolation goal – easy fields which the Celtic goalie was nevertheless punching clear nervously and deflecting for unnecessary corners – my father started to take a genuine interest in the proceedings for the first time. Behind me an irate Celtic fan was spraying spit all over my bobble hat, while bastarding and fucking his adjectival way through Connaghan's litany of weaknesses (weren't seated supporters in the more expensive grandstand supposed to be better behaved?). I was petrified that Airdrie would score, that my father would disgrace himself by standing to applaud the goalscorer, that he would get a 'moothful a' heedies', and that it would all be my fault when he died on the operating table.

'Dad, you're not going to cheer if Airdrie get a goal, are you?'

'Cheer? *Cheer*? I'm going to give that foul-mouthed eejit behind us a two-fingered up-yours and then I'm going to shout "Away the Airdrie Diamonds – gem of a goal"' (but whispered so that the nutter behind couldn't overhear).

The stark truth is that my father would have been too *scared* himself to react to an Airdrie goal, except possibly for a self-satisfied smirk, but I didn't know that at the time. With tears welling I asked to leave before the final whistle, just to get him out of there, and on the walk home I realized for the first time that my daddy wasn't the perfect paterfamilias I'd always loved unconditionally and without qualification.

The further from the ground we got the cheerier he became, until close to home he bought me a bar of Bournville chocolate, which he let me eat before the tea that was waiting for us – the Saturday night heart-attack special of pork chop, chips and onions (all fried). As I swallowed the bitter chocolate without really tasting it – to finish the thick slab before Mum saw it – my father explained that one of the reasons he didn't want me going to football matches was rude drunks like the one behind us in the stand.

I had been shocked and appalled by the ferocity of the language, and I could see my father's point when he commented that such behaviour in a theatre or cinema would have got the miscreant ejected, if not arrested. I'd always admired my father for his restrained language and above-board behaviour, but when he told me his Singapore anecdote again, on the concrete steps outside the front door, I began to feel somewhat ambivalent towards him. The gist of the story was that when docked in the Malaysian harbour port for three days he gave up his right to two nights' shore leave – to which he was entitled as an engineering officer – because the able seamen were drunken rabble-rousers, like the moron behind us, who'd have attempted to drag him into 'dens of iniquity'. Instead of getting drunk in a seedy nightclub, and whoring the night away with nubile Oriental prostitutes, he'd stayed in his cabin reading paperback Westerns and sipping iced Johnnie Walker Black Label (and this even before becoming engaged to my mother).

The moral of this tale, I suppose, was that your average football supporter with shore leave in an exotic Third World city would spend his time drinking cirrhotic cocktails and sticking his pecker in venereally diseased orifices. Ruffling my hair as we walked up the carpeted hall stairs, I remember thinking that a few bar crawls and some sexy massages might have done him some good. No wonder he was unpopular on-board ship and never kept in contact with any of his sea-going companions. They probably thought he had a fire poker up his ass.

Then again, he lived on his nerves, and if solitary relaxation with a trashy novel and a wee drink was his way of coping with uncouth subordinates and unreliable coal-fired engines, what of it? If only George Connelly could have found a similar coping mechanism. Unable to bear the pressures of the modern game, and his celebrity status, Connelly should have been an all-time Celtic great, the natural successor to Billy McNeill.

But after fighting alcoholism, unsuccessfully, refusing to board a Berne-bound plane at Glasgow Airport along with the rest of the Scottish international party (after having surrendered his passport!), going AWOL from club training, confessing that he'd rather have been a long-distance lorry driver than a professional footballer (to the disbelief of all long-distance lorry drivers everywhere), breaking an ankle in a suicidal tackle against Berne at Parkhead (just to get out of the 1974 World Cup squad?), after all this Celtic finally lost patience with their wayward genius and sacked him in 1975, when Connelly should have been at the peak of his career, aged 26.

Tragic is the only word to describe Connelly's decline, a descent into the ditches of *road-digging* made all the more poignant by this quiet Fife man's apparently nerveless debut as a 17-year-old, when in front of over 60,000 people he entertained the crowd before a Cup-Winners' Cup tie with Dinamo Kiev by keepie-upping his way round Parkhead's red baize running track – without the ball ever touching the ground. Thrown in against teams like Rangers, Fiorentina and Czechoslovakia, in vitally important games, he strolled through each 90 minutes. But after being voted Scottish Football Writers' Player of the Year in 1973, with the attendant increase in unwanted publicity and pressure, his world started to come apart at the seams. Surprisingly, he played on the losing Celtic side in *seven* major cup finals, including the European Cup final of 1970.

A born loser? Maybe, but he's the only Celtic player I ever wrote a fan letter to (c/o Falkirk FC, which he joined in the summer of 1976 only to be booted out by Christmas). I never got a reply but I hope he got the letter. In it I simply thanked him for all the pleasure he'd given me over his few short years at Celtic Park.

However, Jim Craig, my other hero, was ambitious and determined, but despite being the sole reason for Celtic winning the *Quiz Ball* trophy on television I never sent *him* a fan letter (which would have needed forwarding to South Africa in 1972, where the ex-right back emigrated to practise his dental skills on kruggerand-rich Afrikaners; but only for a year, after which Craig returned to Britain to play for Sheffield Wednesday, restoring his moral integrity in the eyes of his many admirers).

Celtic 0
Inter Milan 0

(European Cup semi-final second leg, 19 April 1972)

The Goalkeeper's Fear of the Penalty is as nothing compared to the *Striker's Trepidation* at the prospect of having to score from 12 yards, with only a nothing-to-lose-but-potentially-heroic figure to beat. Professional footballers should score from the penalty spot nine times out of ten, but the more important the kick the less the odds favour the taker.

Sometimes the outcome is obvious, and all football fans have experienced the 100 per cent certainty of success or failure before a ball has been blootered or placed. Everyone I know who attended this game, and who saw the goalless semi-final go to a penalty shoot-out decider (even after extra-time), swear that they *knew* Dixie Deans was going to miss Celtic's first kick, after Mazzola had opened the scoring with the same ease as he had exhibited five years previously in Lisbon. Watching the TV highlights on STV without knowing the score, I knew too, even from behind the cushion-bagged sofa, a prone viewing position normally reserved for episodes of *Dr Who* when the Daleks were 'exterminating' their way through a conveniently stairless Universe. Nevertheless, precognitive forewarning was not the same as being psychologically forearmed. As the ball ballooned over the bar

65

75,000 hearts in the stadium sank, as feelings of *déjà vu* and despair mixed horribly. If forced to put an unopened pay packet on one Celtic player to score, Deans would have been the unanimous choice – a prolific goalscorer memorably described as 'a rogue elephant of a centre forward' (with, we all assumed, not a nervous bone in his bulky body).

All the other penalties were successfully converted, so that Celtic went out of the competition 4–5 on aggregate. And Deans was inconsolable, because he knew that he had *bottled* his penalty attempt. A great diving save from Vieri would have been hard enough to bear, but to have wilted under the pressure and blown a European Cup final place was something altogether more painful.

'If only' mantras can destroy sanity if overplayed inside anyone's head, but football supporters chant them with religious regularity. 'Might have beens' and 'what ifs' can also be applied to this game, by the score, one of the most sinisterly seductive being: What if Deans had remained on the bench instead of replacing Dalglish as a second-half substitute (Stein had expected the Italians to play for a penalty shoot-out, and in readiness therefore Deans was introduced to the play especially for this eventuality)? At Seamill, in preparation for possible penalties, Deans had been knocking them in as if genetically programmed to do so. However, if Dalglish had played out the 120 minutes and taken Celtic's first penalty, he would probably have scored, at least judging by his penalty conversion in his first 'Old Firm' match the previous August, when the 20-year-old was so confident that he bent down to tie a non-loose lace tighter before beating Peter 'Lighthouse' McCloy from the spot (in a League Cup game at Ibrox in front of over 70,000 spectators).

It's probably worth pointing out that even if Deans had scored, Celtic may well still have lost. Having missed, there was *less* pressure on Celtic's other nominated penalty takers – Jim Craig, Jimmy Johnstone, Pat McCluskey and Bobby Murdoch (whose final successful penalty was utterly academic) – but if Deans had scored who's to say Craig *et al* would have followed suit? I think we can assume that the Italians would have scored five times whatever, since during this period they were renowned for their penalty-preference personalities, and Celtic had Evan Williams doing his ball-dodging routine on the goal-line, with his uncanny ability to go the wrong way four times out of five.

Stein's choice of penalty takers after Deans is interesting in that two defenders – Craig and McCluskey – were preferred to two goal-scoring forwards, Lou Macari and Bobby Lennox. The paradox of defenders being preferred to specialist goalscorers when penalties have to be taken continues to this day for many teams and it's a tactic that I've never been able to comprehend. Jim Craig, for example, in normal open play rarely if ever found himself in the middle of the opposing box with only the keeper to beat. Is it simply that defenders have a lesser weight of expectation on their shoulders to hinder them in their no-nonsense run-ups (defenders after all do tend to favour the blooter method)? Are forwards caught in a surrealistic, slow-motion nightmare, amazed and appalled at having an almost infinite amount of time to do something which they normally have to accomplish in the blink of an eye without even thinking?

The psychology of penalty taking is still barely understood by either its exponents or students, but converting the damn things is definitely more of a mental rather than a technical dilemma. There are only three basic options: sidestep the ball to the right *or* left of the keeper, as near to the post as possible without actually hitting it, ideally sending the keeper the wrong way too, *or* alternatively blast the ball and beat the keeper with unstoppable power, even if he does get a staved finger to it. Decide – and then bloody well do it.

Albert Camus, Algerian goalie and French Existentialist, never took a penalty but it would have been interesting to watch him try (if, say, a penalty shoot-out against a Structuralist XI went all the way to the respective goalkeepers during sudden death). Would Camus have beaten an upright and non-diving Russian Formalist like Vladimir Propp? And if a penalty shoot-out is inherently meaningless and absurd, would Camus have exercised his will effectively by scoring, thereby bringing individual meaning to the experience? Or would he have deliberately ballooned the ball over the crossbar, thereby defining himself through negative action? And what would he have made of that old Romantic bourgeois Hamish McAlpine,[1] the Dundee United keeper who used to take all of his side's penalties whenever one was awarded during regular 90-minute matches? Come to think of it, Camus taking a penalty at Tannadice doesn't bear thinking about. He'd probably have stood over the ball for 30 agonising seconds, before whipping out a revolver and shooting a suspiciously dark supporter in the George Fox Stand (since United fans are known colloquially as 'Arabs').

In the Rotterdam final Inter met Ajax and were soundly thrashed 2–0, both goals coming from one Johan Cruyff.

FOOTNOTES

1 Goalkeepers taking penalties has a certain bizarre logic – who better to know the most difficult type of shot to stop? – but like most teams Celtic have never had one of these gamekeeper-turned-poacher eccentrics, which is probably just as well since most Celtic keepers have had great difficulty in just getting *goal-kicks* out of their own box. In 1967, however, Celtic's quarter-final opponents Vojvodina had a goalkeeper who took penalty kicks – Pantelic – and although the Yugoslavs didn't get a penalty over the two legs, a missed one at Celtic Park would have been a sight to see, especially if the Jungle had a home goal to cheer straight from any such miss, with Pantelic stranded in the centre-circle in a futile attempt to race back. The corrugated roof would have come off.

McAlpine I remember with affection, since the Tangerine Terror often missed his penalties, necessitating a desperate sprint, long-legged but stiff-backed, the length of the pitch to get back in position. McAlpine lost a lot of bad goals, but never, I think, directly as a result of one of his own penalty misses.

Celtic 6
Hibernian 1

(Scottish Cup final, 6 May 1972)

If I'd been a neutral Martian watching this, the Red Planet would probably now have an extraterrestrial branch of the Hibernian Supporters' Club, since romantically inclined football fans have a tendency to adopt well-beaten teams when trying to figure out allegiances between two unknown clubs. And since this game Hibs have always been my 'second team'. Part of the attraction was the aesthetics of their strip, the romance of their name and their free-flowing style of play (although for the most of this match it was in a backwards direction).

Dixie Deans was man-of-the-match, notching a superb hat-trick and redeeming himself for the missed penalty against Inter. Watching his second goal on TV, described hysterically by commentator Alex Cameron, even my father had to concede that it was 'a priceless example of tanner ba' football', although he couldn't resist describing the Hibernian defence as 'headless chickens trapped in full-beam headlights' (*sic*). Deans went past the Hibs goalie Herriot, bore down on goal *along the by-line*, cut back to give himself an acute angle, beating a defender and Herriot *again* in the process, before poking the ball into the empty net. I celebrated by copying his forward roll of joy, crash-landing on to my father's slippers and knocking the lightbulb of the Dolans' downstairs ceiling lamp out of its plastic socket as a result. An amazing crowd of 106,103 were lucky enough to witness this epiphanic goal in person.

No wonder Celtic fans worshipped Deans (who like Kenny Dalglish was originally a Rangers fan!). And to think that if Stein hadn't signed the undisciplined rogue from Motherwell in 1971, when he was serving yet another suspension, Deans would probably have dropped back into the head-banging and testicle-tugging nightmare of Scottish junior football. All heart and honest brawn, Deans was the first Celtic forward who became an especial hero, and I was devastated when he was transferred to Luton in 1976. His character is best summed up by one of his last performances for Celtic, against St Johnstone, when he lost two front teeth. Up until doing the research reading for this book, I'd always believed that Dixie had *swallowed* the dislodged teeth, but according to *An Alphabet of the Celts* by Eugene MacBride, Martin O'Connor and George Sheridan (Polar Publishing, 1994) he merely spat them out before playing on with blood gushing from his mouth. Whether swallowed or discarded, the teeth incident illustrates a wonderfully macho determination (I know that if I lost just one front tooth I would have been rooted to the centre circle, blinking away venal tears, with the yellow tooth mounted on an open but trembling palm – even if the opponents had been St Etienne rather than St Johnstone).

Jim Craig played his last game for Celtic against Hibs, before retiring prematurely early to pursue his dental career in South Africa. But if he'd stuck around for the St Johnstone game in 1976, it would have made for interesting viewing – with prostrate and toothless Deans surrounded by concerned colleagues, and Craig pushing his way through the mêlée with cries of, 'Make way, make way – I'm a dentist.' Then picking up the bloody stumps and chasing after Deans shouting, 'Dixie, I can save them – we've got the technology . . . at the Glasgow Corporation Clinic . . . for emergency bridge work.' 'Fluck off, Cwaig – A dinnae sshhore goals wi ma teeth.'

Craig was almost as unique as a penalty taking goalie, because he was one of the few professional footballers to possess a university degree – namely, a BDS in Dentistry from Glasgow. Relatively few 'intellectuals' are attracted to association football in Britain, unlike France for example, and their rarity value is not something to be thankful for (Britain, of course, is the only country in Europe where 'intellectual' is a term of disparagement). Football is essentially a working-class preoccupation, and one of the few escape routes to wealth and fame for cerebrally challenged proletarians, but the lack of educationally qualified footballers is still quite frightening. Although the 'intellectualisation of football' (supporting) is a welcome recent phenomenon, the social and occupational divisions between an amateur rugby team and a part-time football club are still strictly stratified. Your average rugby squad will consist of doctors, lawyers, surveyors, teachers, lecturers, scientists and policemen, with one token farm labourer from the Borders. The average football team, however, will include the unemployed (residual), criminals (hardened), plumbers (cowboy), lorry drivers (HGV), barmen (saloon), electricians and engineers (but not electrical engineers), security guards (underpaid), printers (but not self-employed), labourers (casual) and miners (being retrained as typists), with possibly a token student (in *Further* not *Higher* education, doing, say, an HND in Arc-Welding). Such social demographics lend real weight to the cliché about rugby being a game for hooligans played by ABC1s and football a game for gentlemen played by lumpen proletariats (Marx would probably insist that football has replaced religion as the opium of the people). Celtic-playing intellectuals are as thin on the grey-matter ground as they are for most other teams, and 'Cairney' is certainly the *summa cum laude* graduate of modern times.

John Cushley deserves an upper-second mention, since no other 17-year-old on the Celtic books in 1960 had Highers in English, History, Latin and Spanish. He graduated from Glasgow University with an MA in Modern Languages in 1964, combining his studies with his bridesmaid role of perennial reserve centre-half to Billy McNeill. In August of '64 Cushley's language skills were called on by his employers in a scenario that would make a wonderful period comedy for BBC Scotland's Drama Department (Andrea Calderwood please take note). Shot in black-and-white, it would star John Sessions as the youthfully naive Cushley and Brian Cox as Celtic's ageing manager Jimmy McGrory. The plot would detail Celtic's ludicrous attempt to sign the great di Stefano of Real Madrid, in a wild goose chase worthy of Max Sennet or Billy Wilder.

The unlikely duo flew to Madrid, with a rumoured £30,000 in used fivers stuffed in a net shopping bag (Mrs McGrory's), and the pair must have attracted a few curious glances in International arrivals: 21-year-old Cushley in Carnaby Street clobber and 60-year-old McGrory in heavy black overcoat and Homburg hat. The dialogue between the two Scotsmen – one a future author of *Mechanised Book-Keeping* and the other a shy, uneducated man from the Garngad district of Glasgow – and the mercenary, arrogant Argentinian must have been hilarious, with Cushley's interpreting abilities pushed to limits not normally approached in the language labs of Gilmorehill.

Seated around a pool or on a balcony, in the shade of aromatic acacia trees, ordering dinner must have been a social nightmare for McGrory, who may well have embarrassed his young interpreter by complaining, all be it politely, that the *gazpacho* soup was 'stane cawld'. Would there have been enough pesetas in the legendary Biscuit Tin to pay for the expensive meal?

Out of contract with Real, and destined to sign for lowly but ambitious Espanol, did 'the great Alfredo' seriously discuss terms?

'Would Celtic supply him with a house with pool, Mr McGrory?'

'Eh, well now . . . Tell him he could buy a big hoose in Helensburgh, John, beside the seaside . . . '

'Like the Costa-del-Clyde, Signor di Stefano, the Scottish Riviera, Côte-de-Rhu . . . What kind of automobile would the club provide, Mr McGrory?'

'Whit *kind* a motor? . . . Jings, A dunno whit the Board will say tae that wan . . . Tell him a wee runabout jalopy – *maybe.*'

'Would he get to pick the team without interference, Mr McGrory?'

'Whit! A don't get tae pick ra team withoot interference.'

'Oh, jolly good, right, gracias, Signor di Stefano . . . He'll let us know, Boss . . . '

'Help ma boab, where's he goin' wi' the £30,000, John?'

'Oh . . . Well, he called it his "discussion fee", Mr McGrory . . . Mr McGrory! Mr McGrory! . . . Here drink this Perrier water, Mr McGrory . . . You fainted there, Boss . . . '

'In the name a the wee man, whit will Kelly say? Nae di Stefano and nae £30,000 . . . Dearie, dearie me . . . '

Craig, however, is the brain-box par excellence, and a very pleasant chap, too. I met him for the first time in January of '95, when we were both in the studio of Scot FM's Saturday afternoon sports programme *Dugout*. Craig was neither drunk, dishevelled, dense nor derogatory – quite the opposite in fact – and it's very disappointing when idealised icons of one's youth don't live down to their self-destructive stereotype. George Connelly, on the other hand, when he pressed the auto-destruct button, set off a chain of nuclear proportions.

Connelly and Craig represent the two extremes of Scottish character: the Caledonian romantic (doomed to destroy himself) and the Calvinistic pragmatist (determined to better himself). In both Celtic mythology and Presbyterian dogma, acceptance of the concept

71

of predestination is not unusual, with the saints and the sinners, the elect and the damned, doomed or anointed from birth. It is tempting to think of Connelly and Craig, the Jacobite and the Redcoat, as mere pawns moving in predetermined ways, but their respective fortunes were also the result of their free moral choices, and for which they either suffered or prospered. While Connelly gave himself up to the slippery slope, Craig strove to climb the ladder of success, 'to get on' in life (finishing university and marrying an attractive and intelligent daughter of Celtic director Jimmy Farrell) – a case of the Bohemian and the Bourgeois?

In historical terms, Connelly played Bonnie Prince Charlie to Craig's Duke of Cumberland. Going AWOL from the Scottish squad heading to Berne was the equivalent of turning back at Derby in 1745 (when he could have had it all!). The efficient massacre at Culloden – which was just good 18th-century politics – resembles Craig's year in South Africa and his subsequent successful career as dentist and media pundit (although this tortuous analogy is being somewhat harsh on Craig, and I certainly wouldn't stretch it so far as applying 'Butcher' Cumberland's nickname to Craig's dental technique).

In retrospect, however, and after considering the above, I'm still glad it was George Connelly I wrote to and whose rosette I chose instead of James Philip Craig's. After all, who can resist a *tragic* hero?

Glasgow Rangers 3
Moscow Dynamo 2

(European Cup Winners' Cup final, 24 May 1972)

From Nuremburg to the Nou Camp, from defeat by efficient Germans to victory over enervated Russians. And depending on your sectarian point of view, 'the Barcelona riot' saw Rangers fans behaving like brave Wehrmacht warriors defending themselves honourably against Stalin's advancing army of atavistic animals *or* disgracing themselves and their race like the Waffen SS or Gestapo let loose in a beautiful and civilised Jewish 'ghetto' in Warsaw or Budapest.

Archie Macpherson, who was there, has commented that the Rangers fans 'had been turned into a street gang. It has been suggested that this was their own intrinsic response to provocation, that only they would have responded in such a way. It is a theory that dangles irresistibly in front of you, awaiting confirmation from outside the prejudiced Old Firm context.'

Such objective confirmation will not be found in the next few pages (and anyone who wishes to read an impartial and reasonable analysis of the riot should refer to the 'One Disaster after Another' chapter of *Action Replays*). I may be – I am – guilty of viewing the riot through green-tinted binoculars, but up-close the behaviour of the Hun hordes was, I believe, a disgrace – judged by any reasonably unbiased criteria.

Because Celtic and its supporters are *not* ecumenical saints without a trace of prejudiced bigotry in their Fenian blood, there is a simplistic tendency to lump both sides of the 'Old Firm' together in the sectarian dock, with both deemed to be equally guilty of religious intolerance, socially unacceptable behaviour and anathematic attitudes. This is not the case, however, and because of Celtic's justifiable claim to the moral high ground – or at least ground of *higher* morality – their support tends to monopolise the allegiances of, for want of a better description, liberal-humanist-intellectuals (*especially* if they are ostensibly Protestant in their background or upbringing).

This indiscriminate parallelising is often applied to the events in Lisbon and Barcelona. For example, the bald facts are that both Celtic and Rangers won a European trophy and that both sets of fans invaded the pitch. But there are very important differences. Rangers Cup-Winners' Cup win was in a palpably inferior competition to Celtic's European Cup victory. Celtic supporters invaded the pitch but their most destructive act was to dig up pieces of the newly consecrated turf, and their entry on to the field of play was restricted to *post-*match celebrations. Rangers fans invaded the pitch prior to, *during*, and after the 90 minutes of supposedly sporting spectacle, and they ripped up not only grass divots but wooden seating, which they used as makeshift clubs, machetes, spears and javelins. Sore heads in Lisbon were due to over-indulgence in sangria; aching skulls in Barcelona were the result of impacting with police truncheons and long-handled batons. Celtic fans had been pleasantly pissed; Rangers fans were tanked up and psychopathically paralytic. The Lisbon final ended with a lap of honour and a wave of human happiness; the Barcelona riot ended with hundreds injured, dozens arrested and one *dead*.

Also, in pure footballing terms Celtic attacked in entertaining waves until they overwhelmed one of the most formidable teams in the world; Rangers, after being three-up on a demoralised and mediocre team, ended the game hanging on for grim death, and would have conceded an equaliser – and possibly a winner – if not for the unorthodox and lucky heroics of keeper Peter McCloy and the bloody-minded leadership of captain John Greig.

Celtic fans are supposed to be ignorant, unemployed C2DEs (of peasant Irish extraction), but they savoured the atmosphere and attractions of cosmopolitan Lisbon and endeared themselves to the local populace. Rangers fans like to think of themselves as respectable working-class C1s and upwardly mobile AB professionals, but they turned the Nou Camp into a re-run of the Battle of the Boyne and inflicted more damage and terror on the Catalonian capital than ETA terrorists managed in over a decade.

The thin light-brown line of Franco's policemen has been accused of starting the violence, and of inflicting it with over-the-top authoritarian relish (Catholic Fascists being the worst kind of Protestant-bashers, of course). In their defence it should be said that they didn't (over?)-react at all until Rangers fans had been on the pitch in frightening numbers *four* times, restricting their attempts at crowd control until after the final whistle, when the presence of Rangers supporters on the pitch made the touchline presentation of the trophy impossible. Also, as quasi-military enforcers of law and order – and suppressors of legitimate Catalonian nationalism, it has to be admitted – each policeman carried a revolver, none of which were fired at the red-white-and-blue hordes as they attacked, retreated, reformed and attacked again. Batons, jackboots and bare knuckles constitute a restrained response to such public disorder, I would suggest.

Until Rangers signed Maurice Johnston in 1989 they never fielded a Roman Catholic player (knowingly, that is, because a few non-practising 'left-footers' are rumoured to have slipped through the 'What school did you go to?' recruitment policy). This determination to play only eleven Protestants was – and still is to a degree – the main moral objection to the imperial Ibrox institution, discrimination which operated by any other employer in Govan would have been not only immoral but illegal. The defence from Orange apologists is that such exclusiveness is part of the Rangers tradition, a defence which apartheid South Africa often had the effrontery to put forward.

The appalling behaviour of the Rangers fans in Barcelona reflected a different mind-set from Celtic supporters, because anyone who supported Rangers in 1972 either had to turn a convenient blind eye to the religious bigotry of the club, or more likely was willing to immerse himself wholeheartedly in the ethos of enmity which the club deliberately fostered. In 1972 Rangers appealed almost exclusively to manifest bigots, the kind of unthinking morons who sported tattoos of 'No Surrender' on one arm and '1690' on the other, with William of Orange atop his white charger needle-and-inked on to their pigeon chests. To put it with succinct mildness, Rangers and its rabid following were uncivilised barbarians, die-hard dinosaurs with tiny reptile brains in an age of technological sophistication and social conciliation.

'But Celtic are traditionally Catholic,' whine the Billy Boy Bluenose brigade. Yes, but not dogmatically or exclusively so. And by having Protestant managers, players and supporters Celtic have managed to create a club character which avoids the worst excesses of bitter sectarianism.

In a pathetic effort to shift the sectarian spotlight on to Celtic, apologists for Rangers teams which are fielded without a St Christopher's cross round any neck often cite the fact that the Irish tricolour flys over the roof of the Jungle terracing (as if this is a comparable crime). This is true, a gesture in commemoration of Celtic's Irish origins, but they always fail to mention the fact that attached to other flagpoles are the Scottish Saltire, the Stars and Stripes and the *Union Jack*.

And, yes, Celtic do let Roman Catholic priests into their ground free of charge – but Church of Scotland ministers and Orthodox Jewish rabbis also get in for nothing, if suitably attired in their working clothes.

As for the 3–2 scoreline in 1972, it still rankles with Celtic supporters, but at a hard push most will admit that on the balance of play Rangers just about deserved to win. What really sticks in the throat, however, is the fact that the result was allowed to stand by UEFA and that Rangers were allowed to keep the Cup. The morning after the riot even the Rangers players thought they could be in big trouble – the Russians had lodged an appeal to UEFA headquarters in Geneva, but the Swiss Gnomes who heard it were not noted for their pro-Communist leanings; indeed, pro-Calvinist sentiments were more to the fore. Rangers did not have the Cup taken away from them even after some of the worst violence in football history, whereas in 1984 Celtic were forced by UEFA to replay a Cup-Winners' Cup game they'd already won, after an Austrian defender at Parkhead pretended to have been hit on the head by a bottle and/or coin. Rangers escaped the punishment of having to replay the final – although they were banned from defending their title the following year.

Celtic, too, in 1968 almost never got the chance to compete in Europe, despite qualifying as Scottish league champions, after incurring the displeasure of UEFA (but for quite different reasons to those which led to the non-participation of Rangers, and which highlight the moral distance which separates the two clubs). In protest against the Russian invasion of Czechoslovakia, Celtic refused to play their first-round tie against Communist opponents Ferencvaros of Hungary. Celtic were about to be thrown out of the competition themselves, before other Western teams finally followed their lead and withdrew from ties against teams from behind the Iron Curtain. UEFA were then forced to re-draw the first round, at which point all the Soviet-bloc teams withdrew in a protest of their own (except for Czech champions Spartak Trnava, which would have been a wonderfully emotional and good-spirited tie if Celtic had drawn them instead of St Etienne).

Celtic 1
Ayr United 0

(Scottish League, 30 September 1972)

My father took me to this run-of-the-mill home game to atone for the embarrassment he'd caused the day before, when he waited outside the boys' gate of Carntyne Primary with the engine running to pick me up. Getting a run home from a parent in an ordinary family saloon would have been mortifying enough, but the sight of a Glasgow Corporation double decker bus shuddering away in neutral almost caused me to instantaneously combust in shame. Sitting downstairs with Jimmy the conductor, it seemed like an eternity before the bus started to move off, my father in the driver's cabin waiting until every giggling member of my class had time to press their noses against the window opposite my seat, where they pulled grotesque faces, made ding-dong noises and tried to imitate Inspector Blakey's 'I'll get you, Butler!' catchphrase from *On the Buses*. Just when I thought the social torture had reached its peak, one inspired sadist jumped on the open rear platform and paraphrased the playground catchphrase to: 'I'll get you, Bennie!'

As the bus finally began to grind forward, a running posse formed in its wake, and the more adventurous leapt for the platform pole, hauled themselves on board, and then squatted down with their backsides inches from the accelerating tarmac. At which point I got up and stamped on their pole-gripping fingers until they dropped off and rolled away like windswept tumbleweed.

Why couldn't my father have taken his No 38 straight back to the Cranhill bus depot at the end of his shift, instead of re-routing to pick me up? By the time he dropped me off at home, six years of carefully constructed ontological identity had collapsed.

My father – the Scottish Stan Butler (Reg fucking Varney).

Primary 7A . . . 999
Primary 7B . . . 998

(Carntyne Primary Domino Cup, 1972–73)

The final year of primary education was a glorious orgy of kick-about football, from dawn to dusk, played on makeshift pitches in school playgrounds, public parks, back gardens, back streets and church halls. Those of us lucky enough to be in 7A even had the girls' empty playground to ourselves every school day between three and four p.m., when the much-loved Mr Strachan permitted the boys out to play seven-a-sides, on a marvellously uncongested concrete playing area (the girls did knitting, embroidery, basket-weaving, flower-arranging and spelling bees, depending on the day of the week, while the male pupils of Miss Cratchet's 7B spent the final hour doing *maths*, when not nipping out on toilet passes to press their envious faces against the corridor windows overlooking the girls' playground). None of us knew how the 60-odd intake was divided up each year into two classes, A and B – it wasn't based on alphabetical order or intelligence quotients – but we were eternally grateful that six years earlier we'd been selected for Miss Birrel's 1A; otherwise *we'd* have ended up enduring 7B's football-free curriculum. And although we revelled in our good fortune, its arbitrary nature genuinely unsettled us when we thought about it, because we couldn't imagine school life without our daily fix of free-flowing football (as compared to break-time matches, when moves had to be constructed through an obstruction course of younger pupils playing tig, kick-the-can, hide-'n'-seek, conkers, marbles and other juvenile irrelevances).

These were definitely the happiest hours of my life, and my grown-up classmates of today probably share this sentiment, because there was never any aggro or argy-bargy, just good-natured and unbridled enthusiasm. The picking of players went like clockwork, too, with 12 of us just pleased to be picked by one of the unofficial captains (the two best – or most aggressive – players), while our 15th man, Georgie Esslemont, stayed indoors with the girlies, by choice, weaving his baskets and knitting his scarves into, respectively, surrealistic sloping cones and never-ending woollen worms.

The games flowed up and down with rarely more than two goals separating the sides, and with Strachan refereeing them we tended to play to our positions, instead of crowding round the ball *en masse* like iron filings chasing a magnet or flies congregating over dog shit. And no one was bullied into being goalkeeper every day, since Strachan made us take equal turns.

Strangely, Strachan wasn't a football fan himself, and he refereed from a standing position beside the water fountain, dressed as always in a dark three-piece suit and heavy black tortoise-shell spectacles. Like Mr Chipps I think he just liked to see us happy. But he was no mug or easy touch, since our truancy rate was zero, while Miss Cratchet's charges absconded so often that she eventually married a Corporation truancy inspector.

7B did of course get to play football in break-times – morning, lunch and afternoon – and their opponents were invariably Strachan's Superstars. If our seven-a-sides were training bounce games, with the emphasis on entertainment, the 15-a-side encounters were win-at-all-costs battles, waged from Monday through Friday for a plastic domino trophy (awarded weekly at the end of the Friday dinner hour to the team with the highest cumulative score).

On a typical Friday, when the dinner bell rang, I grabbed my satchel and sprinted the mile home, where I wolfed down a jelly piece and glass of milk, while trying not to choke on regurgitated strawberry jam as the *Watch With Mother* brigade of *Andy Pandy* and the *Woodentops* dangled and jerked their way across our black-and-white TV screen. Neither *Playschool* – 'Oh, the square window but who cares?' – *Trumpton* – 'Pugh, Pugh, Barney McGrew, Cuthbert, Dibble and GRUBB!' – or *Bill and Ben* – 'Weeeeed. . . .' – held my attention for long, and I was soon 'Flobalobbing' goodbye to my mother and dashing back up the hill like Muffin the Mule with his testicles tied together with a set of clackers. I would find out the score and join the deprived diehards from 7A who ate school dinners, as they played down the slope of the boys' playground (for some reason we *always* played down the slope). As time passed more home-lunchers would reappear to join the fray – from both sides – while the playground became more and more congested with little kids (some of whom played parallel games, while others attempted to play against the cross-flow, but needless to say we 11- and 12-year-olds had right of way).

When the bell rang that was the final whistle. Normally we were two or three ahead for the week in what resembled a basketball or cricket scoreline – although different cumulative scores could run in tandem for days, because of arithmetic discrepancies and disputed goals.

In the picking-of-teams pecking order for our extra-curricular seven-a-side games, I was normally chosen before any embarrassment could have me shuffling awkward feet, but I was rarely the boy-of-the-match or the player who enjoyed most possession. In the 7A–7B stramashes I liked to think of myself as a useful attacking full-back, but the glory of goal-scoring I normally left to others – bigger if not better players. One lunch-time, however, I became a fully fledged star, scoring 16 goals and relishing the unaccustomed space in midfield (a strange form of religious mania had infected the boys and girls of our year, and each Monday lunch-time ever-growing numbers of converts attended the bible-study group held in the gymnasium, until both teams were depleted in terms of numbers and ability). With all the ball-hoggers on their knees, I took the opportunity to run up something approaching a record score. Sitting in class, mentally wallowing in my achievement, I decided to commemorate my staggering tally in hard statistical form.

An A4 piece of white cardboard was procured from the art supplies cupboard, and I drew up a bar graph, each class member having a cross-hatched bar to the level of the number of goals scored. Rather than title the graph I left it ambiguously blank, refusing to tell those who asked what it represented. For the rest of the week, I memorised all our goal-scorers and updated the graph each day. By Friday morning I was still in the lead, just, but no one had yet tumbled to the graph's significance (not even with my 16–2–0–0 results for the four days that week). Interest was nevertheless intense and I eventually had to divulge what the graph was measuring.

When they knew what it was, it had to be passed around class, so that everyone could stare for minutes at a time at their statistically analysed performance and think: 'I've scored a goal, therefore I exist.' It was a thing of beauty, outlined painstakingly in pencil and coloured in using felt-tip pens. Statistics have a magical fascination for sports fans, and when I got the graph back I was delighted to see that there wasn't so much as a dirty thumb print to spoil its look, and someone usefully suggested that I cover it with tracing paper to protect it, which I did by sticking plasticine dots to the top edge, so that the tracing paper could be lifted back to show an unknowing guinea pig his results in this experiment of empirical analysis.

But during that dinner hour's final competitive game of the week, a funny thing started to happen – the experiment became subject to deliberate fraud and interference on the part of the subjects. Needless to say, everyone stopped being generous with goal-creating passes, individuals became obsessed with scoring all by themselves, and all collective effort by a team of supposedly co-operating individuals ceased. Our tactics were limited to long-range shots from impossible distances and selfish dribbling when surrounded by opposing defenders.

Predictably, 7B – who couldn't understand why our players kept stopping to count on their fingers – came from a dozen or so goals behind and won the Plastic Domino Cup for the first time that term. But none of my class-mates cared – they just queued in front of my desk, bad-temperedly, waiting to submit their tallies. This continued for almost a week, until occasional fraud on the part of the disgusted investigator became a factor, when I started to fiddle my goal tally upwards (at home at night, by just one or two goals a day). When I eventually pulled level with the leading goalscorers, a lynch mob was formed, and I was interrogated with my head down a urinal, with a flushed cistern for every goal I couldn't justify and that no one else could recall. After that, people played with pencils and bits of paper, on which they noted *all* goalscorers. 7B retained the Plastic Domino Cup three times in a row.

In retrospect I suppose I should have incorporated 'assists', but it's not a word or concept that I recall appearing in tabloid sports journalism with any great regularity in the early '70s. But would it have made any difference? Somehow I don't think so – as an experiment in the socio-pathology of materialism and greed it would probably still have gone horribly, horribly right . . .

The above child is definitely the father of the present man, and even today I can spend a ridiculous amount of time poring over statistical histories of Celtic and player-ratings in newspaper form guides. Part of the appeal of football-related statistics, then and now, is that they stop my mind wandering into depressingly profound areas. Sports trivia is a useful antidote to the virulent angst contracted when thinking about unanswerable Big Questions.

I vividly remember suffering pre-teen *ennui* at ten, playing in goal but slumped against a red-brick pillar/post, literally stunned at the realisation that when I had lived the same number of years again I would be a man of 20, a full-grown adult, with mature hopes, fears, experiences, memories, responsibilities and genitalia. At a very virginal 15, this doubling-up calculation acted like a massive dose of bromide (injected through the dorsal vein of my penis so as to avoid tell-tale track-marks on my arms), and I stayed awake night after night lying on my back, instead of my erotically sensitive tummy. At 20 I suffered great Dostoevskian despair (although in retrospect the depth of feeling was too shallow to drown in), thinking that in another 20 years I would be a Methuselahtic 40, with more behind me than in front. At 30, which I distinctly remember dreading when I was 15, if I multiplied by two the answer was a barely conceivable 60.

'Me – 60? I'm sorry, officer, you must have the wrong person. Look, my driving licence doesn't expire until 2032. Your calendar must be fast – I don't make it 2022.' (At least now, aged 34, I can still fantasise about being discovered by a Celtic scout taking a Sunday stroll through Holyrood Park, or getting a game for Meadowbank Thistle[1] and scoring a hat-trick against Celtic in the Scottish Cup – who would ideally score four in reply before signing me for five figures – because nowadays professional footballers can play on into their mid-30s, like Gordon Strachan who has just retired from international football aged 37.) But in only six years I'll be 40, double which is fucking 80! Christ, this isn't funny anymore. And 40 will be a real watershed in the relegation battle of life, because multiplying by two after this is hopelessly optimistic. Still, maybe not . . . Doubling 50 and getting an attainable lifespan is just within the realms of possibility (but will it be long enough to see Celtic win the European Cup again? Would immortality be long enough?). But after 50 . . . 60 times two = !!! Equals 120! Jesus-jumped-up-fiddling-Christ.

Thinking of growing old at an exponential rate never made, or makes, me feel any better. It's definitely not a good idea from the point of view of robust mental health, nor is it strictly accurate, because our ageing process follows a pattern of growth that is linear – one year at a time, the increments of change remaining constant. The doubling-up way of considering my mortality as a Celtic fan means that the sands of time collecting at the bottom of the Celtic Egg-Timer of Life (£4.99 including postage and packaging from the Celtic Shop) are growing to the exponent two: five, ten, 20, 40, 80, 160! Plotted on a graph this gives a curve which starts off relatively flat but soon begins to accelerate upwards at an amazing rate (ie time passing faster as you get older and Celtic get worse). Now, at 34, if I look above my head, the gradient of the line is almost fucking vertical. But worse to come, at about 38 the line begins to double back on itself – ie the Law of Diminishing Returns comes into operation – and one's quality of life stops increasing in steady increments; each additional year – without a league championship – becomes less and less enjoyable, until eventually one's Quality of Life Points (QUOLPS) become *negative* and the line arches back into the top-left quadrant, where it disappears off the graph paper altogether into infinity (where the Huns' league-winning sides appear to be heading).

By the year 2001 artificially intelligent, fifth-generation, fibre-optic computers will probably be solving exponential equations for light relief with their plugs out, but I'll still be growing old *exponentially*. As the human race enters the third millennium, and Celtic add 21st-century pages to their 19th and 20th-century history, I'll be hitting the big Four-O (40 simply being 20 times two); not over the hill, since I never reached the summit, but slipping back down towards the Valley of Death. My sweet bird of youth has *already* flown the coop, leaving behind years of wasted revelling, dreaming high thoughts and postponing fulfilment. When and if I reach 40, I'll be facing my own mortality in an increasingly polished mirror, illuminated by a garish fluorescent strip-light, while callow fans of 18 will only see reflected a very vague outline, softly back-lit, a likeness so indistinct that they can dismiss it from their unformed minds.

Oh to be turning 20 in the year 2000 – a seminal date if ever there was one – with an adult life and a new century about to blossom into full bloom. Luckier still will be those just being born – the bastards! – bursting into life in tandem with the new millennium. God, in 2000 AD ten-year-old kids (one of whom could *conceivably* be mine) will be staggered to learn that I grew up in the *1960s*. Okay, I might not remember much about them, in very great detail (apart from 1967's European Cup win and Neil Armstrong landing on the moon in 1969), but I *had* learned to talk by the time Lee Harvey Oswald had learned to shoot straight, and I did 'live' through the Swinging Sixties. At least the Suez crisis was before my time, but how wonderful it would be to be turning one in 2001 . . .

Jee-*zuz*. I'm envying *unborn* Celtic supporters now. What's so damn special about the year 2000 anyway? It's just sitting there at the end of the decade/century/millennium, waiting, and when we arrive it's probably going to be a massive anti-climax, with everyone demanding their money back: 'Look here, God, this Universe you sold us – it's fucking expanding!' It's not the end of the world (which would, however, really bugger up reincarnation). And it's not as if 2000 is the year when the ageing process somehow magically freezes, leaving 21-year-olds grinning like idiots, all milky white teeth and pink gums, while those over 60 spit blood from haemorrhaging gums and grind their dentures together in ill-disguised bitterness.

But what difference does it really make what age I am at the turn of the century? Morbid Victorians – some of them Celtic supporters! – must have had similar feelings of dread about approaching 1900, but they're all now DWEMS (Dead White European Males), no matter how young they were in 1900, except possibly for children who were too young to conceptualise along these lines, as are all those who lived through 1800, and 1700 and 1600, and as I'll be soon enough when 2000 is just another page in the history books. Time just rolls over everything in its path, and come 2100 students of the past will have great difficulty in relating to the people of our era as ordinary humans who once lived, breathed and went to home Celtic games as they do. Just as I find it difficult to take seriously the *Victorians* who formed Celtic, most of whom seem over-the-horizon distant, but who at one time were at the cutting edge of Western civilization, the time-spatial vanguard of Scottish mankind, now relegated to obscure reference books, dusty libraries, and overgrown graveyards. 1995 is now the tip of the temporal iceberg, but flakes of time-snow continue to fall steadily, until in a few relatively short years it will disappear beneath the surface of history – out of sight, if not completely out of mind. For a very long time now, humanity has consisted more of the dead than of the living – and this is now true of all those who have played for and supported Celtic – and the crushing weight of the departed grows heavier and heavier. Soon – how soon? – I'll be adding my own minuscule but sentimentally treasured contribution . . . I wonder if I shall reach the point in life where of the Celtic supporters I have known more are dead than are alive?

Death, the unreverberate blackness of the abyss – the final frontier, to go where all men have gone before, into the infinitely deep six-foot grave, with eyes wide shut. Never to experience *anything* ever again, while the Universe continues to expand regardless, with suns going supernova, white dwarfs collapsing, black holes swallowing red giants, civilizations rising and falling (completely unaware that you ever existed), Celtic Football and Computer Club competing in the Inter-Galactic Super Cup . . . right to the absolute end when intelligent life has reached the 'Omega Point' of godlike omnipotence, omniscience and omnipresence, having gone everywhere go-able and done all things do-able . . .

And even at this particular synapse of time and circumstance, life is no series of 3–0 victories away from home – more like mid-table mediocrity/security . . . Good God, Ref, approaching 35 – ie, the official start of MIDDLE AGE – having missed every train I should have caught . . . Not only does time accelerate as you get older, but after 30 or so the only trains running are expresses, which don't even slow down, never mind stop, at stations called Thirty-Upon-Something. If you don't have a seat on a gravy train by this time – in other words, a definite destination in life and career – there are only two options available. One, return to the Waiting Room, after having purchased a one-way single ticket to God Knows Where – the last service on the timetable, *stopping at all stations*. Or alternatively, risk breaking your fucking neck by jumping on board one of the expresses as it hurtles through dry-ice, foggy, lucky-to-survive-the-Beeching-cuts Thirty-Upon-Something, in order to escape from Christopher Lee, Peter Cushing, Donald Sutherland and AN Other (a graduate of the Pinocchio School of Acting) and their excruciatingly bad dialogue – all of whom are playing three-card Tarot for human souls in the Waiting Room, furnished by Amicus Horror Interior Decoration Ltd, as they await Dr Terror's sometimes delayed but never cancelled Train of Death . . .

Hmmh . . . Thinking, fantasising and worrying about football trivia to an obsessive degree may not be the healthiest way of harnessing one's mental resources, but it does beat banging your brain against the brick wall of unknowable metaphysics . . . And the preceding tangential ramble gives some idea of the miasmic maunderings that my mind tends to indulge in when not concentrating on football (or work!). Reality may well be a crutch for those who can't cope with drugs, even if the opiate is an obsessive interest in football.

Being a Celtic supporter is the only role in life that gives me any sense of communal identity, that gives me a feeling of being part of something bigger and more important than myself, that links me in any kind of deep emotional bond with other human beings. What are the alternatives – to be Scottish, or a Socialist, or an Existentialist, or an Esso employee, or an élitist intellectual, or a nihilistic misanthrope, or an alienated atheist? Being a Logical Positivist is a source of some comfort, but only intellectually. In the final analysis being a Celtic supporter means that I am not and never will be totally alone, or beyond the understanding of other similar human beings.

FOOTNOTES

1 Dreams of being discovered late in life by Meadowbank Thistle will be well and truly shattered in season 1995–96, when their chairman plans to move the club out of Edinburgh to the New Town of Livingston, 20 miles away. Their name will also be changed to Livingston FC, since Meadowbank's Commonwealth Athletic Stadium will no longer be their home.

This is slightly annoying for me personally, since if I am not reporting a game or watching Celtic I won't be able to decide on the spur of the moment at five minutes to three to walk the short distance to see a senior game of Scottish football. My disappointment, however, is as nothing compared to the despair and despondency of local Thistle fans, who are quite rightly outraged at the move, such lock-stock-and-barrel transfers to different urban conurbations normally being the reserve of American football, baseball and hockey proprietors.

On 19 March 1994 the diehard fans' patience finally snapped during a home game with Cowdenbeath, in what became known to regulars in Meadowbank's Golden Gates pub as the 'Afternoon of the Long Knives'. A handful of fanatically devoted fans were frogmarched from the stadium by Rock Steady stewards/security guards for voicing their disapproval of chairman Bill Hunter, unaffectionately known as Mr Blobby. Comments directed within-earshot of Hunter included:

'This is a dictatorship, Blobby!' (accompanied by a National Socialist salute).

'Blobby! Blobby! Blobby! Out! Out! Out!'

'You're living in dreamland, Blobby!' (To which reported quote Graham Spiers in *Scotland on Sunday* Sports Diary hilariously added, 'Actually, it's Prestonpans?')

Meadowbank Thistle may only average 400 supporters, but no 'hard-headed businessman' like Blobby – sorry, Hunter – has the right to buy and move the club out from under them. If the new stadium in Livingston gets built, maybe Hunter will be able to persuade Mrs Thatcher to come and open it – 'the syphilitic-ridden whoor', as my father used to call her. Affectionately.

Celtic 3
East Fife 0

(Scottish League, 21 October 1972)

My father was extremely nervous and ill-at-ease throughout this game, our attendance at which was a last-minute impulse on his part, designed to soften the blow of some bad news. I was just relieved that by the time we had walked back as far as Parkhead Cross he hadn't worked up enough brass neck to give me some kind of embarrassing introductory sex talk; instead, his humming and hawing had been leading up to an explanation of his forthcoming court case, for dangerous or reckless driving. With two endorsements on his licence already, for minor traffic offences incurred while in charge of a moving double-decker bus, one more would mean a driving ban and getting his jotters from the Corporation.

He explained that he could probably get off the charge by following the advice of his TGWU-appointed lawyer, who wanted him to blame the running of a red traffic light at a busy road junction on blinding glare from an autumnal sun (no one was even mildly injured in the prang with a milk float). But like George Washington, whom he actually quoted, my father couldn't tell a lie *under oath* in a *court of law*. It was a matter of principle – and anyway, on the day of the accident the *prevailing atmospheric conditions* had been *overcast*, so he could hardly have been *blinded* by the glare of a *non-existent* sun, could he?

My father's refusal to perjure himself in the sheriff court was, I thought at the time, 100 per cent stubborn honesty, even if it meant losing his job. Looking back, his over-active conscience can be seen as an inculcated knee-jerk reaction from a 'respectable' member of the proletariat, cowed to respect some highly dubious authority figures. I wouldn't want to push this Marxist-Leninist interpretation too far, however, since he was by nature the most scrupulously honest and generous of men. In this case, though, I think his overly active but uncontrollable imagination got the better of him, inducing visions of Prosecution lawyers armed with meteorological weather reports for the cloudy day in question, with hostile witnesses from the Meteorological Office lined up to testify that there were no recorded incidents of sunshine in the Glasgow area over an eight-hour period. And so on, in Kafkaesque fashion . . .

I think he was a bit hurt by my obvious indifference, but he certainly got the reaction he sought when he came to the 'kicker' of his confession. While banned from driving for six months, his income would be seriously affected, and we'd all have to make sacrifices. One of which would be no more Celtic games until he got his old job back, or a new one.

Copious tears flowed, as I imagined him 'letting himself go' and becoming structurally unemployed. Would that afternoon's goals from Harry Hood, Dixie Deans and Bobby Lennox be the last I'd ever see a Celtic team score? At least Stan Butler would have turned up in the dock with an eye-patch, complaining of a burned retina at the very least . . .

Celtic 2
Uijpest Dosza 1

(European Cup, second round first leg, 25 October 1972)

My father's P45 was in the post, and therefore my hopes of persuading him to take me to this, my first European match, were dashed. Stuck in my room, I heard the roars when Dalglish scored just after half-time, and then again in 75 minutes. At two up I decided I could bear to listen to live radio commentary on BBC Scotland, but this proved a surreal and confusing experience. Celtic were in fact only one up, Bene having scored for Uijpest Dosza in the first 20 minutes. Eventually the commentator – David Francey? – referred to 'Bene's crucial early strike' and I was flabbergasted. I knew the origin of my surname was in the North-East, where Bennies, Benvies and Benzies take up a significant portion of the Aberdeen telephone directory, but what was a Bennie doing playing for the Hungarian champions (when France was the medieval source of the Bennie clan)? Were we distant cousins? Why was he getting more of the ball than any other player?

The commentator was pronouncing Bene like the Scottish surname, rather than *Ben-ay* in the Continental manner, but there was no excuse for such ignorance. As I later learned, Ferenc Bene was a famous centre-forward who was joint top scorer in the 1966 World Cup. No Bennie has ever played for Celtic (although one Robert Bennie of Airdrie played for Scotland in 1925 and '26), and I was warming to the sound of old Ferenc Bene, since as an eleven-year-old I was beginning to loathe my surname. Famous people with the same name in the '70s were the comedian Jack Benny, the motel idiot Benny in *Crossroads* and Benny the Ball in Top Cat's cartoon gang. In addition, any mentally retarded failure or minor gangster in American movies is – and was – invariably called Benny (for example, *LA Law*). But even although I didn't believe it at the time, there are worse surnames beginning with B, some of which have actually played for Celtic (eg Battles, Baines, Bauchop, Biggins and Bogan!). Today I've grown into the name and I actually quite like it: it's basically value-free and not outrageously embarrassing, but distinctive enough in print to stand out and be remembered.

Getting confused about the presence and pronunciation of Bene was just part of the confusion that an eleven-year-old naturally goes through. At the same age, switching on the TV to see Queen's Park Rangers playing was a similar brow-furrowing experience: why were Rangers (Glasgow) playing in Celtic's green-and-white hoops (on a black-and-white TV screen)? Learning about the procreative act from a medical textbook, and the importance of male ejaculation in the process, I spent many smug hours thinking how inconvenient it must have been for married couples wanting babies to have to wait until the man needed to empty his bladder (for a few years I assumed that sperm was urine micturated out of an erect penis).

In the second leg Bene scored twice in a 3–0 win, and Ferenc is now running the Bene Chip Shop in the Royal Mile – although he doesn't like talking about his glory days as a Hungarian internationalist. I just say to him: 'Hey, Ferenc! Give me my fish supper the Glasgow way: with salt "n" vinegar, not salt "n" sauce' (the latter being the Edinburgh style).

Hibernian 2
Celtic 1

(League Cup final, 9 December 1972)

As a Celtic supporter I've often been accused of having it too easy, that my experience of following a fantastically successful team bears little relation to the experience of people who support ordinary teams, like Hibs say, whose natural condition is one of continuing disappointment. But even in their heyday, Jock Stein's teams had their fair share of unexpected defeats, and this was the third successive League Cup final failure (with another to follow in 1973). The Scottish Cup, too, punished any hubristic arrogance, and failure in these competitions was made all the more piquant by the tendency to lose in finals, as opposed to earlier rounds when expectations were less pronounced.

Although not on a par with the Famous Five team of the '50s (Smith-Johnstone-Reilly-Turnbull-Ormond), defeat to a team which had players like Brownlie, Stanton, Blackley, Cropley and Duncan was no disgrace. But the main effect on me watching the television highlights was a renewed determination to get my hands on a Hibernian strip (my Celtic top was attracting too much flak from passing Huns and I naively assumed that a Hibs kit would allow me to melt anonymously into the background – it didn't; when finally procured for me I was still assaulted on a regular basis by thugs with a working knowledge of Hibernian's Catholic origins).

Aesthetically, the 1972 strips of both teams were a joy to see, and to be seen in. A bit like the surname Bennie, Celtic's green-and-white hoops have the potential to appear a bit naff, but in the early '70s the shirts weren't defaced by advertising logos for CR Smith or People's. They had smart round necks instead of hideous button-down collars, and the width of the hoops hadn't yet started to grow, almost imperceptibly year by year until today when they look more like geometrically angled bands (the increase in band width being necessary to accommodate the CR Smith name, club crest and Umbro-manufacturer's logo, a dog's dinner of advertising graffiti that is far too congested and cluttered to please a discerning eye).

In 1973 small V-necked wing collars were introduced, and this was a small but not unattractive innovation. With white shorts, numbered in green, and white stockings, the basic Celtic strip is a wonderful piece of design, immune to most 'improvements', but it has suffered from some recent and utterly tasteless interference.

UEFA's insistence on black numbers on the shirt backs for European matches may make identification easier, but they ruin the simple symmetry of the hoops. Variations in shorts and stocking

89

colour is always a sartorial disaster, with green socks in particular destroying a normally tasteful combination of two primary colours. Today's strips are also fashionably baggy, which any weight-conscious clothes designer will tell you is not a flattering look when combined with horizontal, fattening-to-the-eye hoops (especially in the case of Paul Byrne). Lightning-type flashes, shoulder segments, numbers on sleeves, elasticated V-necks, cross-over necks, sewn-on CR Smith panels (as opposed to embossed lettering), elasticated sleeve collars, club insignia on the centre of the breast bone and shirts with latent underlying geometric patterns have all undermined a design classic (not to mention the switch from cotton to acrylic and other man-made fibres).

The current vogue for away and *third* strips is simply a marketing exercise to exploit the blind loyalty and bad dress sense of committed (and committable?) fans. Celtic's away strips have been as offensive to the sensibilities as most other clubs – with the possible exception of Greenock Morton's red *tartan* away strip sponsored by Buchanan's toffee – but the current 1994/95 ensemble change strip looks to have been designed by a blind monkey on an Apple Mac painting programme, with hideous black, white and green *stripes* and *panelling*. A third strip was unveiled in February of '95 – a green, white and yellow monstrosity which Celtic and Umbro were selling for £36.99 – but the Scottish League refused to give permission for it to be worn against Hearts at Tynecastle, restricting its epilepsy-inducing appearances to four home fixtures at Hampden Park.

My parents were delighted by my request for a Hibs strip – my father was back in work as an engineer with Teacher's bottling plant in Glasgow – because they thought it would be less inflammatory and because they thought it would be significantly cheaper. Celtic strips, or tops, have always cost about a third more to buy than their Rangers equivalents, but having since worked in the rag trade I now know that this wasn't because of a cartel of Masonic sports outfitters. A plain blue Rangers top is significantly cheaper to produce because unlike the Celtic shirt two different colours don't have to be combined, with the resulting increase in costs associated with the necessary extra stitching and dye-running precautions. The Hibernian strip was relatively good value, but I had to wait almost two years before getting one, since stocks of the Edinburgh club's kit were not kept in Greaves or other sportswear shops in Glasgow at the time.

Rangers 3
Celtic 2

(Scottish Cup final, 5 May 1973)

Another ruddy cup final defeat, and the Huns had secured their first Scottish Cup trophy since 1966 (and even although they 'won' the European Cup Winners' Cup in 1972, they did not qualify for that tournament as Scottish Cup *winners*, but as runners-up to Celtic, who won the league and cup double in season 1970–71). Under Jock Wallace, Rangers were a physically intimidating, tremendously tall and frighteningly fit team who battled for every ball, and in this match at Hampden they drew inspiration from the presence of Princess Alexandra in a makeshift royal box. The fact that Celtic contrived to lose to John Greig and his fellow bruisers was an indication that the Lisbon team was not being followed by a squad of similar quality. 'Transitional' would remain the term most often used to describe Lisbon's successors, although there was no shortage of talented individuals coming through the scouting and nursery systems.

One member of the so-called Quality Street Gang was little Luigi 'Lou' Macari, a player who was talented enough to bear comparison with Lions like Chalmers, Wallace, Lennox and Johnstone. However, he was not deemed committed enough to play for the love of the jersey, and after a protracted dispute over money he was transferred to Manchester United for a Scottish record fee of £200,000 in January of 1973. This might not necessarily have been the beginning of the end of Celtic as a major European force if they had bought a replacement player of similar ability (and price!), but instead, the money received from Old Trafford was frittered away on 'bargain' buys: namely, goalkeeper Ally Hunter for £40,000 on 24 January (from Kilmarnock), £35,000 for winger-cum-full-back Andy Lynch on 7 February (from Hearts) and £50,000 for midfielder Steve Murray on 1 May (from Aberdeen). Of the three, only Hunter played in the Cup final and he lost three goals! If Macari's financial demands had been met and he had played in the final, the scoreline may well have been reversed. And from this point on Celtic's transfer-dealing record bears comparison with my father's second-hand car buying and selling, with rust buckets being purchased for over-inflated sums before being sold for scrap a few years/months/days later.

Apart from Tom Forsyth's painful winner – when a Derek

Johnstone header hit one post and then trundled agonisingly along the goal-line, before rebounding off the other and being stabbed in by the stumbling defender with his exposed studs – George Connelly's 2–2 equaliser sticks in the mind. After Greig deliberately handled on the line, Connelly strode up to take the penalty, watched by a total crowd of 123,000 and facing whistling and jeering from the Rangers end. Celtic had been failing to convert penalties all season, and the pressure on Connelly must have been like taking a spot-kick at 20 fathoms. Nevertheless he despatched it past six-feet-plus McCloy with aplomb (and Connelly was the man who would begin to crack up with the strain of being a celebrity just a few *weeks* later).

Finally, reading Ian Archer's report of this game in the *Glasgow Herald* I was surprised to find out that the founder of Glasgow Rangers was a Victorian oarsman by the unlikely name of Moses McNeill, which sounds to me suspiciously Roman and/or Irish in origin.[1]

FOOTNOTES

1 For 'Old Firm' fans names are very important – for pigeonholing people – and although Saussure has argued that there is no necessary connection between the signifier (a word) and the signified (a thing), I'm not sure I can accept this. Without unity of the sign, judging people by their monikers sight unseen becomes problematic, especially if every signifier has several signifieds. For example, it would mean that someone called Mason Boyne could be elected Pope without raising eyebrows, never mind shackles, or that a footballer christened Jesus Fergus O'Leary could be the next Rangers centre-forward without Union-Jack burning protests.

The day before writing this chapter I heard an anecdote in the Raith Rovers press box/rabbit hutch which illustrates the above point. A well-known tabloid journalist was manning his paper's telephone hot-line, for readers' opinions, when a tired and emotional caller enquired about Celtic's new striker Pierre van Hooijdonk (signed for £1.2 million in January 1995).

'Hey, is Hooijdonk a Catholic name or what?' (Presumably a question from a bigoted Celtic fan seeking reassurance.)

'No, it's a fucking anagram!' replied the disgusted journo, before slamming the phone down.

Scotland 2
Czechoslovakia 1

(World Cup qualifier, 26 September 1973)

After leaving primary school in June, I almost ended up crossing the sectarian divide by going on to attend a Roman Catholic secondary or high school. There is no such educational division in

England or Wales, with the exception of fee-paying institutions for the sons and daughters of well-to-do Catholics, but in Scotland local councils finance separate Catholic schools, which are administered by Catholics themselves. Whether this kind of religious apartheid promotes social intolerance, or is merely a reflection of it, is a moot point. I personally must admit that from the ages of five to 12 I never really concerned myself with the fact that my regular playmates from downstairs, Kathleen and Elizabeth, went to a different primary school.

At 12, however, my summer holiday was spent taking religious instruction from a specialist priest, with a view to converting into a Papal left-footer and progressing on to a school like St Aloysius, Holyrood Secondary or John Paul Academy.

Like most working-class parents, mine were happy enough to let their offspring attend the *nearest* State school, but my mother put her left foot down when Smithycroft Secondary proved to be my closest comprehensive. Situated next to Barlinnie jail, a university of crime into which many ex-pupils progressed, its catchment area included Carntyne, Riddrie, Dennistoun, Provanmill and the notorious Blackhill. My mother regarded Smithycroft as a nursery or preparatory school for the Bar L and was determined that I wasn't going to come under its malign influence. Instead, enquiries were made about the possibility of enrolling me at a Catholic school – my mother's mother was a Catholic from County Donegal – but to be accepted I had to be a card-carrying, *bona fide* devotee of the Church of Rome.

To meet the necessary criteria, I immersed myself in learning the Catechism, as well as studying the rites and rituals of the Roman Church, and I was anything but an obdurate catechumen. I learned by heart the Lord's Prayer, the Hail Mary and the Our Father. I also learned that I would be going straight to Purgatory when I died, because I had not been officially baptised, although I didn't think it prudent to confess this to my instructor.

Surprisingly, my father went along with all this, but on the condition that I kept my theological and educational options open over that summer. This meant that on Sundays I had to attend mass at the chapel, morning service at the church, the Catholic Youth Fellowship and the Church of Scotland bible class – a very long day which didn't end till late in the evening with question-and-answer sessions in which my instructor would try to catch me out on my Catechism.

In the end a Catholic education was denied/spared me, when my father found out – or someone told him and he believed it – that I would be taught exclusively by nuns, or 'shrivelled spinsters of the soul' as he called them. And although I succumbed to agnostic atheism before the onset of puberty, I don't feel my cramming for conversion was a waste of time, because even today I prefer the fiery heart of Catholicism to the gimlet eye of Calvinism, even if both are rationally ridiculous. During the dialectics of the Catechism I once asked how, if God can see through walls, He doesn't see through the bathing goonies that nuns wear when taking a bath? At the Church of Scotland bible class the theory of evolution was tacitly accepted, but my Sunday school teacher couldn't explain where the cut-off point was for primate parents and humanly immortal offspring.

I would have avoided Smithycroft more effectively if the time and trouble devoted to religious instruction had been used to study for a scholarship to a school like Allan Glen's. But if I'd become a scholarship boy at 'Dirk Bogarde's *alma mater*' (which is how the *Evening Times* always refers to the actor's three unhappy weeks there), I wouldn't have got to go to the Scotland-Czechoslovakia game which saw Scotland qualify for a World Cup for the first time in 16 years.

Twelve of us in first year were lucky enough to have our names drawn from a waste-bin during PE, and we got to stand in the schoolboys' enclosure at Hampden. Celtic had five players in the team – Hunter, McGrain, Connelly, Hay and Dalglish – but my pride in the Celtic contribution palled in the 34th minute when Ally Hunter in goal deflected an innocuous cross-cum-shot from Nehoda into his own net. For the rest of the game, and indeed for the rest of his career, Hunter's self-confidence was shattered into a thousand neurotic pieces, and whenever the Czechs attacked on the break I found it hard to breathe, never mind look.

A Scottish victory would have guaranteed qualification, and they got back into the game just before half-time with a headed goal from man-mountain Jim Holton. It was pandemonium in the schoolboys' enclosure, and within seconds there was a high-pitched chorus of 'Six foot two/Eyes of blue/Big Jim Holton's after you . . . '.

In the second half the tenth-of-a-million crowd roared themselves hoarse, but their heroes were definitely struggling to get a winner (and Hunter in goal could only watch as a cross from Pivarnik rolled along the top of his bar). In the 64th minute Willie Ormond replaced Dalglish with Joe Jordan – the Leeds United *reserve* striker – and because of Hunter's disgraceful performance, I was too embarrassed to voice my suspicions of anti-Celtic bias.

It would be years later before I saw the winning goal clearly – I'd have had a better view if I'd stayed home to watch the game live on TV – but I did catch a glimpse of Jordan rising to head the ball towards goal with 15 minutes left. I knew that it had beaten Viktor as the famous Hampden Roar deafened my eardrums and the terraces exploded with waving scarves and unfurled Lion Rampants. I was actually crying with joy and relief, and the 14 minutes remaining suddenly transmogrified in my brain from a rapidly running-out time scale to an almost infinite stretch of slow-moving nano-seconds. But Scotland held out to qualify for West Germany, and I've never again experienced such a *pleasurable* wave of raw emotion as I did that night as a schoolboy attending my first international.

Celtic 4
Basle 2

(European Cup quarter-final second leg, 20 March 1974)

This game was the first time I had been to Parkhead in season 1973/74, although my devotion to the club was by no means waning. Having started at secondary school, and having joined the Boys Brigade, I was playing in organised football matches most Saturdays.

Because of the miners' strike many games were rescheduled for Sundays, with early kick-offs to avoid the necessity of using floodlights. But persuading my father to take me on a Sunday was problematic, because he was now working for the Gas Board and on alternate weekends was 'on call'. (After finishing work as a bus driver, he quickly got the job with Teachers, in their Glasgow bottling plant, and his job was to make running repairs to the conveyor belt, which management insisted could never be switched off, as it would cause a bottleneck in the production process; hence he had to effect repairs while the cogs, pistons and ball-bearings of capitalism continued to turn above him as he lay on his back; and hence his voting Labour and then Communist in 1974's two General Elections.)

On 27 January, my 13th birthday and a Sunday, we did head off in the direction of Celtic Park, but we only got as far as Duke Street and missed the two-thirty p.m. kick-off. A middle-aged alky had staggered out into the flow of traffic heading for Parkhead and was knocked down by a Volkswagen Beetle containing *six* drunken Clydebank fans. I clearly remember the man lying in the middle of the road with an ever-increasing pool of blood expanding outwards from the back of his skull, with the Beetle skewed to a halt and with its front boot having sprung open. After standing over his victim, the lachrymose driver sat on the ledge of the open boot and buried his face in his hands.

Like other passing pedestrians I just stood and gawped, but my father got me to run to the nearest phone box to call an ambulance. When I got breathlessly back, his new Dunn & Co tweed jacket, purchased the day before while shopping 'in town' accompanied by my mother, had been rolled into a pillow and placed under the injured man's head (he'd been moaning about being uncomfortable). I was both appalled and impressed at this humanitarian gesture, which was typical of my father, but I knew my mother would be furious when presented with the blood-soaked garment, since it had cost almost ten pounds.[1]

By the time the ambulance and police had departed, it was too late to attend the match, and we walked back home with my father carrying the bloody jacket under one arm, taking a short-cut across some waste ground close to the greyhound track. Still dreading my mother's reaction, I was nevertheless full of admiration for my father, who had gone back up significantly in my estimation (although there was no way I'd sacrifice a good day-old jacket for a dying drunk – then or now). Desperate to show some dutiful affection but unable to articulate such an emotion, I decided to ask a question which would allow him to display his superior wisdom.

'Dad, what are those big windowless towers that you always see on bings?'

'Oh, those corrugated-iron constructions with the ladders up to the single entrance . . . ?'

'Aye, Dad. Who builds them and what are they for?'

'Em . . . Well, son . . . I assume they're gang huts – that one over there for the Carntyne Powrey and the other one for the Dennistoun Tongs. Judging by the graffiti, like . . . Just like the Towers of San Gimagnoano that I showed you in the encyclopedia . . .'[2]

My mother, to her credit, suggested that my father phone the Royal Infirmary to enquire after the condition of the knocked-down drunk. But since he was dead on arrival there was no question of sending him a dry-cleaning bill (and as my mother predicted the stains were to prove permanent anyway).

Because I'd missed out on the 6–1 Scottish Cup thrashing of Clydebank, which would have been my main birthday present, I got to go and see the second leg against Basle, who were 3–2 ahead after the first leg in Switzerland (a country my father described as a *superior* sort of Scotland, misquoting Sydney Smith either deliberately or unknowingly). There was a massive crowd of over 70,000 and once again we ended up in the Jungle terracing – this time without the benefit of a crush barrier to be crushed against. Because Bradford, Heysel and Hillsborough were still to happen, we were packed in like sardines. On numerous occasions I was lifted right off my feet, and I was so scared that when the Swiss cancelled out two early openers from Dalglish and Deans I only felt relief because it reduced the swaying of the crowd.

When at half-time my father decided enough was enough and that we were leaving, I was delighted. But only secretly. He had to drag me out kicking and screaming, and when we got home he took a leather belt to my underpanted behind for the second and last time. But I deserved it, because I had started shouting: 'Help me. Help me – he's no' ma da!' Feeling guilty, no doubt, after my *gentle* thrashing, he let me watch the TV highlights. Celtic levelled the tie on aggregate (5–5) by scoring a 3–2 winner in the second half. In extra-time they got a fourth, from Steve Murray,[3] and we were through 6–5 on aggregate.[4]

FOOTNOTES

1 With regard to 1974 prices, Tom Campbell and Pat Woods in their *A Celtic A-Z* quote the then admission prices to Celtic Park: Upper Stand 70p; Front Stand 60p; Ground 35p; and Boys 20p. Even taking into account the hyper-inflation of the 1970s, the cost of attending football matches has soared, the rate of increase outpacing the Retail Price Index to a significant degree. To watch Celtic in season 1994/95 meant breaking a £20 note, and if you bought a programme, a pie and a Bovril there was barely enough change to get a bus back to Easterhouse. Before moving to Hampden in '94, Celtic Park had a *one*-pound *off* concession for the unemployed, but they had to be in the ground an *hour* before kick-off to take advantage of this generous offer. Transfer inflation has also been subject to South-American-type indices, and today an average Premier League player costs about one million pounds.

2 My father's explanation of the corrugated black towers which spring up almost overnight on waste ground in Glasgow's deprived areas was a crock of shit – needless to say. In reality they serve as *pigeon-lofts*. Or they did. Maybe today the pigeons have to share with gang members, alcoholics and junkies.

3 Steve Murray deserves at least a footnote as a closet intellectual, even although as a teenager he failed a Higher necessary for acceptance on to a university course in pharmacy. But he studied

for it at night class while playing for Dundee, and while at Celtic was enrolled on an Open University course in maths and science. And he did turn down a second international cap – for a friendly against West Germany in Frankfurt – in order to concentrate on his studies. Hence his nickname of 'Back Seat', from sitting at the back of team coaches on the way to away games reading set textbooks. But instead of becoming a teacher as he hoped, he went on to manage Forfar and Montrose, before being sacked as Dundee United assistant manager in 1989. I like to think of him today as a mad scientist working in his garden shed, amongst an array of test tubes and Bunsen burners, close to discovering a chemical vaccination against necrotising fascitis or AIDS – or even something more important to his fellow man like a cure for baldness or impotence.

4 In *The Glory and the Dream* Campbell and Woods make powerful use of a statistical and historical comparison: 'The pessimists noted that 11 years previously Celtic had eliminated the same club [Basle] 10–1 on aggregate in the Cup-Winners' Cup.'

Celtic 0
Atletico Madrid 0

(European Cup semi-final first leg, 10 April 1974)

A few days after the Basle game, where I thought I was going to die, I damn nearly did die. Bicycling down Marfield Street towards Shettleston, and a difficult away fixture in the Subbuteo Cup against Pukka Paterson, the broad road was devoid of any traffic and for once I had both hands on my Chopper handlebars. Nevertheless I fell off – either through hitting a pot-hole or having the chain come off – and I didn't even have time to brace myself for the expected injuries of scraped skin and bruised joints. Relieved not to be in any stinging or throbbing agony, I picked myself up and came face-to-face with a retired couple, standing ashen-faced on the garden side of their half-trimmed hedge. The old woman disappeared under the hedge in a dramatic swoon.

Only when I saw the amount of blood did I realise why she had fainted. I was literally covered in blood from head to foot, and when I patted the back of my head with my right hand it felt horribly soft and wet. Ignoring the old man's offer to call an ambulance, I put the chain back on and started to pedal home. At this point my main worry was the ruined school shirt I was wearing – newly-bought that Saturday in C&A and which I should have changed out of – and I just wanted back to get the row over with.

Passing the bus-stop at the bottom of our street, I saw a fellow member of the first year first team, Roddie Campbell, standing there. With a safety-conscious look over my shoulder I cycled across to the other side of the main road, where Campbell finally noticed me (he went on to be a teacher, I believe, but only of PE). His handsomely square jaw dropped as he took two involuntary steps backwards and looked as if he was about to keel over. Then I began to get *really* scared for the first time, and I pedalled furiously for home as stunned shoppers dropped their net shopping bags in my colourful wake. More blood couldn't have been pouring from my body if I'd severed a jugular vein or carotid artery.

Fighting back panic I *squelched* up the carpeted, red Axminster hall stairs, and found my mother peeling potatoes at the sink. 'What are you doing back so early?' she asked without turning round. Preferring to giggle hysterically rather than greet pathetically, I said quite cheerfully: 'I've been shot in the head by the Purple Man.'[1] When she turned round, drying her hands, she shoved the Culzean Castle tea towel into her mouth to stop herself screaming – although muffled sobs still managed to escape. My lunatic grin was fast giving way to a trembling lower lip.

After my father had brought her round with smelling salts, my mother perched me on a stool and examined the back of my skull with trembling fingers. 'You're definitely going to need stitches,' she said – brutally – with all the medical certainty of someone who used to work in the Royal Infirmary (as a typist). At the prospect of stitches in my head I broke down and started blubbering like a baby (and after a negative skull X-ray at the Royal's Accident and Emergency Department, an unsympathetic nurse cut off large shanks of hair and a nervous junior doctor inserted 16 stitches).

Landing head first on pebble-dashed tarmacadam could have put me into a permanent vegetative state, and I was lucky not to have been injured more seriously. However, like good plotting in a novel, the above incident has not been inserted gratuitously into this narrative, because within a year its consequences were to cost me a place in the First XI and in the long term may have prevented an *averagely* successful career as a professional footballer (with Raith Rovers, say, if not Glasgow Celtic).

Relieved at not having lost his only son, my father agreed to take me to see Atletico Madrid with surprising alacrity. I was pleased that he was actually looking forward to the match, which was explained by the fact that he thought Atletico were from the same attractive mould as Real, whom he'd watched with real exhilaration at Hampden 14 years previously. He didn't know anything about Atletico's history or reputation, both of which should have warned the media of what the Spanish champions were capable of.

Atletico de Madrid struggled to survive in its early years, and its existence was only assured when the Fascists won the Civil War and it amalgamated with the Aviation Club (members of which had spent the war dropping high explosives on George Orwell, a Wigan supporter presumably). Early in their career they had been managed by Helenio Herrera. In season 1971–72 Austrian Max Merkl had been at the helm, and he turned the club into an élite military training camp. By 1974 Atletico's manager was Juan Carlos Lorenzo, the notorious figure who had coached the 1966 Argentine World Cup squad and whose players Alf Ramsey had described as 'animals'. In Spain, Atletico had the reputation of being the dirtiest team ever to play in their first division.

We sat in the Front Stand and it only took seven minutes for the Spaniards to get the first of their *seven* bookings, when the Argentinian winger Ayala had his name taken. Within a minute Jimmy Johnstone was poleaxed by Diaz, the *same* full-back who had kicked Jinky all over the pitch during the first leg of the World Club Championship at Hampden in 1967, when the South American hit-man had been playing for Racing Club of Argentina. By the end of the game, Atletico were reduced to *eight* men, Turkish referee Degan Babacan doing his best to punish them for their cynical tactics.

I remember the scar on my skull throbbing as I watched the proceedings in mounting disbelief, anger – and fear. Even my father was on his feet, pointing at unpunished miscreants in headshaking outrage.

Some indication of Atletico's cynical disregard for the laws and spirit of the game is given by the following match facts: of their two *substitutes* one was booked and the other was red-carded (the third player to go off), while their *goalkeeper* was booked for time-wasting; for Celtic only Dixie Deans and Jim Brogan went into the referee's book (for retaliation).

After the final whistle, things went from bad to worse. Walking towards the tunnel Johnstone was punched in the face by Eusebio, and the little winger fell to the ground dazed. Thereafter a punch-up brawl ensued, with the Glasgow constabulary doing its best to keep players and officials from both sides apart. I remember standing on tiptoes, on my seat, and seeing Ayala in track-suit top goading Billy McNeill on for the Spanish equivalent of a 'square go'. Only a thin line of policemen with caps askew kept them apart.

In retrospect Lorenzo's plan probably was to incite a riot amongst the 70,000 Celtic supporters, but not one of us reacted by vaulting the perimeter and getting Celtic banned by UEFA. And as for Atletico's punishment? Well, they had to do without the three dismissed players for the second leg (which was *standard* procedure, for God's sake, and two of whom were only fringe players drafted in for their sacrificial dispensability). Also missing from the return match were three of the four other booked players (since they had reached the necessary number of cautions in the tournament for *automatic* suspensions). Playing on a neutral ground or in front of an empty stadium would have been the most lenient punishment imaginable, but Latin-loving UEFA simply imposed a token fine on Atletico.

Two weeks later Celtic went down 2–0 in Madrid, in front of a rabid home support whose enmity was almost palpable. And poor Jimmy Johnstone had an even more torrid time than during the first leg, having received by telephone at the team hotel a death threat which everyone in the Celtic party took seriously. By kick-off the non-specific threat had developed into a detailed rumour – a South American ex-gaucho sniper was in an upper-tier stand, or on the roof, with a rifle fitted with a telescopic sight and re-bored to fire armour-piercing dumdum bullets, with a possible accomplice in or on the opposite stand to provide crossfire indemnity against missing (the red-headed blur on 16mm footage of this game is Johnstone running about at pace *at random*).

The result of this semi-final taught me an important lesson: namely that the good guys don't always win (but that it doesn't always matter). And at least Atletico lost to Bayern Munich in that year's final.

FOOTNOTES

1 'The Purple Man' was an early urban myth, a floridly coloured sex pervert who we first yearers passionately believed haunted the 'Riddrie Rocks' and who supposedly leapt on unaccompanied children with his Afghan hound. In reality the Purple Man was probably just a Pomeranian dog-walker, with a bad case of impetigo or rosacea.

Celtic 3
Dundee United 0

(Scottish Cup final, 4 May 1974)

Had Celtic lost this, yet another cup final, Jock Stein would have had a ready-made excuse: a viral infection which decimated the squad after they had decamped to their traditional big-match headquarters, down the Ayrshire coast at Seamill. This was a closely guarded secret prior to the final, and almost every player was affected to some degree.

Less than a month after Atletico and less than an hour before kick-off against Dundee United, neither I nor my father were in the best of health. We were both toiling to climb a steep hill on the approach to my Aunt Barbara's, in douce Knightswood, with my mother and kid sister leaving us progressively further behind (my father would have driven us all in his new Gas Board van, having served his driving ban, but the week before he had been reported and reprimanded for giving my mother a lift into Duke Street to do the weekly shop, a contravention of regulations made worse by the fact that he should have been at home 'on call' for emergencies at the time – although he was only out of the house for less than half-an-hour). He was peching for breath – in the middle of his first mild coronary (or 'heart episode/spasm') – and I was seeing lightning flashes in the midst of travel sickness – caused by a shoogly bus – and my first migraine attack.

We both made it to the semi-detached house of our destination, where Aunt Barbara revived us with, respectively, malt whisky/salted peanuts and Irn-Bru/salt-'n'-vinegar crisps (which in medical parlance must have been *contra-indicated* in big red capital letters for our respective attacks). While my mother interrogated my father about a suspected tight chest and deduced stabbing pains down the left arm – symptoms he vehemently denied having while fighting to catch his breath and struggling to flex the affected arm – I sucked all the salt off the potato crisps and quenched the resulting thirst with greedy glugs of Scotland's other national drink (which is still the most effective migraine cure that I know to this day – if taken early enough).

At three o'clock I switched on the wide-screen colour TV, the most up-to-date model available from Radio Rentals and the main reason I'd agreed to come on the visit (we still had black-and-white in 1974!).

Neutrals, if they remember it at all, recall this game as a one-sided bore – Celtic scored twice in the first 25 minutes – but Celtic didn't have to play that well to beat a young United team who froze on the biggest day in their history. Nevertheless, as any football fan will tell you, being two goals up is never a comfortable-enough cushion to relax against, and the migraine started pounding again in the second half when bloody Connaghan was forced into action by Andy Gray, after which a goal-bound shot from Archie Knox – the current Rangers No. Two – 'hit McNeill involuntarily on the head'. One United player played with white boots, and combined with a '70s glam-rock haircut and a Frank Zappa moustache, he looked like a reject from the Glitter Band or Mud.

Dixie Deans scored a third in the final minute, and the adrenalin released in my brain knocked the migraine on the head (or possibly a remission was affected by throwing up with relief and excitement into a basin balanced on my lap).

Walking back down the hill, towards the distant bus stop, my father and I were even more taciturn than usual, brooding as we were on our medical prognoses. My father had managed to convince my mother, and possibly himself to a degree, that he'd suffered nothing more life-threatening than bad indigestion. But whereas he was exhibiting classic signs of denial, I was in the throes of rampant hypochondria. I was convinced that the bike accident had left me with a brain tumour, and my only consolation was I'd seen Celtic break their cup-final-losing hoodoo (even if it was the last cup final that I'd ever live to see).

Scotland 1
Yugoslavia 1
(World Cup finals, 22 June 1974)

Summer holidays alternated between Millport, on the Isle of Cumbrae opposite Largs, and St Andrews on the east coast. In 1974 the Bennie clan followed in the wake of the Scotland squad, who'd been based in Largs prior to beating England 2–0 at Hampden in May. We travelled down from Glasgow by train, and while waiting for the ferry to take us to the town of Millport strolled along the front. The owners of every rowing boat for hire assured us that their craft was *the very one* that Jimmy Johnstone had been set adrift in by Sandy Jardine, in an early-morning attempt to register the first single-handed red-haired winger to cross the Atlantic/Firth of Clyde/Cumbrae Slip without oars (or depending on the newspaper reporting the story, with a *single* oar, which the wee man allegedly raised above his head while shouting, 'Scotland! Scotland! Scotland!'). At approximately six a.m. the coastguard had been alerted to Johnstone's plight – adrift and drunk – and they'd rescued him before landfall had time to disappear over the horizon from his tearful sight. The Flying Flea's teammates watched the proceedings with great hilarity, especially since the aeroplane-phobic Johnstone couldn't swim to save his life.

I watched Scotland's final game on the nearly deserted side of the island, in an atmospherically run-down beach-hut café in Fintry Bay, along with about 50 other sunburnt and peeling Glaswegian holidaymakers. I'd cycled round to Fintry on my own, in glorious 70-degree-plus sunshine, and while waiting for the game to start I'd taken my melting CurlyWurly and ice-cold Kia-ora (an orange-*flavoured* drink) and walked barefoot along the beach in contemplative mood. A win for Scotland would have guaranteed qualification for the second phase and put the seal on what had been, on balance, a wonderful vacation (I always complained bitterly about having to make do with Millport or St Andrews but I would not have been keen to experiment with Majorca instead, as some of my classmates' families were beginning to).

I sat down cross-legged and reviewed the one-and-a-half weeks that had passed.

The biggest plus was successfully negotiating, without applying the brakes at any point, the Hill of Death, a cycle ride from Cumbrae's second-highest point straight down a steep and twisting road, finishing in free-wheeling exhilaration in the town's Kames Bay, during which I overtook a Cortina pulling a horse-box at a speed approaching 40 mph (a form of psychological torture, after my accident, akin to getting back on a bucking bronco after having been unsaddled and landing in a rattlesnake pit).

But although my nerve still held – I hadn't been back on a bike since the accident in March – an unexpected consequence was beginning to affect my health (in addition to migraines, which I suspect I may have been prone to anyway). Looking through binoculars bought on a day-trip to Largs – proper ones made in Switzerland – I found it impossible to read the names of passing ships for entry into my *Observer Book of Ships*, no matter how long I fiddled with the magnification and focus. I knew something was seriously amiss when my six-year-old sister offered to read the names for me – using her telescope, which had been bought in Maples toy shop in Millport and which was made of plastic. Over the coming year my eyesight would deteriorate to the point where I couldn't read the blackboard from the *front* of the class and I had to get bottle-bottom-thick spectacles (they may have had contact lenses in the mid-'70s but I'm sure the only people who could have afforded them were professional footballers). Visual problems, of course, are associated with brain tumours and I was convinced I was going blind because of one, rather than heading towards extreme short-sightedness. It was only when the optician took my case history that the connection was made between my accident and sight problems (an apparently not uncommon consequence of serious blows to the head).

Apart from incipient blindness, then, the holiday's other major worry was the behaviour of my father on the second Sunday. Being away from home for two weeks meant two weeks without his coupon being collected on Thursday nights (Littlewoods didn't have standing-order forecasts in those days). He knew his regular perm numbers, eight from ten, by heart and any normal person would have avoided the pools results section of the *Sunday Post* like the plague. But not my father, with whom I pleaded on the second Saturday night not to check his numbers. He promised not to do so, but when I got up on the Sunday morning I *knew* he had – he'd made breakfast for everyone and was in high good humour, because – he couldn't resist telling me – 'my numbers didn't come up, so I haven't missed out on becoming a millionaire'. He really couldn't understand why I couldn't face eating my egg roll, which he scoffed, or why I was trembling with anger, frustration and, admittedly, relief.[1]

Watching the actual game was a bitter-sweet-bitter experience. Miljan Milanovitch's men only needed a draw to progress – and they played for it cynically and effectively. With less than ten minutes to play the Yugoslavs scored on the break, a powerful header from Karasi giving David Harvey in goal no chance. The atmosphere in the café went as flat as the warm lager dregs in the cans consumed earlier (the Fintry Bay café was normally unlicensed but crates of Tennents lager had been laid in specially for the occasion), and as Karasi scored the bathing-beauty Tennents models were crushed in-hand and underfoot in frustration at every table.

Sectarian recriminations then began to flare up, as the Scotland bench tried and failed to attract the attention of the referee in order to throw on Johnstone as a late substitute. Celtic fans were of the opinion that Willie Ormond wasn't trying hard enough to catch the official's eye – and that Johnstone should have been on from the start (if not for anti-Celtic bias in team selection). Rangers fans were beginning to take comfort, loudly and vocally, from the fact that Celtic's most famous winger would never get to play in a World Cup final game, when Joe Jordan got a last-gasp equaliser. Stunned silence and then noisy ecumenical reconciliation.

At the final whistle, café patrons dejectedly climbed down from their vantage points on chair seats, table-tops and roof beams. With Brazil scoring a late third goal against Zaire (whom we had only beaten 2–0, before drawing 0–0 with the holders of the Jules Rimet Trophy), Scotland were out of the competition on goal difference, the first *unbeaten* team in World Cup history not to qualify for the second phase.

As I cycled the three miles back to town, my heart swelled with pride. And there was always the next World Cup in South America to look forward to winning. Plus season 1974–75, when Celtic would be going for a world-record beating tenth League title in a row (instead of having to share the honour jointly with nine-in-a-row MTK Budapest and CDNA Sofia) was just a couple of months away.

As the sun began to set, I stopped and watched the Sleeping Warrior of Arran fade from view. My life was really only just beginning and there was a lot to look forward to, as an adult man and as a football fan. The Sleeping Warrior would reappear as ever in a few short hours, bathed in glorious early-morning sunshine.

The next day broke overcast and humid, and when I finally ventured out of the holiday flat with my bike and ball it began to spit rain. Finely at first, accompanied by sheet lightning, before a thunderstorm hit the island . . . It reached its ferocious peak as I turned for home into the teeth of a howling gale, at the most exposed point of Cumbrae: the northerly Stinking Bay. It was to be an uphill struggle from here on in . . .

FOOTNOTES

1 Because of his 'heart spasm' – which had finally been confirmed by an ECG – this was the first holiday during which my father didn't go swimming, in spite of almost Mediterranean temperatures. Years later we sat watching late-night television together, when the 1968 movie *The Swimmer* came on, starring Burt Lancaster as a man who swims his way home using the pools of rich friends. It was one of the few films that held my father's undivided attention. He turned up the volume and watched it entranced. Then he told me that he had gone swimming in every outdoor pool in Scotland, accompanied by my mother in the early months of their courtship, with my father on a Triumph motorbike and my mother in the attached sidecar. When I asked why, he responded cryptically by saying: 'Parents have more complicated pasts than most children realise.'

EMBARRASSING
THE HOOPS
1974–1989

Celtic 6
Hibernian 3

(League Cup final, 26 October 1974)

Prior to this classic cup final, in which the football played was every bit as impressive as the scoreline suggests, I'd seen Celtic win about half-a-dozen times at Parkhead, without the opposition getting even a consolation goal to cheer up my long-suffering father (who had reluctantly agreed to let me go on my own once I reached the age of 14). I remember almost nothing about these run-of-the-mill league and league cup games – neither match incidents nor personal circumstances – and I will therefore resist the lazy temptation to regurgitate the press reports. In his contribution to the *My Favourite Year* anthology, Ed Horton correctly states that 'there is a paradox in football's literature: the closer you get to the game itself, the less compelling your narrative becomes'.[1] Collections of dry match accounts only ever sell as *reference* works – to obsessive fans, sports journalists and writers about football – and if such tomes are going to be transformed into popular literature, authors have to leaven the facts, descriptions and statistics with the yeast of their own personal experiences and prejudiced perjuries.

One consequence of the above paradox must already be clear to the reader of this book: of the matches so far covered, the author has been notable for his physical absence from the majority of them. The point, however, is that I remember them as if I was there, so much emotional nostalgia having been invested in them. If everyone remembers where they were when John F Kennedy was shot – I was in my pram – so do football fans when recalling unattended but memorable matches.

While Dixie Deans, for Celtic, and Joe Harper, for Hibs, were scoring hat-tricks during this league cup final, I was wandering lost and bewildered through the Gorbals, having been mugged on a parentally unauthorised expedition to Hampden to see the game. The scoreline of 'Celtic 6, Hibernian 3' invariably stimulates this particular remembrance of things past, and even now I can feel the sharp tip of a Stanley knife (or possibly an unmanicured thumb) in the small of my back. Panic-stricken I handed over all my money – over two pounds! – and sheepishly obeyed my assailant's gruff instructions to walk 400 yards without turning round, believing his threat that he would be watching and would catch me up and cut my 'fuckin' Adam's apple from ear to ear' (*sic*) if I disobeyed. Thereafter I remember sitting on the bottom steps of one of Sir (*Sic*) Basil Spence's monstrous tower-blocks in the 'Hutchie E' housing complex, listening in snotnosed despair to the roar of the 54,000 fans further down Cathcart Road as they cheered each of the nine goals.

I had been persuaded to attend the final, against my better judgment, by Baby Albert, whom my father and I first met a month or so earlier when Baby Albert demanded ten pence for 'watching' my father's Ford Escort, after he had parked it in London Road while we were on our way to a Celtic-Hamilton Academical quarter-final first leg. If the money had not been forthcoming we would have returned to find the car with slashed tyres, scratched paintwork or shattered windscreen. After the game, my father was relieved and delighted to find his rust-bucket washed and waxed, and I was appalled when he gave Baby Albert his remaining five pence, plus a ten-pence tip for the unrequested car-valeting service. As I sat in the passenger seat, radiating resentment and disapproval, my father and his blackmailer conversed chattily, until my father offered him a Kensitas Club cigarette. And Baby Albert was at least a year younger than me! The next evening, a Thursday, I was none too pleased when Baby Albert arrived to share our mince-and-tatties tea, presenting my father with a 'new' battery for the Escort as a token of his appreciation. I was even more incredulous when my father took me aside and told me to let Baby Albert have a shot of my beloved Hornby train set, because young Albert was 'a homeless orphan in constant pain from rickets'. He finally left the house with a Great Western Railway locomotive (broken but purloined) and money from my mother for Vitamin D tablets.

We kept in touch, however – he used to call from the pay phone at the 'orphanage' – and it was his idea to go to the game, while pretending we were 'in town looking at the shops'. Baby Albert had been mugged jointly with me, but his Faginesque background stood him in good stead as he lied about having no money to hand over. And to his credit he offered to give me half of his own saved money (which, however, would not have been enough to get us *both* into Hampden). I rejected his offer, tearfully, as derisory. I also rejected his suggestion that I use his money to pay my way in at the gate, while he cadged a 'lift over' a turnstile (which I'm sure he would have managed, through a combination of cheerful cheek and being able to pass for an under-12).

As for getting home, we walked, squandering his remaining money on chips, fritters, ginger and sweets. Trudging along Duke Street in the cold dark, I was plunged into even deeper depression by the sound of a juke-box or radio being played in a pub we were passing. I slumped in the entranceway and wedged a swing door open with my foot. The potency of pop music is powerful poppycock and the strains of that week's Number One, *Sad Sweet Dreamer* by Sweet Sensation, moved me to the edge of tears once more.[2]

Visions of Isobel Hodge, whom I would have seen in person that Saturday morning if not for the disastrous detour south of the river, swam before my eyes. She had been my girlfriend in first year, and although I had broken it off – to show how masculine and independent I was becoming! – we still met each Saturday morning as part of a group that got the No 42 bus to go swimming at the modern pool in Easterhouse, where I ignored her with the completeness of the still hopelessly infatuated. Or to quote and paraphrase slightly the Duncan Thaw character in Alasdair Gray's *Lanark*: '(*I*) looked loftily round the (*pool*) with an absent-minded frown hoping she would notice (*my*) superior indifference.' This simulated indifference went on for another *four* years, until the end of secondary school, by which time she had developed into a quite stunningly beautiful redhead.[3] But as I wallowed in the sentimental lyrics and lush arrangement of *Sad Sweet Dreamer*, I could think of nothing but how my lost two quid, spent correctly and charmingly in the pool cafe, could have won back her affections.

Baby Albert disappeared into the pub, and with his last few coppers won enough on a slot machine to buy a bottle of Pomagne cider (which some paralytic adult presumably bought for him from the off-licence booth). We both got drunk quickly and I made the mistake of telling him about the object of my emotionally repressed desires. After he expressed the withering opinion that she was probably winching some lifeguard with a motorbike at that very moment, we ended up fighting in a vomit-filled gutter.

FOOTNOTES

1 'Going Down? Oxford United 1991/2', *My Favourite Year*, Ed. Nick Hornby (Gollancz-Witherby, 1994).

2 '70s pop music played in the background normally fuelled football-fantasy daydreams to the extent that I would come out in goosebumps, zonked on a physiologically measurable adrenalin high. The intellectualisation of pop music criticism, however, is not by any means easy-listening. As a post-graduate I once listened to a seminar entitled 'Jumping Jack Flash: The Role of Radical Rock in Revolutionary Politics'. The Marxist academic's central thesis was that the political watershed marked by the Paris riots of May '68 had been reflected at the time by politico-popico changes in the arrangement of the Hit Parade. The dramatically different Number One hits in April and June were representative, *he argued*, of a radical shift in popular

political opinion over these crucial three months, April beginning with *What a Wonderful World* by Louis Armstrong and June finishing with *Jumping Jack Flash* by the Rolling Stones. In May itself *Young Girl* by Gary Puckett and the Union Gap knocked Armstrong off the top, an example of irresistible historical forces at work, which saw American cities on fire by August, when *Fire* by Arthur Brown topped the charts. Mary Hopkins' chart success with *Those Were the Days* in September was merely a reactionary spasm by the bourgeoisie (ie Paul McCartney), clinging desperately to their ill-gotten gains as capitalism threatened to collapse under the weight of its own contradictions.

I was sorely tempted to ask the speaker about the social significance of *Ob-la-de ob-la-da* by Marmalade taking over at Number One on 1 January 1969, but I was genuinely concerned that he'd take the question seriously and link the Scottish male vocal group's only Number One with the rise of structuralism and the search for a truly objective symbolic language, only for the attempt to collapse in the mid-'70s when Marmalade made their last chart appearance with *Falling Apart at the Seams*, which scraped into the Top Ten for one week at Number Nine in 1976. (Okay, I made the above example up, but examples of equally pretentious and pompous pop music theorising abound – in the musical press and academia.)

3 After leaving school, I saw Isobel Hodge one more time – in 1980, on the top deck of a No 38 bus, during the commuter evening rush hour. Apparently she hadn't become a model, although as a 19-year-old with her looks she could well have done. I had just started working for Esso, and although I had worked there long enough to put on two stones in weight (thanks to three-course business lunches washed down by pints of lager) I hadn't yet used my first salary cheque to buy a decent suit. Instead, my office clothes consisted of tan brogue winklepickers, polyester flared trousers (with extensive 'bobbling'), beige Marks and Spencer sports jacket (Extra-Long), drip-dry pin-striped shirt, nylon kipper tie and enormously large Elton-John-type spectacles. In addition, I'd just had a really bad haircut. She actually started to mouth a friendly 'Hello', before I made it die in her pretty mouth by storming past her seat with a lecherous look of non-recognition. Only six weeks later, say, I would have been mature, and presentable, enough to overcome the years of repressed conditioning that West-of-Scotland males have to submit to – to the extent that I could have said something sensitive and soul-baring like, 'Hi, Isobel. How are you?'

Celtic 3
Airdrie 1

(Scottish Cup final, 3 May 1975)

The last game I attended together with my father, sitting in the gods of the South Stand. Rangers had just prevented Celtic making it 'ten-in-a-row' in the league, by winning the last-ever old-style Scottish First Division (before reconstruction and the introduction of the Premier League).[1] Although there had been plenty of warning signs, the failure to make it ten came as a terrible shock to the all-conquering, utterly complacent Celtic legions. The league run-in was an unprecedented disaster, with only four wins in the last 15 matches, a collapse made all the more painful and incomprehensible by a start to the campaign which only included two defeats in 20 matches. Everyone knows that empires rise and fall, but the rapidity of decline in the final stages invariably unnerves the erstwhile forces of domination. Celtic finished eleven points behind Rangers, and four behind Hibernian, and in the run-in Jock Stein must have felt like Eugenius at the end of the fourth century as the Roman empire collapsed under him – with a series of shock defeats at the hands of the Huns (Rangers), the Visigoths (Motherwell), the Ostrogoths (Hibernian), the Franks (Dundee United) and the Vandals (Airdrie).

A Cup double was some consolation, and although Airdrie made a game of it, and were never sacrificial lambs, the result was never in any real doubt – thanks to outstanding performances from Kenny Dalglish and Paul Wilson (who scored two fine goals).

Wilson suffered racial taunts from the opposition throughout his career, which must have been especially irritating since he was born in Milngavie, went to a good Catholic school and was not especially coloured (just extremely swarthy). My mother thought he was a dead ringer for Rudolph Valentino, which probably prompted my father's jealous observation during the final that Wilson looked like 'a Eurasian macaroon' (sic). Wilson's name occasionally crops up in pub arguments about Celtic's first 'coloured' player, along with Paul Elliot who was signed from Pisa in 1989. In actual fact the first black Celt was Gilbert Heron, a Jamaican American, who played for the first team in the early '50s, at a time when Rangers were importing blue-eyed, blond-haired Aryans from Scandinavia in job lots.

FOOTNOTES

1 The ten-team Premier League was formulated by a conspiracy of anti-Celtic forces in response to Celtic's seemingly unstoppable domination of Scottish football, and it was given a considerable boost when Celtic won their ninth championship in a row and Jock Stein jokingly suggested his club would have to consider applying to the English First Division. Clandestine meetings were held in top Glasgow hotels, with representatives from the Scottish League, the Scottish Football Association, the Press Association, Glasgow Rangers FC, the Scottish Conservative Party, the Church of Scotland, the Glasgow Chamber of Commerce, the Chief Constables Association, the Masonic Order, the Strathclyde Passenger Transport Executive and organised crime in attendance. Masonic actuaries had compiled detailed dossiers which showed that although Celtic had a better record than Rangers against *both* Scotland's biggest clubs, like Aberdeen, Hearts and Dundee, and the smaller teams like Arbroath, Dumbarton and Morton, Rangers were closer in parity if results against the also-rans were excluded (the rationale being that a great club like Glasgow Rangers had trouble motivating themselves against runt-like rubbish). The only other possibility considered was to handicap Celtic, to a greater degree season after successful season, by deducting points from them before a season had even begun.

The fact that Celtic lost their monopoly of the league championship a year before the introduction of the Premier League is probably due to the motions passed at the above meetings in 1973–74 demanding that Scottish Grade One referees 'redouble their efforts to push back the green tide of Fenian formidability'.

Also, the fact that Stein was in an almost fatal car crash in July 1975 suggests Masonic skulduggery, too. Stein was a fast but skilful driver, and although accidents were commonplace on the notorious A74, the one involving Stein's Mercedes was highly unusual. Driving back from Manchester Airport, at the end of a holiday in Minorca, the Mercedes was hit head-on by a car travelling the *wrong* way on the Glasgow-Carlisle dual carriageway. The car was a Peugeot. Peugeots were the make favoured by Glasgow's kamikaze gangster assassins in 1975, as popularised by the French movie star Alain Delon.

Rangers 1
Celtic 0

(League Cup final, 25 October 1975)

Because of Jock Stein's car crash in the summer, assistant manager Sean Fallon took over team management for season 1975–76. Given his record – Celtic failed to win anything for the first time since 1964 – it's surprising he wasn't co-opted on to the board of British Leyland as a non-executive director.

On a personal level, I had been dropped from the school First XI and reserves, leaving me free to attend most home games at Celtic Park on my own. There I whipped on my spectacles at one minute to three, before removing them smartly at 20 minutes to five. I would then make my way home, following a route that never deviated, through shudderingly unfocused outlines and wobbly haloes, having read in the *Reader's Digest* or *Sunday Post* that myopia could only be cured if eyeglasses were not worn continually, thereby allowing defective vision to be 'exercised' and gradually improved.

Baby Albert occasionally joined me, at my usual vantage point in the Celtic End, if his car-parking extortion business was providing adequate cash flow. We went to the final together, and this time only missed the first 15 minutes, due to confusion on my part about the time of the early kick-off (it was one p.m., not two o'clock, a move forward in timing designed to cut down on drinking and the resulting hooliganism). Nevertheless, the majority of the 50,000 crowd were not noticeably abstemious, and for once my platform shoes proved practical when relieving myself in a toilet awash with urine, although the same claim could not be made for the Bay City Roller-type bell-bottom-turn-up trousers (but without the tartan trim).

The game was a bad-tempered bore, made worse by Alex MacDonald's headed winner in the second half. Baby Albert was too short to see much of the action and he had to ask me who scored. When I told him, he climbed up on my shoulders and started screaming: 'Ya wee fuckin' nyaff, MacDonald! A know where ye park yer motor, ya bass!'

The team lines for this match are, in retrospect, instructive. On the plus side Kenny Dalglish and Danny McGrain were developing into genuinely *world*-class performers (the former through natural ability and the latter by dint of committed application). On the negative side, Peter Latchford was now first choice keeper and the left-back berth was filled by Andy Lynch.

Englishman Latchford as a youth had been tipped to play for England – at basketball – and he came to Parkhead in 1975 as yet another cut-price 'solution' to the team's endemic goalkeeping problems. To be fair, he was popular with the fans in general, with his tendency to save shots spectacularly to make up for losing goals solecismistically (often in the same game), but to me he was always an overweight embarrassment who caused my stomach much dyspeptic discomfort. As a goalkeeper in a ladies' netball team he would have struggled to cut out the most innocuous of crosses.

Lynch was a classic example of what Celtic used to do with disastrous forwards and midfielders whom they couldn't get rid of. He was bought from Hearts as a left-winger, but because of his inability to dribble, cross or shoot was eventually converted into a very ordinary left-back. I don't know why crap front players at Celtic always moved *backwards* in position – it was never tried in reverse – but it seemed almost official club policy. Its one major success was Tom McAdam, signed from Dundee United as a non-scoring striker, who was transformed into a classy and quick centre-half. Lynch, however, fulfilled the role – specially created for him by Stein – of non-attacking full-back without defensive responsibility.

A few days after the final, I was flicking through a book published by Victorian head-measurers – we didn't have a lot of books in the house but our library, such as it was, was an eclectic collection – when I came across a series of line drawings. As the reader moved across and down the page, the chins and noses of the profiled heads receded and elongated, respectively, until the final deformed caricature of a head was deemed to be indicative of congenital imbecility. I knew where I had seen this profile before. I wrote his name in pencil under the most stretched head, and if the current proprietor of the Inveresk Guest House in Glasgow would like a framed copy to hang above reception, I'd be happy to dig it out of my mother's loft.

Johannes 'Shuggie' Edvaldsson, an Icelandic internationalist, was signed in 1975 and he played in the final too. An excellent utility player, Edvaldsson was bought from Holbeck of Denmark, one of the last successful transfer-ins for many years to come. Other so-called 'bargain buys' would embarrass the hoops for many years to come, a view confirmed by Bob Crampsey in his excellent biography of Jock Stein, *The Master* (Mainstream/Coronet 1986/87): 'From now on the curious signings would begin to outnumber the good . . . ' From a supporter's point of view, read *crap* for 'curious' and *competent* for 'good'.

In March of 1976, Celtic paid Ayr United £90,000 for winger Johnny Doyle, to fill the gap left by Jimmy Johnstone, who was now playing for Sheffield United. Doyle had all of Johnstone's wild temperament but without an iota of the dribbling skill. Undeniably popular with the Celtic faithful – Doyle was 'Celtic daft' – he was the natural successor to Andy Lynch (following the same front-to-back career structure). But Celtic-daft Doyle, with the emphasis on daft, didn't live long enough to become an All-Time Celtic Genius. His entry in *An Alphabet of the Celts* baldly states: 'Aged 30, he was electrocuted in a domestic accident.' A favourite Hun joke circa 1981 was: 'How many Celtic players does it take to change a lightbulb?' Answer: 'Two. Johnny Doyle – and someone else to remove the body.'

With established star veterans retiring, or moving on and down, it was just as well that youngsters like Roy Aitken, Tommy Burns and George McCluskey were beginning to push for regular first-team places . . .

Scotland 6
France 12

(Five Nations Championship, 10 January 1976)

If Smithycroft Secondary had had such a thing as a prospectus, the range of its sporting activities would have made for impressive reading (as long as the academic results were hidden away at the back in a small-print paragraph):

> Athletically inclined boys at the 'Croft are well catered for, and can choose to participate in rugby, rowing, golf, soccer, track-and-field athletics, tennis, gymnastics, hockey, cross-country running and swimming (the school boasts a heated indoor pool, thanks to a generous bequeathment from the Strathclyde Education Department). Our boys – and girls! – benefit from a curriculum designed to keep them off the streets, and the discipline of competitive physical sport helps channel adolescent energy into non-delinquent areas. And although not many of our boys leave our institution armed with abstruse academic qualifications, we like to think of our *alumini* as practical *doers* rather than esoteric *thinkers*. Special scholarships are available from the Scottish Probation Service and various juvenile courts. The school motto is: *It wisnae me!*

Coach trips to Murrayfield, twice a year, were another innovation implemented by our sports-mad mad headmaster (who also spoke fluent Latin, which was optimistically introduced to the syllabus). We invariably disgraced ourselves and muddied the 'good name' of the school, and at this particular match we incurred the wrath of the supervising teachers by cheering the French on to victory. Herded together in the schoolboys' enclosure, we nevertheless made the 80 minutes of play sheer hell for the becapped and short-trousered public schoolboys who surrounded us. If they replied in the negative to the question 'Are you related to Bill McLaren?', they had their school caps gobbed in and their exposed back legs thwacked with 12-inch steel rulers. In the high-pitched history of the schoolboy enclosure at Murrayfield, our school contributed the only recorded police arrests (but only for drunk and disorderly behaviour and toilet-roll throwing). On the coach trip back to the notorious East End of Glasgow I had to sit on my own at the front, because Celtic had won 3–1 away at Motherwell and I was rubbing my Blue Nose classmates up the wrong way. It was a perfect end to a perfect day.

As my myopia got worse through third year, so I moved out further along the back division of the school rugby team. Eventually I was banished to the wing, which was fine by me, since our team was incapable of passing the oval ball out that far without dropping it (the rugby XV was made up of those not good enough for either of the football XIs and those who were serving Glasgow District Schools

Football League suspensions; the split was usually about 50–50).

Although our rugby XV never won a game – they never finished a match with 15 players – other schools with rugby-playing traditions hated playing us. Our forwards based their play on the indisciplined French pack of the mid-'70s, and if they had bothered to acquire an even rudimentary understanding of the rules they would have been frighteningly effective. I suppose you could say that they played a rucking-and-mauling game. Or maybe fucking-and-bawling, as eight Jean Pierre Rives wannabees attempted to stamp their authority all over the opposition – literally.

I played my last game of school rugby as hooker, and I won my fellow forwards respect early on by winning a scrum against the head. I achieved this impressive feat by kicking my grammar school opposite number in the goolies, and back-heeling the ball out before he caused his side of the scrum to collapse. We nearly won this game, and I came off the pitch dazed but exhilarated. Not being able to see properly was hardly a major problem in the scrum and I was quite keen to continue in my new position. But a school medical a week later resulted in my transfer to the rowing team.

I was diagnosed as having head lice. When I gave the letter to my mum she took it as a personal affront and I got boxed round the ears! Foul-smelling lotion from the chemist (not local) and a nit-comb eventually de-infested my scalp, but my mother was convinced I'd contracted the little parasites from rubbing shoulders with the great unwashed in the scrum (she could well have been right) and I had to tell my sports master that my mummy wanted her little boy to do a non-contact sport. Hence my switch to rowing.

Celtic 1
Dundee United 1

(League Cup, 1 September 1976)

With Jock Stein back behind the manager's desk, Celtic won the cup and league double, although they lost to Aberdeen in their *13th* successive League Cup final. In the UEFA Cup we went out in the first round, but to the European giants of Wisla Krakow. In season 1976–77 I attended every home league game at Parkhead and never saw Celtic lose – an impressive record, but with melancholy memories for me personally, since attending Celtic games during fourth year at school was the nearest thing I had to a social life. That and going to the public library to study for my 'O' Grades. My sex life consisted of browsing in and borrowing books from the Art and Travel sections (but many of the selected picture books featuring Renaissance nudes and African tribeswomen were 'unreadable' because of stuck-together pagination). At this point football served to fill a girl-shaped hole in my life.

At half-time Stein introduced new signing Pat Stanton to the crowd. The 32-year-old Hibs captain got a rousing reception and I was delighted. He was a magnificent defender and I still had my old Hibernian top at home (even if it was full of holes and becoming a very tight fit). Stanton played superbly in every league and Scottish Cup match that season, before sustaining the injury that ended his career in the very first game of season 1977–78 (against Dundee United).

Rangers 0
Celtic 1

(Premier League, 24 November 1976)

This was a Wednesday-night fixture at Ibrox, with recorded highlights broadcast on BBC1 Scotland after ten o'clock. In order to watch it 'as live' I would normally have had to have been on red alert against hearing commentary on Radio Scotland or score updates on Radio Clyde, as I studied in my room.[1]

I came into the living-room in blissful ignorance, however, having 'studied' for three hours in Trappist silence, without a radio or record-player having been switched on (normally, to my parents' bewilderment, I studied the plays of Shakespeare, irregular French verbs and the inert properties of ticker-tape trollies with Tiger Tim's radio show blaring away in the background, with a black-and-white portable flickering away in the foreground with the sound turned down). The absence of background music and lack of silent programming was due to my total immersion in a dog-eared and broken-spined paperback copy of *The Catcher in the Rye*. I had been given it that afternoon, during double English, by one of my Modern Studies teachers, Mr Jeyes, who had been standing in for our regular English teacher, who was taking one of her regular 'sickies'.

While he caught up with marking of his own, he allowed us to read anything that took our fancy from either the class or school library, the stock of which ranged from Enid Blyton to Sir Walter Scott. Lethargically page-turning *Hergé's Adventures of Asterix the Gaul* (a joint publishing exercise by 4D, who had mixed Tin-Tin and Asterix during one of their library-book restoration periods), Jeyes looked up and noticed my bored distraction. I was invited up to his desk, where he rummaged in his battered briefcase. As he presented me with his own copy of JD Salinger's classic novel, his eyes sparkled with rekindled teaching idealism (which Smithycroft had knocked out of him soon after he left Jordanhill Teacher Training College).

I looked at the orange Penguin cover as if it was a poisoned chalice.

'It's not set on a farm, is it?'

From the first paragraph I was hooked, and when I got home I could hardly wait to get my tea eaten and my chores done. Once in my room I was so engrossed in Holden Caulfield's stream-of-consciousness that I completely forgot to switch the radio on. Here was the book I had, without knowing it, been waiting on. Although not *about* me specifically, it had obviously been written *for* me in particular, encapsulating as it did my teenage condition of boredom and anxiety. It was also so rib-achingly funny that I had to put it down every few pages to recover.

When my mum told me the football was starting, I seriously considered giving the 'Old Firm' highlights a miss, especially since Celtic hadn't beaten Rangers for almost three years. But if I watched the game, the pleasure of reading the book would be extended.

Early on the referee awarded Celtic a penalty, after John Greig scythed Bobby Lennox down in full flight. The linesman, however, decided that Lennox had dived and waved the referee over to the touchline. Relieved that his chances of getting a good supervisor's report had been restored, the Mason in the Black gave a free-kick to Rangers – against Lennox for play-acting. Lennox was carried off to hospital with a fake broken leg.

This is the first 'Old Firm' game which I viewed objectively enough to realise that the standard of the football being played was at best mediocre, and at worst miserable. The atmosphere was as highly charged as ever, but as is often the case in the 'World's Greatest Club Game' the quality of play suffered in inverse proportion. The winning goal was described by Archie Macpherson as 'stunning', but in reality it was more of a speculative effort from 25 yards resulting from a lack of any other possible options. Scored by Joe Craig, a supposed replacement for Dixie Deans and bought from Partick Thistle for £60,000 (he only lasted two years at Parkhead), it was the kind of strike that could equally well have sailed over the bar or sliced away for a shy – Craig just turned and blootered it. I was delighted to see it go in but far from convinced it was deliberately executed. Even this soon, could Literature be changing my priorities and developing my critical faculties? Possibly, but not so that anyone else would notice, least of all Mr Jeyes, who was on the receiving end of brutal, Glaswegian, male understatement.

On the Friday I ran into him in the corridor – I couldn't have taken avoiding action, because being a circular building the corridors were proportionately curved and you therefore couldn't see teachers coming (they just appeared without warning coming round bends) – and Jeyes stopped me to ask what I'd thought of *The Catcher in the Rye*. I actually *wanted* to say that it was brilliant, fantastic, wonderful, etcetera, and that I'd always be grateful to him for introducing it to me (I'd have gotten round to it eventually, I'm sure, but reading it as an adult wouldn't have provided the same *frisson* of recognition). I think Mr Jeyes not only hoped for an enthusiastic response but half-expected one – even from a male pupil in 4B. As I rummaged in my bag to find the book, I tried to find the right words to express my delight and gratitude. Thrusting it at him, as he beamed in expectation, what I did say was:

'Ucch, it was okay, sir . . . Better than Enid Blyton at least . . . Bye!'

FOOTNOTES

1 Since it was my 'O' Grade year, my nine-year-old sister Lynn was moved out of our shared bedroom, into the living-room and on to a sofa bed, in order to give me the privacy necessary for swotting-until-you-go-blind revision. At the start of primary school she had been a loyal Hun, but by ignoring her and not rubbing her Blue-Nose nose in Celtic's success I had at some point converted her into a devout Tim; so much so that at the age of nine or ten she declared her future vocation as a 'Caramelite nun' (*sic*).

Celtic 2
Dundee United 0

(Premier League, 26 March 1977)

I attended this game with Baby Albert, and we were not looking forward to our first look at Roy Baines, yet another cut-price goalkeeper (actually, the Morton goalie was part of a swap deal, which took the mercurial talents of Andy Ritchie to the Greenock club, plus £15,000; almost inevitably Ritchie developed into 1979's Scottish Player of the Year, the year in which Baines was sent back to Morton with his goalkeeping tail between his legs!).

With the score at 0–0 United got a dubious penalty, and the Dundee club's eccentric goalkeeper Hamish McAlpine wandered up the park to take it. He proceeded to miss, or to be fair Baines saved, and 37,000 excited Celtic supporters enjoyed the spectacle of McAlpine rushing frantically back towards his own goal. United's Plan B then went into operation as the Tannadice Terrors of David Narey, Paul Hegarty, Tom McAdam and Walter Smith (the current Rangers manager) hacked down every Celtic player who was rushing to get into position in the United half.

Celtic won the game with goals from Joe Craig and Ronnie Glavin (a successfully converted penalty!). New hero Baines kept Latchford out until mid-April, when he let in three goals against Motherwell at Fir Park in a 3–0 defeat, two of which were og's from Andy Lynch! Three days later Baines missed the 1–0 victory at Easter Road against Hibs which clinched the title but, incredibly, Lynch retained his place (the first indication in my mind that Jock Stein had lost 'something' and would never be quite the same after his horrendous car crash).

Celtic 1
Rangers 0

(Scottish Cup final, 7 May 1977)

This was the first 'Old Firm' final shown live on television, and I decided to watch it from the comfort of an armchair. Played in torrential rain it was a truly awful game, made memorable only by referee Bob Valentine of Dundee momentarily forgetting which way Rangers were shooting and awarding a penalty against them. Inexplicably, Dalglish was not keen to take it and I almost fell off the pouffe on which I was sitting, hunched forward a foot away from the screen, when the Rangers keeper Kennedy threw the ball to Andy Lynch, who placed it on the spot as if his blood had just become infected by a Mexican jumping-bean virus. Lynch – who had only taken two penalties in his life, for Hearts, and who had missed both of them. If Kennedy had dived the right way he could have saved the shot with his eyes shut.

Celtic hung on for the next 70 minutes, playing a decidedly unattractive defensive game, with the result that Alfie Conn became the first player to collect Scottish Cup medals for both Rangers and Celtic. Stein had bought him earlier in the season from Tottenham Hotspur, as a 'ready-made' replacement for Dalglish, whose transfer requests were becoming ever more frequent and urgent. At the time the Hun hordes were screaming blue murder for the return of their old favourite, and Stein's move for the occasionally brilliant but normally anonymous Conn was partly motivated by a mischievous/malevolent desire to put the Blue Nose hooters out of joint. Conn was a disastrous buy at £65,000 – both in financial and footballing terms – and within two years he had to be offloaded to Derby County on a free transfer. His eight goals worked out at almost £8,000 for each successful strike. From the day of Conn's signing to this, buyers and sellers in the transfer market have been able to see Celtic coming from miles away, with their tendency to trade potential cash cows for the proverbial handful of beans (see *Dalglish, Kenneth – transfer to Liverpool*). And vice-versa, of course (see *Cascarino, Antony – transfer from Aston Villa*).

With a league and cup double, and Dalglish still on the books, the summer of '77 was a pleasant one for all Celtic supporters. On a personal level, May had provided a sporting triumph of my own, even if official recognition had been denied. In the Glasgow Schools' Rowing Regatta, my racing-four crew had 'won' the Under-17 400-metre dash. However, any entry in Smithycroft's imaginary prospectus highlighting the achievement would have ended with the mysterious qualification of 'Withheld' – because of some breach in toffee-nosed rowing etiquette.[1]

On the academic front, my 'O' Grade results were initially thought by the school to be a computer error, and were only accepted as accurate after checking with the Scottish Education Department (six A Band One 'O' Grades, plus a failed F in French).[2]

FOOTNOTES

1 A year or so later I submitted a play called *The Crab Catchers*, based on my rowing experiences, to a playwrights' competition for teenagers. Although it didn't win, one of the judges sent the MS back with a note praising it. He also suggested I re-write it, bringing out the 'latent homosexual desires of the nubile young rowers', a revision that he was generously willing to help me with personally. I didn't take him up on his offer, since

the many reasons for my personal unhappiness and poor self-image didn't include latent homosexuality.

2 Incredulity at my exam results were perhaps understandable, since not only were they the best in the 20-year history of the school but were among the best in the whole country, fee-paying schools included. Their impressiveness is largely explained by the fact that I had nothing else to do, apart from football and golf, except for swotting like a demon for them (but admittedly in a house without heating, lighting, floorboards or running water, since my parents refused to be decanted during council modernisation work).

Celtic 0
Dundee United 0

(Premier League, 13 August 1977)

The first game of the season and the scoreline summed up perfectly the footballing year which was to follow, as well as painfully symbolising my continually thwarted relations with members of the opposite sex. Watching from the back row of the Upper Stand, I had a bird's eye view of the pigeon-shit pattern of play that Celtic would henceforth be forced to adopt, now that their greatest ever player had flown the coop. Three days previously Kenny Dalglish had signed for Liverpool, and although it constituted a British club record fee of £400,000 it was nevertheless utterly inadequate financial recompense for the loss of 'the finest club footballer in Britain over the period 1970–85' (Bob Crampsey). No amount of money would have compensated for the loss of Dalglish (whom could we have bought to replace him?), but with their usual disastrous but immaculate timing the Celtic board managed to off-load their most valuable asset just before the financial Big Bang hit the British transfer market.

I was gutted when Dalglish was transferred, and all of his posters in my bedroom were taken down and shredded. Blind club loyalty he may not have had, but for seven years Celtic supporters had had the pleasure of seeing a footballing genius play week in and week out, and in every game Dalglish never gave less than the clichéd 110 per cent. We may have missed out on his development from a very, *very* good player into a truly great one, but we had still been privileged to see Dalglish scoring great goals, laying on memorable assists and covering every blade of grass with the grace of an Arab thoroughbred and the heart of a Clydesdale workhorse. He may have grown up in a Govan towerblock overlooking his beloved Ibrox, and it may have taken

Sean Fallon two teeth-pulling hours to get the taciturn 16-year-old to sign forms for Celtic, but in his time at Parkhead Dalglish regularly transformed ordinary sporting contests into extraordinary exhibitions of performance art.

With Dalglish gone, and Stanton and Conn seriously injured in the opening match, Stein would have needed to be at the height of his powers – physically, psychologically and tactically, while cajoling the best out of a technically limited and mentally brittle squad under pressure from the 'New Firm' of Aberdeen and Dundee United – to keep Celtic to the fore of Scottish football. Instead, the Big Man stumbled through his last season on increasingly clay-like feet, until Celtic finished fifth in the league, performing woefully in all competitions and winning nothing. Even with £400,000 in the proverbial Parkhead Biscuit Tin, Stein was plain bloody-minded in his refusal to pay more than £100,000 for potential new recruits.

The players he did bring in would not have got a game for the *reserve* team of the late '60s, the only exception being Tom McAdam from Dundee United (£60,000). John Dowie was a Rangers 'S' form *reject*, recruited from Fulham (£25,000), a midfield mucker who dug holes for himself and his team-mates. Joe Filippi from Ayr United (£15,000 *plus* the excellent young Brian McLaughlin) was brought in to replace the injured Danny McGrain, but soon lost his place to the og-specialising and mentally retarded looking Alan Sneddon, who had learned his football trade in the cauldron of the Ayrshire Juniors. Robert Kay was a free transfer from relegated Hearts, a flat-footed full-back who had *once* played a blinder against Celtic at Tynecastle. The final piece of this ill-fitting jigsaw was Frank Munro, an on-loan liability from Wolves. Made *captain* on his *debut* against St Mirren, Munro's first significant contribution was to blast an own goal past a bewildered Latchford. Stein immediately made arrangements to sign the overweight Munro on a permanent basis.

Celtic ended up with 36 points from 36 games, an awful record which I would nevertheless have been pleased to transpose to my own personal league table of romantic involvements. This actually existed in documentary form, in an A4 binder labelled 'Sex Statistics' (which I rediscovered in my mother's attic while rummaging about looking for old match programmes, as research material for this book). The rating system I adopted was as follows:

    * = terrible, stuttering performance (ie hyperventilation)
    ** = strained but not suicidally embarrassing

*** = fairly normal conversation
**** = good; smooth and amusingly urbane repartee (hee-hee-hee)
***** = HOT DATE!!! (ie penetrative sexual intercourse)

I continued to keep these records up to date until Christmas, relegating and promoting the female objects of my desire each month. Needless to say I never showed my 'sex stats' to anyone, five-star entries being confined to the explanatory index (see above). As well as star ratings out of five for each conversation entered into with a member of the opposite sex, two points were awarded for each example of social contact, regardless of the outcome. And for each day, Monday to Friday, one of that month's five selected girls *had* to be talked to – otherwise she lost two points (a sort of inverted joker system).

I also kept records in a folder titled 'Seed Catalogue' but there is no way I'm reproducing extracts from that particular document either (suffice to say that I was a keen but wasteful bedroom horticulturist, spilling copious amounts of seed on unfertile ground; and by necessity I was also an efficient but nocturnal laundry-by-hand specialist).

On Tuesday 11 October I had a talk with the Careers Officer about my future. He asked me what I *wanted* to be, and got a bit huffy when I suggested professional golfer or private detective. I then wound him up further by asking what qualifications were necessary to become a Careers Officer (answer: none, and even he couldn't have grown up *wanting* to become a Careers Officer). When I eventually made a serious suggestion – journalist – he dismissed it out of hand, reminding me gleefully that it was an extremely competitive job arena, even for graduates. With my 'O' Grade results I could have been studying for Oxbridge Entrance Examinations, but he had probably never had cause to recommend these to anyone during his many years of bureaucratic time-serving. He even advised me that studying English Literature at Glasgow or Edinburgh universities was no longer an option because I had failed 'O' Grade French.

'To further my interest in economics and business studies' (quoting from his notes on the Interview Sheet), an interest which had apparently grown from nothing during the course of the interview, I was given an application form and prospectus for Glasgow College of Technology, which he added was an institution I could apply to without the disadvantage of having to fill in a 'complicated and bothersome' UCCA form. Other pupils had their hopes and dreams similarly slapped down and redirected – simply because of our social class and educational catchment area – and if I sound bitter it's because I am.

Celtic 5
Partick Thistle 2

(Premier League, 22 April 1978)

Although this was an entertaining and easy home win, Baby Albert and I left the Upper Stand trembling with anger and frustration. We had been sitting just behind the directors' box and directly in front of us sat two ex-Celtic players, both of whom had been competent pros and regular squad members in the good but not great Celtic teams of the early- and mid-'70s. During the first half, when Celtic had raced into a 3–0 lead within the first 20 minutes, they had barely paid any attention to the proceedings on the park, preferring to puff on stubby cigars and sip from a shared hip flask (one wore a sheepskin coat with a fur collar and the other a purple suede overcoat). They remained bored and indifferent until midway through the second half when Doug Sommer took advantage of sloppy Celtic defending to get one back for the Jags, immediately after which they perked up considerably. Caustic comments about the current team followed, along with resentful asides about the inflated wages then being paid at Parkhead. In their cups they assured each other that in their heyday they would never have let a struggling team like Thistle back into the game. When Joe Craig put Celtic 4–1 ahead a few minutes later they slumped despondently back into their padded seats – which they enjoyed for free, while Baby Albert and I were using almost all of our disposable income to see the game. I was so outraged that I wrote a complaining letter to the club's official newspaper *The Celtic View*, naming the two footballers, but it was never printed (the publication wasn't known to supporters as *Pravda* for nothing).

The only mitigating factor in favour of this pair's indifference was that they weren't actually on the playing staff any more. Danny McGrain, who was a long-term injury casualty for most of season 1977–78, is on record as being disgusted with the attitude of some of his fellow professionals on the park during this year, shock defeats and insipid draws affecting their self-satisfied and complacent off-field demeanour not one jot. The fact that McGrain was also struggling against diabetes makes his frustration and commitment to the Celtic cause all the more admirable. The old – ie younger – Jock Stein would never have tolerated such pre- and post-match apathy about the club's predicament, and he really did have to go. The appointment of Billy McNeill as manager, after a successful year at Aberdeen, was widely welcomed by the support, although most would agree that Stein was treated shabbily by being offered a 'non-job' as a director with special responsibility for the Celtic Pools. The initial acceptance by Stein of a position which was beneath, and probably totally unsuitable for, him is an indication of how far the Big Man's pride and abilities had declined.

As manager of the anti-heroic Leeds United, he lasted one day longer in the job than Brian Clough's controversial 44, before accepting the offer of becoming manager of the Scottish national team. This appointment of a legendary but increasingly cautious figure was a knee-jerk reaction by the SFA to the flamboyant but disastrous tenure of Ally McLeod, who began June of 1978 as the nation's most admired 'character' and who ended the month as the most reviled individual in the country (outwith convicted child molesters serving sentences in solitary confinement).

Holland 2
Scotland 3

(World Cup finals, 11 June 1978)

During the hysterical build up to the finals in Argentina, almost every male pupil in the school was convinced that Scotland and Ally's Tartan Army were capable of 'going all the way'. A sizeable contingent of fifth-years actually attended the hubristic Hampden happy hour, paying hard cash to witness McLeod and his players doing a lap of honour in an open-backed lorry. Commercial sponsors used the Scottish World Cup squad to promote everything from motor cars to alcoholic beverages, a combination of products that many of the players were not averse to indulging in simultaneously (the advertising copywriter who came up with the slogan of 'Running rings round the opposition' for Talbot cars never worked in the industry again, except for a short spell at the end of June as a freelance poster remover).

I was sent to Coventry for a week for suggesting that the 'Inca pensioners' of Peru were no pushover. When they won 3–1 in Cordoba I was at least psychologically prepared for the outcome. The 1–1 draw with Iran in the same stadium left me gobsmacked, gutted and gfued (generally fucked up). That evening Andy Cameron's *Ally's Tartan Army* and Rod Stewart's *Olé Ola*[1] were removed from the Radio Clyde playlist and smashed on bended knee (on air). Into the early hours and beyond World Cup sports programmes and news flashes replayed one particular image over and over – the now infamous recording of McLeod on the bench, burying his shiny head in skeletal hands, before looking up pleadingly like Patrick Troughton's priest in *The Omen*, the one whose photographic negatives had mysterious smudges over them, moments before he is impaled by a falling spiked railing (Troughton, that is, not McLeod, although the Tartan Army of 500 or so would have been hurling more than verbal abuse if a wrought-iron fence had been available to them). This pathetic image of McLeod was reprinted the following day in most of the papers, although no sub-editor dared to caption it with the most appropriate description, namely, *Ally McLeod: fucked up and far from home.*

If political support rose significantly for the SNP during the 1974 World Cup finals, and would actually have swept the country to independence if the team had succeeded in winning the tournament, then participation in the 1978 finals had a similar knock-on effect, although in reverse. But I'm not referring to the SNP, even if its opinion-poll ratings did plummet, but to the SED (Scottish Education Department).[2] The worst 'Higher' results since the damn things were introduced coincided with the late-night football in Argentina, examinations having been scheduled for late May and June. Some of the academic results for Smithycroft's fifth-years in particular made the 1–1 draw against Iran look like a good point won away from home.

If mass hysteria had swept the country prior to the finals, the results against Peru and Iran plunged the male population into a malevolent mob mentality, which was turned on innocent members of the home-based Tartan Army (crime rates soared and the SFA offices in Park Gardens had their double-glazed, one-way-mirrored, bullet-proof windows panned in).

One or two days after the Iran debacle – a Thursday or Friday –

I was walking up the road to either the Riddrie Public Library or the school (but not for a Higher exam). Whatever my destination I was dressed in full school uniform and I had to pass a group of deserters from third year (Blackhill and Provanmill Cannon-Fodder Infantry), who had gone AWOL from woodwork, car maintenance or remedial English. I probably betrayed a victim mentality by moving my Adidas bag – full of revision notes – from my carrying right arm to my chest, where I clutched it like a Jewish baby in a concentration camp line-up. Noticing this Clark-Kentish gesture they swung down from the tree they had been swinging from – it was actually a wall – and decided to investigate the contents of my bag. If I had allowed it to be opened, my revision notes – which were superb examples of concision and comprehensiveness – would undoubtedly have been cast to the four winds, if not set alight and urinated over. I therefore clutched the bag even tighter to my chest, put my head down and marched determinedly forward.

As I walked, staring fixedly ahead, they started to take turns in pushing and shoving me. Then kicks aimed at my backside started, followed by punches, or dunts, between the shoulder blades. Punches then rained down on my head and face, followed by kicks to the small of my back, administered after run-ups. I was then covered in spit, coming at me from all directions. The good adult burghers of Riddrie crossed the street to avoid the unpleasant scene which was developing in front of them, and in the semi-detached houses that we were passing Venetian blinds snapped shut and net curtains swished drawn.

When my tormentors followed the lead of their dominant pack leader and started to pick up half-bricks from a small area of waste ground, I knew that I was in danger of becoming too brain-damaged to sit any more Highers, never mind pass them. The chief grunt gave me a shouted warning from behind, just in time for me to turn round and duck my head. Otherwise the half-brick would have hit me full in the face (or on the back of my head).

Switching the bag back to my right hand I turned again and ran as fast as my hollow legs would carry me, breathing through my mouth since my nose was gushing blood. If not for the weight of the bag – it had all my revision notes for every subject, plus books – and the metal segs on the soles of my black brogues I may have been able to outrun them and thereby reach the sanctuary of the school administration block, but I could *feel* them catching me up. They caught me as we drew level with the start of a block of street-level shops, when the foremost thug grabbed the collar of my blazer (ripping it in the process). With conscienceless ferocity he told his cronies to get me on the ground, and delegated the smallest runt to get hold of my Adidas bag. Surprisingly, I wasn't frightened, and my thinking was amazingly cool and detached. I knew what I was going to do – if I was able – and my last articulated thought before doing so was that 'No jury in the land will convict me after this provocation'.

I dropped the bag, swivelled round, got my right leg wedged behind both of his, grabbed him with both hands by the lapels of his vinyl jacket, and then shoved him back and up with all the force I could muster. He crashed through the plate glass of a greengrocer's window, ass backwards, with his arms and legs outstretched in front of him, as a cartoon character would have been depicted in similar circumstances. After a breathless 'Ah, mammy daddy' he burst into tears, as various fruit juices trickled damply over his head and down his front and back (a fluidity that must have felt like the warmth and stickiness of blood). I leaned over to examine the new window display and once I was satisfied that no shards of glass had severed his jugular vein or pierced his heart, I turned back to retrieve my Adidas bag.

It was a hundred yards down the road, in the possession of the little delinquent assigned to grab it (my other assailants were still rooted to the spot in gobsmacked shock). Cold calculation gave way to red-mist fury, and I picked up a large shard of glass in the shape of an elongated 'V'. Gripping it so tightly that it cut into palm and fingers, I chased my quarry for over three miles, even ignoring the discarded bag which he 'papped' when I got within slashing distance of him. By the time I caught up with him completely – in Govanhill south of the river – I still had my bloody weapon but no longer the unthinking willingness to use it on him. Instead I just stared him down until he wet himself with worry about what I *might* do.

Although I got my revision notes retrieved for me, and no criminal charges were ever brought, *I* was the one thought to be in the need of the services of a child psychologist!

No child psychologist accompanied the Scottish World Cup squad, although they could probably have used one as McLeod's lack of authority led to petty squabbling amongst the players over pocket money, bed times, substance abuse and heavy petting sessions with Latin *au pairs*.

To progress further in the competition Scotland had to beat mighty Holland by three clear goals. Watching on TV I couldn't help myself getting wildly excited about the possibility when Archie Gemmill scored the goal of the tournament to put Scotland 3–1 ahead. This, however, was getting too close even for the laid-back Dutch team's comfort and they promptly strolled up the park for Johnny Rep to unleash a *stoppable* shot from 30 yards (Alan Rough in goal, of course, remained rooted to the spot in case the ball's trajectory had a last-gasp swerve back towards the centre of the goal sneakily built into it). Scotland again went out of the World Cup on goal difference, but it was an ignominious rather than glorious failure. Much was made of the fact that Scotland managed to beat the previous and future World Cup finalists in their last game, but it was a match the Dutch were *happy* to lose, since it left Peru as Group 4 winners and therefore qualifiers for the tougher Group B, which included host country Argentina and favourites Brazil. The moment Scotland looked capable of overtaking the Dutch, the exponents of Total Football[3] simply put their collective feet on the accelerator and disappeared over the Group 4 horizon.

FOOTNOTES

1 Rod Stewart can be forgiven for the excremental *Olé Ola* because of the lyrics in his 1977 hit *You're In My Heart*, which include the following affectionate reference: 'You're Celtic, United, etcetera. . . . ' No Top Ten hit has ever alluded to the romantic associations of Glasgow Rangers FC.

2 When the brown envelope from the SED dropped through the letterbox in July with my Higher results, the certificate read AABBC (grades which would have been good enough to do any undergraduate degree at Glasgow or Edinburgh except for Medicine, being one A or B short). On the other hand, I would still have been accepted for Glasgow Tech without the two A grades. My parents' reaction was a surprise and led to the first row with them in which I used the dreaded F-word as a verbal re-enforcer. Their first comment was a synchronised and spontaneous: 'Hmm . . . Only a B for English – that's a bit disappointing, isn't it?' 'No it *fuckin'* well isnae! Chrissake . . . ' 'Don't you dare speak to your mother like that just because you fluffed English.' To give my father his due he did try to get me to investigate the possibility of applying late for university, or of taking a year out and applying for the next academic year, but I went ahead with the Business Studies course partly because it had a year's work experience as part of its structure, and partly – it has to be admitted – to annoy the hell out of him.

3 The Dutch version of Total Football, where their players were expected to play anywhere on the pitch, as well as they would have done in their nominal positions, had its Scottish equivalent in 1978. The Scots players were dragged all over the pitch by Peru and Iran, and performed equally ineptly out of position as they did in their usual berths.

Celtic 2
Liverpool 3

(Jock Stein Testimonial, 14 August 1978)

If this narrative was following the usual fictional would-be-writer's-rights-of-passage structure, the summer after leaving school would be a lazy lacuna of eclectic book-reading in fields of sun-ripened rhubarb, as the young working-class hero looks forward eagerly to the mind-broadening experience of attending the Yooni, where he will become the faithful sidekick of a charismatic older student who will encourage the tyro writer to hammer out short stories on a second-hand Adler typewriter, and which will be published without a single rejection letter in the *New Yorker/Horizon/People's Friend* (à la Stingo and the mad genius Nathan Landan in William Styron's *Sophie's Choice*, which in the summer of '79 I was fatalistically amused to see contained an embarrassingly risible 'Uncle Bennie' in the second chapter).

Instead, I was dreading the dry syllabus of my chosen course, which included *sociology*, and not enjoying my vacation employment. I lasted two nights in a Finefare supermarket, before crashing a forklift into a stack of newly arrived plastic advertising hoardings, shattering the NEFAR lettering of all six. Working in the meat market for two months was physically demanding and stomach turning, but it put more money in my pocket than I knew what to do with, even after handing over 'my keep' to my mother. One of the offal merchants gave me a copy of his New Authors edition of Archie Hind's *The Dear Green Place*, since he knew I was going on to college, and although I thought it was pretty good – especially the descriptions of animal killing and on-the-hoof carving – I handed it back to him with a comment of typically Glaswegian understatement: 'Bit of a cattle-slaughterer's A-Z, isn't it?'

I paid Baby Albert into the Upper Stand for Jock Stein's testimonial against Liverpool, and Dalglish got a very warm reception from the fans. Especially those in the Jungle, who gave him an absolute roasting every time he touched the ball. Dalglish had obviously made the right decision in going to Liverpool – he was voted Player of the Year in 1979 – and I took out my frustration at my wrong choice of academic institution by screaming blue murder at him (so much so that a steward threatened to eject me if I didn't shut up). Years later, when Charlie Nicholas deserted Parkhead disloyally early, I felt more sympathetic than angry, his decision to go to boring and methodical Arsenal reminding me of my own disastrous career choice.

Sickened by the scoreline, even if it was only a friendly, I realised that football was not going to tail off in importance as the main source of meaning, inspiration and identity in my life, which I had thought (hoped?) it might when I became a student. Celtic would now have to fill a university-shaped hole in my life. With melancholy resignation I accepted that I was going to grow into an *adult* obsessed with football, the highlight of whose week would be football on Saturday afternoons – just like the socially deprived nutters in the Jungle.

At the end of September, instead of buying a duffelcoat or overcoat for the forthcoming academic term, I purchased a padded anorak with detachable hood. The former attire would have been *de rigueur* for a posing undergraduate in leafy Hillhead and bohemian Byres Road, but the latter would be more practical for the Celtic End or Front Stand at Parkhead . . .

Hibernian 2
Celtic 2

(Premier League, 18 November 1978)

This was the first away game outside Glasgow I ever attended, and it sticks in the memory because of the traumatic travel arrangements. Two days earlier I had sat my driving test, and it was a matter of family honour that I passed it first time at 17 years of age (to have failed would have stigmatised me as an immature homosexual, as far as Hun relations in East Kilbride, Kilbirnie and Fife would have been concerned). After a summer of paternal tuition I was unlucky enough to be allocated Riddrie Driving Test Centre, as opposed to the less demanding Shettleston equivalent (this may have been yet another urban myth, but it was commonly believed that no 17-year-old males ever passed first time at Riddrie; I certainly believed it). Coughing up most of my vacation earnings for an intensive course of professional lessons, I tried to unlearn my father's bad habits. My instructor initially tried to frighten me into signing up for 20 two-hour sessions, but I made do with a masculinely minimal ten.

My examiner was a typically petty bureaucrat, who clipped his nasal instructions through pursed lips and who sported a military-type tash. I called him 'Sir' throughout the examination, a respectful form of address which I hoped he would appreciate (I also wore a collar and tie). Kangarooing, slightly, down Smithycroft Road at the start, my chances of passing were almost ruined by a thin squall of rain – if it hadn't quickly blown itself out the examiner would have had no choice but to abandon the test there and then, since I suddenly realised with a horrible sliding feeling in my intestines that I didn't have a clue where the switch on the dashboard of the dual-control Datsun Sunny for the windscreen wipers was. The shock induced, however, and the relief felt when the rain stayed off, actually helped me forget my nervousness, which was extreme.

For the next 30 minutes I drove with the aggression and risk-taking panache of a 60-year-old office clerk in a Volvo equipped with a sewing-machine engine, changing down gears so I wouldn't have to overtake buses stopping to pick up arthritic passengers. Heading back to the test centre only one major difficulty remained: a sharp 340-degree turn from Gartcraig Road into Lethamhill Drive. Despite crawling round so slowly that I almost stalled, I managed to mount the pavement with the two nearside tyres.

Parked outside the test centre, slightly closer to one kerb than the other, I scored 100 per cent on the Highway Code questions. The examiner was obviously still swithering, so I threw in a final obsequious 'Sir'. To which he responded by saying that although I had a lot of minor faults, I was obviously the kind of young man who would work conscientiously to correct them. 'Yes, Sir!' I confirmed as he wrote out my pass certificate. As I waved the precious piece of paper at my waiting instructor, his jaw dropped in a rictus of stunned surprise.

The next day, a Friday, I took the Marina into college and tried to park it in the Strathclyde University car park, a manoeuvre which required me to reverse into a single confined space. After much to-ing and fro-ing, I still wasn't parked properly. A final attempt at reversing was accompanied by the hideous screech of metal against metal. I'd slash-scratched the new Austin Princess next to me, from front wing to rear bumper. Blinking away tears of panic, I lurched out of the parking bay praying that no attendant or servitor had seen me, inflicting further damage to the bodywork of some Head of Department's pride and joy. I finally got parked in a deserted residential street just outwith the Glasgow city boundary.

With my fragile driving confidence utterly shattered, I spent all day during lectures and tutorials worrying about the drive home in rush hour traffic (after getting a taxi back to the remote spot where I had parked).

I had planned to take Baby Albert as a passenger on the drive through to Edinburgh to see Celtic at Easter Road, but I fobbed him off with a story about there not being enough room because I was taking some classmates through instead. He didn't believe me because he knew how few friends I had made at college – two, neither of whom were Celtic supporters (Glasgow Tech's Business Studies intake was a bizarre collection of mainly middle-class Tory offspring whose Highers hadn't been good enough to get them into proper university business schools, even with private tutoring and special school crammers).

The drive through to the capital was as nightmarish as expected, with almost as many near misses as the game itself. Standing in the away Albion Road terracing, however, I managed to forget about the stress of the return journey. It was an excellent match, made even more memorable by a goal apiece for Billy McNeill's recent signings Davie Provan (£120,000 from Kilmarnock) and Murdo MacLeod (£100,000 from Dumbarton). These proved to be outstanding buys, and I'd seen the home debuts of both earlier in the season. New Celtic signings start off with considerable goodwill towards them on the part of the supporters, who are desperate to hail new heroes if given good reason for doing so. MacLeod in particular was an instant hit, and his entry in *An Alphabet of the Celts* states that on his debut 'every touch brought ripples of applause'. I remember standing in the Jungle and joining in the warm acclaim, as he dissected the Motherwell right flank with acutely angled balls to Tommy Burns. Although Celtic lost 2–1, I was convinced that our big-bummed and barrel-chested midfielder – 'Wee Rhino' – would be a player to watch, and I enjoyed being part of a crowd whose generous applause visibly increased a new player's confidence with every touch. Although he could obviously pass, tackle and run himself into the ground, his venomous shot didn't become apparent until this game against Hibs. When he left Celtic for Borussia Dortmund in 1987 he was sorely missed but still somewhat underrated, and I was surprised but delighted when the Germans transformed him into a Ronald Koeman-type sweeper.

Celtic 4
Rangers 2

(Premier League, 21 May 1979)

Up until this glorious evening, it had been a disappointing football season and depressing academic year. Football-wise Celtic had crashed out of the ersatz substitute for European competition, the Anglo-

Scottish Cup (to Burnley!), the League Cup (to Rangers) and the Scottish Cup (to Aberdeen). My grades at college were mediocre.

For most of the first term I had been a sex criminal without any convictions, but I finally got myself a record for 'breaking and entering' after kopping of with a babe in the Bubble (Glasgow Tech's inflatable Union bar), my boyishly virginal charm and six-pints-of-lager pogoeing style to the strains of Rod Stewart's *Do Ya Think I'm Sexy* proving irresistible to my piquantly punkish dancing partner (a fellow *virgo intactica* straight from the pages of HP Lovecraft, but one that the cat had dragged in through a hedge backwards after hitting every branch of the ugly tree on the way down). The consummation was an away match at her place with an orgasm score of 0–1, with my early score having more than a hint of offside about it, but in the circumstances the result was more important than the performance, probing foreplay being discarded in favour of a more direct grope-grab-and-guide route to goal.

Up until an hour before kick-off, I hadn't been intending to go to Parkhead (although I still had my ticket), being stuck in my bedroom trying to revise for the Law I exam which was scheduled for the next day, a Tuesday (the game was played on a Monday night as part of a concertinaed back-log of rearranged matches, the original fixture having been postponed because of severe winter weather in January and February, which had decimated the scheduled Scottish football fixture list). The psychological pull of the most potentially dramatic 'Old Firm' derby ever proved too strong, however, and I ran most of the way to Parkhead to join the massed ranks in the Celtic End, reconciled to resitting the exam in September. After all, a failed exam could always be re-sat and passed; whereas failure to attend the game where a Celtic victory would clinch the Premier title would mean missing a once-in-a-lifetime, never-to-be-repeated combination of winning a league championship in the last game of the season *and* depriving Rangers of the very same opportunity in the process (Celtic needed to *win*, in this their last game, whereas a *draw* would probably have been enough for Rangers, who were three points behind but with two games still to be played). Celtic-Rangers. Head-to-head. Winner takes all . . .

If William Goldman had been commissioned by the Great Director in the Sky to script this game, the following plot would have been regarded as believable as *The Princess Bride* (whereas most of the pontificating pundits and paying patrons were expecting to see a footballing equivalent of *A Bridge Too Far*). With Celtic a goal behind at half-time, my thoughts began to stray to the torts and commercial case law that I should have been mugging up on. Less than ten minutes into the second half the Hun hordes in the Rangers End erupted in justifiable fury, followed soon after by an explosion of understandable ecstasy, when Johnny Doyle was quite correctly sent off for aiming a vicious kick at a prostrate Alex MacDonald, which unlike most of his attempts to connect with the ball during the game actually hit its intended target. (In *The Glory and the Dream* authors Campbell and Woods momentarily forget their usual admirable objectivity, describing this incident thus (my italics): 'Doyle, *incensed* after a series of *crushing* tackles by Rangers defenders, *aimed* a kick at Alex MacDonald, another *fiery* competitor, and was promptly sent off.')

The potential psychological benefits of being reduced to ten men are well known to all football followers, but the initial reaction from the Celtic support was one of utter despair and crushing disappointment. The atmosphere was deflating faster than an illicit lover's erection when interrupted by an aggrieved husband brandishing a loaded revolver to a sweating temple. Celtic threw on 35-year-old Bobby Lennox as substitute, but it was right-winger Davie Provan who started to turn the game. In the 66th minute he fed the ball to 'the Bear' (Roy Aitken) in the Rangers box, who in a feeding frenzy of raw hunger headed the ball past Peter McCloy. The equaliser re-ignited the crowd and Celtic responded in kind to the deafening verbal backing. In the 75th minute Aitken was up in attack once more, and although his shot was initially charged down it broke loose to George McCluskey, who almost burst the net with his shot. Then before the utterly berserk celebrations – and I mean absolutely mental! – had time to die down Rangers equalised, Bobby Russell scoring his second. Spontaneous and sickening silence on three sides of Celtic Park, while the Huns cavorted in their own vomit and urine.

At this point I would have settled for the 2–2 draw (after all, Rangers *may* have lost both their remaining games in hand). I felt physically sick and I was beginning to shake all over. Celtic continued to attack, somewhat frantically, with astonishing encouragement from the Jungle, but I was hoarse to the point of speechlessness and gutted to the point of hopelessness. With six minutes left the Rangers centre-half scored a third goal – for Celtic, heading instinctively into his own net for an unbelievable own goal. Apollonian heaven descended on the Celtic End, or an ecstatic Dionysian hell broke loose, and with tears of joy I was hugging and kissing the supporters around me, trying to keep my feet on rubber legs as the crowd swayed back and forwards in uncontrollable delirium.

To the nervous horror of the more composed in the stand, Celtic apparently continued to push forward – with ten men for Chrissake – in the remaining few minutes, but I was too far gone on a higher astral plane to be worried about the advisability of this strategy. When Murdo MacLeod scored a fourth in the last minute, with a 200-yard shot, my eyelids just fluttered gently like an angel's wings, as the overloaded pleasure centre of my brain fused, disconnecting itself from my body with a not disagreeable 'pwoof . . . '[1]

The next day, after sitting Law I – which to my genuine astonishment I passed without difficulty – I wandered the city centre streets in a dreamlike trance, with a moronic grin plastered across my face. I occasionally snapped myself out of it for the pleasure of identifying Hun passersby, who were easy to recognise because of their facial resemblance to high-rolling pontoon players who had stuck on 21 but had nevertheless just lost their life savings to a five-card-trick-trumping dealer.

FOOTNOTES

1 Years later Fat Saul relived his memories of this night with me over a few pints, and if I had stayed home I may well have suffered a similar experience. Fat Saul was unable to attend the 'decider' because of an attack of chickenpox, and he listened to the game at home in Cranhill on the radio. For the final six minutes, after Celtic had just gone 3–2 up, he couldn't bear the commentary any longer – radio being the most nerve-racking way to follow a game – and he switched his transistor off. Nervously fingering his rosary beads he opened his bedroom window for some air and almost fainted when the massive roar accompanying MacLeod's 90th-minute goal carried all the way to Cranhill. Fat Saul was able to distinguish it as a roar acknowledging a goal, but of course he had no way of telling which set of supporters had contributed to the crescendo. Still nauseous from his illness and excitement, he threw up over the balcony. Psyching himself up to turn the radio back on, he said if it had turned out to be a Hun equaliser he was genuinely prepared to follow the contents of his stomach over the balcony railing, even if to have done so would have been a mortal sin. (NB: This story loses some of its dramatic impact when the hearer realises that Fat Saul lived on the first floor and not the third, which I didn't discover until I visited his flat for the first time.) At the time of the 'Old Firm' decider, there was of course no live TV coverage of league games in Scotland, but Celtic fans were deprived of the pleasure of seeing recorded highlights because of a lightning strike by TV technicians, their Masonic shop stewards calling them out in a fit of purple pique. To this day I haven't seen television recordings of the six goals, although Celtic Films have apparently captured them for posterity.

Anti-Celtic conspiracy theorists can also cite the famous 1957 League Cup final, when Celtic scored five second-half goals to make it a 7–1 thrashing of Rangers. A BBC technician supposedly forgot to remove a dust-cap from a lens after half-time, thereby depriving the Celtic faithful of the opportunity to see goals by McPhail (a hat-trick!), Mochan and Fernie.

Luckily an amateur film exists, which Archie Macpherson in his autobiography suggests Celtic ought to show to the composer Carl Davis, while commissioning him to put it to music.

Celtic 4
Partizan Tirana 1

(European Cup, first round second leg, 3 October 1979)

The beginning of the end for Alan Sneddon. One down from the first leg in sunny Albania, 50,000-plus packed into Parkhead for the return leg. Sitting in the Upper Stand I had a clear view of Berisha's garry-owen clearance from just outside his own box. Following the expected flight path I was aghast to see that the ball would land on Sneddon's unsymmetrical cranium, and when it did I was not surprised when he headed the ball over the frantically gesticulating Latchford for a 15th-minute og (if only my July prayers had been answered and Skylab had landed on Sneddon instead of Australia). Playing for Celtic motivates some average players to raise their game significantly, but for others like Sneddon the pressure of expectation almost makes them buckle at the knees. As well as being an overrated liability, I hated Sneddon because he was one of those individuals who inspire intense but irrational dislike, for no coherently justifiable reason – like David Platt of Sampdoria, Arsenal and England, whose bland physiognomy nevertheless has me making a fist of my right hand in furious annoyance (especially since his appearance on a kit manufacturer's poster, posing à la John Travolta in *Saturday Night Fever* with one primatal arm raised). But before the Celtic fans had time to get on Sneddon's hunched back, we were 2–1 up, and went on to win 4–1, despite George McCluskey making his usual copyrighted hash of a penalty. Sneddon was off-loaded to Hibs in 1981, where his ugly mug and suicidal back passes turned Easter Road supporters to rigid stone for almost a decade. In the mid-'80s I asked Sneddon for his autograph, but only because we were both in the showers of the Royal Commonwealth Pool at the time.

In the second round at Parkhead, Dundalk's peasant pig farmers played us off the park and I was relieved to get out of the ground having witnessed an undeserved 3–2 victory, against a team which included the Lawler brothers, Dainty, Flanagan and Muckian. In the second leg in Ireland they must have been inspired by the recent Papal visit, or by the great Glasgow Celtic turning out with five at the back, but the Bhoys held on for a miraculous, and pathetic, 0–0 draw. But having got through to the quarter-finals Celtic beat Real Madrid 2–0, deservedly, at Parkhead, only to go down 3-fucking-0 in the return leg in the Bernabeu. The Real Madrid tie was played in March of 1980, but thereafter the '80s would be a decade when Celtic's interest in European competition always petered out before Christmas.

For Celtic the '70s had started with a European Cup final and ended with the 1979–80 team still in the European Cup and leading the Premier League (which was, however, lost to Aberdeen after a stunning collapse from March 1980 onwards). The '70s may never have had an adjectival equivalent of the '60s 'Swinging' but it was a memorable and enjoyable decade for my football team, and in retrospect a not uninteresting period for me personally (certainly, the '70s formed my character and provided more powerful memories than any other; it is a rather worrying realisation, however, that next year – 1996 – I could in theory be dating females *born* in the 1980s).

Football has always been more important to me than politics, and at a dinner party wake soon after the 1992 General Election I prompted serviette-snuffled sniggers of disbelief when I insisted that I'd have happily settled for every Conservative election victory since 1979 if they had been traded off in Faustian fashion against Celtic winning the European Cup every four or five years. Tory-voting Celtic supporters may be as rare and bizarre as Tory trade unionists, but most of us wouldn't have exchanged Labour Governments through the '80s and '90s if it meant we had to accept the club's actual record of dismal European failure. In fact, if a Tim dictator had pumped one per cent of the Gross Domestic Product into Celtic Football Club I'd have happily goose-stepped along to his Nurembergesque rallies (although I may have balked at a Final Solution for the racially inferior Huns).

In March of 1979, I voted against devolution, mistakenly believing that it would make an independent Scottish parliament less likely. Also, like a lot of apolitical nationalists I naively believed that North Sea oil would be a panacea for *Britain's* economic problems and I wasn't unhappy about sharing the black gold with our English neighbours. In fifth year at school I got 20 out of 20 for a Modern Studies essay in which I seriously suggested that an independent Scotland would be so oil rich that the revenues would have to be spent giving every OAP in the country gold-plated taps for their en-suite bathrooms. Even in first year at college, amidst the 'Winter of Discontent', the beneficial effects of vast oil revenues featured prominently and optimistically in Economics essays. Another argument against devolution that impressed me at the time – and still does – was the horrendous prospect of yet another bureaucratic layer of government, adding a devolved but toothless parliament to district and regional councils (not to mention Westminster and Brussels). For a country that prides itself on its radical traditions and swashbuckling reputation, Scottish voters have a depressing tendency to vote into power the dourest and most stupefyingly dull politicians imaginable.

My parents' MP, for example, was Hugh Brown and he represented the constituency of Provan, the safest Labour seat in Britain after Neil Kinnock's, for 20-odd years. Provan had more social deprivation and sub-standard housing than downtown Naples, and the Honourable Member therefore chose to live in the Glasgow stockbroker belt of Milngavie/Bearsden. His loyalty to the Party was eventually rewarded with ministerial responsibilities – for Agriculture and Fisheries! Neither corrupt nor especially complacent, Brown was merely an anonymous middle-class time-server typical of Scottish Labour MPs at the time.

In retrospect, the iniquitous 40 per cent rule for the devolution referendum was a piece of Unionist figure-fiddling worthy of the SFA's biased dealings with Rangers (see next match report). At the time the devolution debate left me cold, except for some bizarre correspondence in the *Glasgow Herald* and *Scotsman* newspapers, about the correct pluralisation of the word referendum (because Wales had one, too). The two broadsheets followed different style guides, and the letters pages were filled with hilarious epistles debating the grammatical pros and cons of 'referenda' and 'referendums'.

Political apathy is perhaps understandable, because in 1979 a student's financial lot was a reasonably happy one. One could live on the SED grant, and in the summer vacation supplementary and housing benefit were still available. Not that I needed either. Incredible as it may seem to undergraduates of today, two days after signing on as unemployed, the Job Centre telephoned with a definite job offer. For three months I slogged my guts out in a meat-processing factory in the East End, but I earned enough money to go impulse shopping around a Comet electrical discount store on football-free Saturdays.

Celtic 1
Rangers 0

(Scottish Cup final, 10 May 1980)

An enthralling cup final – for a change – which Celtic deservedly won with an extra-time goal from George McCluskey. Most of the press coverage, however, spilled on to the front pages, with pictures, descriptions and condemnations of the 'Hampden Riot' expanding to fill inside pages . . . At its height, mounted policemen – and one much photographed woman – were participating in cavalry charges on the pitch, as rival fans charged and counter-charged, lobbed missiles and fought hand-to-hand in an orgy of drunken violence. Television pictures of the game's bloody aftermath were beamed around the world, much to the chagrin of the Scottish Tourist Board, and a pen-friend in America watched coverage of the 'Scottish Superbowl' in tearful disbelief. I watched the pitched battle develop in front of me from the back of the Celtic End in *stunned* disbelief.

The SFA fined both clubs £20,000, punishments which imply that the supporters of Celtic and Rangers were equally culpable. At the height of the battle, certainly, drunken Celtic fans were inflicting sickeningly gratuitous violence on policemen, pressmen and Orangemen with all the mindless ferocity of their Rangers counterparts, but however childish it may sound it is important to stress that *they bloody well started it*. In addition, the police should have been able to prevent the trouble in the first place.

The boys in blue, however, chose to accuse the victorious Celtic team of inciting the riot when the players ignored SFA guidelines for 'Old Firm' finals by going to their supporters at the Celtic End to acknowledge their backing. In response, hundreds of exuberant Celtic fans spilled over the fence to join their heroes on the pitch. At this point the police should have ushered, or even truncheoned, the Celtic fans back on to the terracing, but they didn't have the manpower so to do. Incredibly, most of the large police presence at the game had been redeployed during extra-time, taking up new positions outside the ground – ostensibly to keep departing fans apart, but with lots of policemen no doubt crammed into their white Transit vans while waiting to 'lift' celebrating Celtic fans for heinous crimes like urinating in public and walking on cracks in the pavement.

The Celtic fans milling about on the pitch and track, including

Baby Albert, were simply indulging in good-natured if over-the-top celebrations. The response from the other end of the ground defied civilised belief, as irate Huns vaulted the fence – with no police line to prevent them – and charged up the pitch with hate in their hearts and broken bottles in their fists. The ecstatic Celtic fans couldn't have been more taken aback if they had been Tommies in the First World War, climbing out of their trenches during a Christmas Day armistice only to be confronted by hordes of Huns in spiked helmets charging towards them with fixed bayonets and mustard-gas bombs.

With the dogs of war released, the pitch soon resembled a real battlefield. To try and describe it succinctly, picture a fight scene from one of Peter McDougall's television plays, but with a cast of hundreds.

Baby Albert tried to get back on to the terracing but was swept back by a new tide of hot-heads jumping the fence in the opposite direction in order to meet the Huns head on. He claimed later that his mild concussion and cut knee had been sustained under the hooves of a rearing police horse, but I suspect he simply fell backwards while trying to reclimb the fence. When some kind of order had been restored, he was carried up the terracing, like a bride crossing the threshold of a new home, by a bearded giant of a young man in a blood-stained Celtic top, who reunited me with my dazed diddy of a friend. The Syringe then gave us a lift home in his company car – a removals van – and he allowed me to rummage through his plastic carrier bag of souvenirs – which included a Rangers top, a flick knife and a police cap (the kind with the black-and-white chequered band).

But rather than end this section on a light-hearted note, it should be remembered that a lot of innocent people were arrested and/or seriously injured. The press photographer Eric Craig, for example, required extensive micro brain surgery.

Celtic 4
Partick Thistle 1

(Premier League, 18 March 1981)

Towards the end of season 1979–80, I remember standing in the Jungle and getting into conversation with two supporters who regularly attended reserve games at Parkhead. Never having been to a reserve game in my life – then or since – I had to take their word for it that Charlie Nicholas was the most exciting prospect since the appearance of Kenny Dalglish. I was sceptical in the extreme, since more verbal mince was spewed out from the Jungle terracing than from any other part of the stadium (the Jungleites certainly provided the highest decibel level of support, led the singing of sectarian songs, and scared the hell out of foreign opponents on big European nights, but their reputation for pawky wit and essayistic erudition was out of all proportion to the actual experience of standing amongst them; for every hilarious *bon mot*, displaced 'snobs' from the stand had to endure a stream of foul-mouthed – and inconsistent – invective[1].)

The prediction about Nicholas, however, was impressively percipient. At the time great things were expected of me, too, since I had just been selected as the successful candidate by Esso for the year-out, sandwich element of my degree, the interviews for which took place in the last term of second year. If the secret of job interviews is to give a totally false impression of one's abilities, I was already something of an expert at 19. A lot of the other college placements were with local companies, who created artificial positions for their guest workers from academia – doing pointless projects or irrelevant surveys – or who used their salaried students as cut-price clerical staff. Esso's placement position offered very generous financial remuneration, but with a degree of responsibility to match. Frankly I was appalled. Having come across as dynamic, gregarious, confident, cool under pressure, ambitious, statistically numerate and telephone eloquent – none of which I was – Saturdays and Wednesdays in season 1980–81 would have to serve as bolt-holes from high-powered, nine-to-five reality.

When the National Union of Seamen went on strike at the beginning of 1981, the pressure at work became intense, as the Marketing Department was responsible for the transportation of all oil-based product in Scotland and Northern England. The Operations Section resembled a WWII general-staff headquarters, as all product was switched from sea tanker to road haulage, with tortuous routes and clandestine pick-up points having to be devised to beat local shortages and flying pickets.

Like many people who are basically shy, but who are not crippled by their wary reluctance, I managed to maintain an outward appearance of spontaneity (rehearsed), self-possession (spurious) and self-confidence (fragile), but during this period external cracks began to show (which I attempted to cover up by mainlining on indigestion tablets during frequent trips to the executive bathroom, where I would take refuge in a locked cubicle, as did a number of other middle managers, none of whom ever flushed the cistern either). Attending football may not have kept me from a nervous breakdown but it was a welcome safety valve for releasing built-up tensions.

Although Celtic only won the Championship, they did so in fine style, and the 1980–81 team was beginning to bear comparison with the Lisbon Lions (an albatross of a comparison which is constantly being hung round the collective necks of improving Celtic teams).

This 4–1 home win against Thistle was a typically impressive league performance, watched from the stand with two friends from college, Michael and Alex, the former destined to become an accountant and the latter a surveyor (the Glasgow Tech Business Studies course being something of a boot camp for boy offspring of the West-of-Scotland bourgeoisie). Having just discovered that Raymond Chandler had been an oil executive early in his career, I bored them rigid with a description of his colourful CV and aphoristic writing style. I didn't reveal my fledgling ambitions to be a writer, except for hints about possibly becoming a 'technical author', because although they were my best friends at college, they were actually friends with other people on the course, most of whom I thought of as close, personal enemies.

As for Celtic's new striking partnership, they were an unlikely combination that Chandler himself would have been proud to have created on the page.

Teenager Nicholas had been a revelation at the start of the season, combining outrageous technical skill with an exuberant personality. He also scored goals with phenomenal regularity, whether stunning strikes on the turn from 20 yards or simple tap-ins from a couple of feet. An ex-Celtic boot boy, Nicholas soon grew up into a glamorous and charismatic entertainer, worshipped by the fans for his freely expressed natural ability. Frank McGarvey, on the other hand, had no natural ability and looked about as co-ordinated as a Gerry Anderson puppet in *Thunderbirds*. He beat defenders by not knowing himself what he was going to do – or knowing and inadvertently doing the opposite. If Nicholas was an aristocratic Don Quixote of a striker, who beat windmilling defences by riding the sails of applause from the crowd, McGarvey was a Sancho Panzer tank of a side-kick who went straight through opposing defences with donkey-like determination. He went on to become the first player to score 100 Premier League goals, and he got one a minute from the end of this match. They complemented each other perfectly and formed an unstoppable striking partnership.

Thistle were so busy trying to snuff out the dynamic duo that they left room for Murdo MacLeod to score two fine goals from midfield, with Dom Sullivan getting the other. Tommy Burns tormented the Jags down the left, while Davie Provan did the same down the right. At the back Roy Aitken and Tom McAdam were a solid partnership. Danny McGrain was still an outstanding right-back, while George McCluskey was always an effective substitute forward. The young Pat Bonner in goal was confident and assured (the goalkeeping equivalent of the golfing yips were still a few years away). The only real weaknesses were Mike Conroy in midfield and Mark Reid at left-back.

The left-back for Thistle in this game was Brian Whittaker, a vastly overrated player who almost signed for Borussia Dortmund under the new freedom of contract regulations in 1980, but the methodical German giants had the good sense to reject him after a trial. He was ordered off in the 35th minute for a vicious double foul on Nicholas, but not before he had Paradise in paroxysms of guffawing merriment. The ball was going out for a shy – in Thistle's favour! – and Whittaker went haring after it to try and keep it in play. He succeeded, by stamping on the ball with his studs, but his momentum carried him over the line and on to the red baize track. An incredulous Provan accepted the teed-up ball and went off with it down the wing. The crowd's amusement was added to when Whittaker just stood watching, in Provan's wake, with hands on hips. In the stand Celtic supporters were weeping with laughter, and I think Provan must have been similarly affected because his cross sailed out on the full. 'Whittaker's a wanker,' warbled the Jungle chorus.

When Whittaker was sent off I made a sarcastic remark about his being the final piece in the Celtic jigsaw if we bought him. In 1983, new manager Davie Hay did just that, using £50,000 of the £650,000 that Arsenal had just paid the club for Charlie Nicholas. Within nine months Whittaker's Celtic career was aborted when he moved to Hearts, where in the words of Chandler he continued to 'look as intelligent as the bottom of a shoe box'.

FOOTNOTES

1 The Jungle is on a par with the Kop at Anfield and the North End at Highbury for the ferocity of the support that it generates, but it was never my favourite or exclusive choice of viewing area. The natives are neither as hostile nor as hospitable as contradictory legends suggest – Jungleites are simply aggressively friendly – but within its dark interior I have been urinated on (from behind), spat on, knocked over, splattered in vomit, punched, lectured at and almost

crushed to death. I have always been somewhat promiscuous with regards to committing myself to a regular area of Celtic Park, but like most working-class supporters who grow attached to middle-class comforts I tended to graduate from the terracing to the stand as I got older (and more affluent). Indeed, if I or a sponsoring company could afford it I would have no hesitation in leaving the *hoi polloi* behind altogether by taking up residence in an executive box. From these self-contained glass cubicles at the back of the main stand, a packed Jungle must have been an impressive sight, a sea of green-and-white scarves raised in salutation and a wall of deafening noise. Before the Jungle became all-seated, it must have been a real pleasure for occupants of the corporate boxes to draw their curtains at half-time in order to partake of alcoholic libations, while the Jungle Tims slavered for a bevvy (booze was banned from all Scottish grounds after the 1980 Scottish Cup final riot; or at least the drinking of it in public view). The social cachet of a place in the north enclosure has varied considerably, however. At one time barefooted urchins were allowed in free with 20 minutes of a game to go, while up until WWII the 'Mickey Masons' paid an extra sixpence for the privilege.

Celtic's renowned travelling support is largely made up of Jungleites, especially for meaningless friendlies or irrelevant testimonials. In 1981 they descended on Portman Road, for the testimonial of Ipswich Town's Allan Hunter. They consumed such vast quantities of lager that the toilets overflowed, and rivers of steaming urine caused the floodlights to short-circuit and cut out.

Juventus 2
Celtic 0

(European Cup first round second leg, 30 September 1981)

Back at college, the decision to travel to this European away game was made immediately after the draw paired Celtic with the Italian champions – in theory at least. Practical travel arrangements were hurriedly arranged following the 1–0 victory over 'Juve' at Parkhead, and even without losing the dreaded away goal Celtic were not favourites to go any further in the competition (this was to be the fourth European tie in a row where Celtic had useful home-leg victories humiliatingly overturned in the away legs).

Initially the plan had been for Baby Albert to pick up a Volkswagen camper, second-hand, from an Australian selling one in Earls Court in order to finance a one-way ticket back to Oz, and then to re-sell it on the return journey from Turin to a newly arrived Aussie ex-pat (for a healthy profit). Instead he got 'an unbeatable deal' on a Ford Transit van, and the Syringe, Fat Saul and I each contributed £20 towards its purchase price. On a dry-run trip to a Scottish away game – Ibrox! – the van broke down on the outside lane of the

Kingston Bridge, when the engine instantaneously combusted. It cost more money to get the damn thing towed off the busiest section of the M8 than it cost to buy it in the first place. The night before leaving for Italy, we were up into the small hours replacing the engine at the garage where Baby Albert worked as a mechanic, and where he'd got 'an unbeatable deal' on a reconditioned engine and a retread tyre (so that we'd have a spare).

We set off for Turin after watching Celtic beat Partick Thistle 2–0 at Parkhead on the Saturday afternoon. I was the only driver who'd bothered to get an International Driver's Permit from the RAC, as well as a warning triangle from Halfords. I also bought foreign currency and travellers' cheques, an Italian phrasebook and a first-aid kit. My fellow travellers contributed a copy of the *Daily Record*, an AA road map of *Southern* Italy (1958), tins of baked beans, an ancient camping stove, three dozen cans of lager and six Irn Bru empties filled with two-star petrol. The spare tyre had to be fitted on the hard shoulder just south of the Watford Gap.

In London's Soho, a woman joined our travelling party. She was called Anne Somers, I think, but she was definitely inflatable. The Syringe kitted her out in an all-green wardrobe – stockings, knickers, bra, mini-skirt, stilettos and blouse – assembled from the Camden/Islington equivalent of the Barras market. She also sported a green crêpe paper wig and her pubic hair – she was an upmarket inflatable woman – was painted green. A taciturn slut, one of our number nevertheless formed a deep personal attachment to her by Calais.

Despite offering a French port official 'une poke sans la dosh', in the back of the van with 'ra burd', we had to cough up more money for some compulsory insurance scam. Anne made a rude gesture with her exposed bottom to the petty bureaucrat as we drove away from the Customs area. Before reaching the outskirts of the town a motorcycle cop with a two-way radio flagged us down and refused to let us continue on our journey until a local garage – owned by his brother-in-law? – fitted headlamp-beam deflectors for an extortionate price. If the two-wheeled policeman had been at all fluent in vernacular Glaswegian, he'd probably have insisted that we got snow-tyres fitted as well.

I had been driving since disembarking the ferry, and I was supposed to take the wheel from Calais to Reims, which were linked by motorway. However, our funds were now so low that to avoid tolls I drove exclusively on B roads, south towards Paris. On the outskirts of the French capital I had no option but to join the Boulevard Periphèrique, the nightmarish 16-lane ring road that encircles the city. My nerves were already ragged from negotiating numerous roundabouts and the priority-from-the-right law. Remembering to go anti-clockwise on roundabouts was bad enough, but giving way to vehicles *entering* roundabouts was doing my head in. The Boulevard Periphèrique did it in completely. At one point I had to move across eight lanes of unpredictable French rush-hour traffic, to avoid barrelling down never-ending slip roads and ramps leading to peripheral towns and Parisian suburbs. Law-abiding lane adherence was not much in evidence – in fact, the French treated the ring road like a Grand Prix circuit – but moving across eight lanes of motorway madness in a right-hand-drive vehicle still required reliable passenger seat assistance. The inflatable woman would have been more help than the Syringe, whose desultory glances in the wing-mirror and apathetic cries of 'Aye, yer awright' were not exactly confidence inspiring.

With gritted teeth, to keep my heart in my mouth, I flicked the indicator stem and moved across following the shallowest angle possible. I can personally and painfully vouch for the effectiveness of Renault and Citröen horns and brakes, as my manoeuvre was accompanied by a deafening cacophony of toots and screeches.

I drove on as far as Fontainebleau, where I fully expected to find that my hair had fallen out and/or turned white. Not giving a toss what my passengers might think, I got out of the van and walked across a pleasant public square, in the middle of which stood a thick-boughed tree. I am not ashamed to say that I hugged it like a passionate bear. With a Pernod in one hand and a baguette in the other, I finally began to unwind. My next turn for driving would not be until Turin, where I would have to find somewhere to park. With a smiling grimace I ordered another Pernod, and another, and another . . .

In central Turin, wisps of steam were beginning to rise from underneath the bonnet. Turning left into oncoming traffic at a busy traffic-light-controlled junction, the electrics cut out and the van stalled. Through sheer mental willpower I got it going again, but steam was now billowing from the engine. Crawling up a steep incline, I looked in vain for somewhere to park. The van stalled again, permanently, and I pulled the handbrake on in despair. But behind me a car pulled out of its parking bay and I immediately let the van roll gently backwards. With one chance and one chance only to get it parked, I fed the steering wheel through my moist palms, before turning it furiously in the opposite direction.

I was parked perfectly, flush to the pavement. Cries of 'Molto bene' and a round of applause came from a gang of youths sitting on steps beside their Vespa motor scooters, including beautiful teenage girls whose three-quarter length jeans revealed shapely olive-toned ankles and calves. From the blood-red scarves and neckerchiefs that both sexes were wearing, I could tell they were Torino fans. Their *bella figura* remained unaffected, but when the Syringe fell out of the back of the van, dressed in a kilt and Celtic top, with the inflatable woman not far behind, their *sang-froid* melted perceptibly. The appearance of blinking Baby Albert and stretching Fat Saul reduced the young Italians to doubled-over hysterics.

Having ridiculed my driving neuroses without let up, my travelling companions now needed my superior social skills, because they were totally out of their depth in sophisticated and attractive Turin (because they knew it built Fiat motor cars, they had been expecting an industrial city like the Big G, whereas all the two cities had in common was a plethora of public parks and a right-angled grid system of streets). With the help of my phrasebook, I introduced myself in phonetically halting Italian to our audience – who couldn't have been more bewildered at our unheralded arrival if we had just staggered out of a flying saucer – and, a few communication problems not withstanding, they couldn't have been more friendly. Luigi spoke a little American English, and he sent Vespas off in all directions (to get water for the radiator, lunch, hostel bookings and *match tickets*, none of which we had to pay for). Hospitality would have been extended to any supporters of an away team playing the hated Juventus, but when I mentioned that Torino were my favourite Italian team because of the 1949 Superga air crash in which most of the Championship squad were killed – and from which the club has never really recovered – their generosity knew no bounds.

Running into and being 'adopted' by a group of Torino fans on the eve of a big European match involving Juventus may seem highly fortuitous, if not downright incredible, but it should be noted that although Juventus are the best-supported team in Italy, they are not the most popular club in the city of Turin itself (in season 1994–95 Juventus transferred a European 'home' leg to Milan, after only getting 20,000 paying customers in a previous round). Part of the local animosity is explained by Fiat's massive financial backing of Juventus, which has underpinned the club's finances for over 50 years, while Torino were at one low point in their history reduced to changing their actual name to incorporate a biscuit brand: 'Talmonte-Torino' (a similar set-up to Glasgow Rangers being subsidised by Murray International Metals and Celtic having to advertise a double-glazing company on their shirt fronts, but at least Celtic have never had to change their name to 'Caramel Log Celtic').

On the Wednesday morning I had to hector Baby Albert *et al* into seeing something of the city. Baby Albert wanted to go and see the Fiat car factory, but I redirected him in the direction of the Automobile Museum, where he got to sit in a toy-like 1914 Opel single-seater. Fat Saul wanted to go into a Standa supermarket to stock up on Italian pre-packed biscuits, having acquired a taste for the industrial quantities of artificial vanilla used in their production. Instead I persuaded him to sample the superb breakfast special served by the Bar Roma, accompanied free-of-charge by all the *grissini* breadsticks he could eat (a policy which they probably had to withdraw after having to re-stock our table three times in 30 minutes). The Syringe was gasping to partake of a liquid lunch, and in the stunning 19th-century Caffe Torino he ordered a fine bottle of red Ghemme, which he ruined in the glass by mixing in ice cubes and glazed cherries (he also drank it using *two* straws – one for him and one for Anne). I took in the cathedral and was disappointed to find that the Turin Shroud was not on permanent display, only a copy in an adjoining chamber of the chapel.

Our tickets to the Stadio Communale gained us entry to the part of the ground where the Italian 'ultras' were congregated, fickle and fidgety fans who wore their scarves in the style of British bank robbers, but topped off with designer Raybans for total anonymity. There was some crowd trouble, most of it directed against Celtic fans, but our inflatable woman defused a lot of tension, and being in the midst of the 'Juve' fans was probably akin to being in the eye of a hurricane. The fact that Celtic were totally outplayed by Juventus, inspired by Liam Brady, also helped to ensure our personal safety. We could have gone out 12–1 on aggregate, rather than 2–1, if not for an outstanding display by Pat Bonner in goal.

In his autobiography *Feed the Bear* (Mainstream, 1987) – ghost-written by Alex Cameron – Roy Aitken says of this tie: 'It would be churlish not to admit that the better team won', before going on to be rather – well, churlish, really – about yet another disappointing first-round European exit. 'Celtic were basically a young team,' he claims. In fact the average age of the team in Turin was almost 24 (and this with teenage Davie Moyes having to replace the injured veteran

Danny McGrain). 'None of us managed even to touch the ball from the time the move started' (describing the opening goal from Virdis in the 28th minute). What Aitken doesn't mention is that *he* started the Juventus counter-attack by mis-hitting a free-kick for Celtic in their half. A brutally effective player in domestic Scottish football, Aitken was a rogue-elephant liability in Europe, and in his time at the club Celtic never progressed further than the quarter-final stage of any European competition. Surprisingly, considering his hard-man image, Aitken possesses a diploma in *piano-playing* from the *London School of Music*, but on the park in European – and 'Old Firm' – matches he tickled the ivories of the opposition with all the finesse of Les Dawson or Victor Borges. Despite his technical failings, which were glaring when counterpointed against Continental opponents, Aitken was a tremendously popular player with the fans, because what he lacked in ability he *almost* made up for in jersey-wearing pride. No one could ever accuse him of not trying or caring.

After the game I was offered a spare place on a Celtic supporters' bus – with its rear window panned in – and I desperately wanted to accept the offer, so that I could curl up on a comfortable if draughty seat and let a professional driver take the strain of the journey home. I eventually declined, and as a reward for my loyalty I only had to take the wheel of the Transit van from London to Glasgow.

On the cross-Channel ferry the inflatable woman was lost overboard, with strong suspicion of foul play (whoever was responsible for Anne's demise took the sensible precaution of rupturing her first, so that there was no possibility of air-sea rescue crews being called out unnecessarily, which probably means I am still the prime suspect in this unsolved case of dollicide).

Celtic 3
St Mirren 0

(Premier League, 15 May 1982)

Going into the final league game of the season, Celtic's hold on the Championship could only have been dislodged if they had lost against St Mirren and Aberdeen had beaten Rangers at Pittodrie. In addition, Aberdeen needed to improve their goal difference vis-a-vis Celtic's by six. Losing 1–0 at home to mid-table St Mirren while Aberdeen thrashed third-placed Rangers by 5–0 wasn't a scenario I lost any sleep over.

Drawing 0–0 with the Paisley 'Buddies' at half-time was disappointing but not disastrous, although the rumoured scoreline from the North-East was both. When the tannoy announcer confirmed that Aberdeen were 4–0 ahead, an oleaginous piece of pie lodged in my windpipe and a mouthful of Bovril was sprayed over two rows of the stand.

'Those motherfucking Huns,' cried a saintly grandmother behind me.

They were obviously lying down and letting Aberdeen walk all over them. The only reason they didn't let in more during the second half was because Celtic finally opened the scoring in the 63rd minute through George McCluskey.

Neither the Scottish League nor the SFA took any action against Rangers, and I suppose from a legal point of view it would have been difficult to distinguish between performances of deliberate ineptitude and inherent ineptitude.

Soviet Union 2
Scotland 2

(World Cup finals, 22 June 1982)

I sensibly decided to follow Scotland's lack of progress in the competition from bars showing their games live on television – but from bars in Maryhill and Scotstoun rather than their overpriced counterparts in Malaga and Seville (supporting Scotland in person in World Cups is invariably a waste of potentially enjoyable summer holidays).

The final game against the USSR, which Scotland had to win, sent me into an alcoholic tailspin. For the first and second last time in my life I drank so much that I blacked out, waking up the next day in a friend's bathtub, which I had apparently clambered into – fully clothed – after using it as an extra-large receptacle for the contents of my stomach. The period in between Souness's last-minute daisycutter of an equaliser and waking up in the strange bathroom was a complete blank, which sobered me up pretty damn fast. Could I have killed a man or raped a woman during my lost hours? I decided not, since drunks like sleepwalkers and hypnotees are not supposed to be capable of behaviour that contradicts completely their moral sensibilities when conscious.

Two moments in particular during the match had been responsible for sending me over the edge into alcoholic oblivion. Firstly, the news flash that the Argentinian garrison in Port Stanley had just surrendered unconditionally. I cornered one punter who had cheered louder than most and who had *tried* to lead three hip-hip-hooray cheers for 'Maggie'. I angrily button-holed him and told him about a *Pebble Mill at One* programme I had seen the previous year in which the Falkland islanders had been protesting to Bob Langley about the withdrawal of the British Antarctic survey ship (on cost grounds). But when the Falklands were invaded by Argentina, Mrs Thatcher had not hesitated in wasting billions of pounds – and hundreds of lives – on the recapturing of the strategically useless islands, largely to help herself to get re-bloody-elected.

The second unbearable moment was when Willie Miller and Alan Hansen collided and collapsed on the touchline, leaving Shengalia a clear run in on Alan Rough and a certain goal (if he could keep his hysterical giggling fit under control, which – being a humourless Russian – he managed to do).

For the third World Cup in a row the sad sacks of Scotland had gone out on goal difference.

Celtic 2
Dundee United 3

(Premier League, 20 April 1983)

Tempers were short and nerves frayed even before the start of this crucial top-of-the-table clash; so much so that Baby Albert, Fat Saul, the Syringe and I had gone our separate ways, after meeting up in the carpark in front of the main stand, and we ended up viewing the game from completely different sections of the ground. Our trip to Amsterdam in September had been a success, mainly because Celtic had put Ajax out of the European Cup thanks to a last-minute strike by George McCluskey. In high spirits our individual cultural itineraries – revolving around sex shops, reefer cafés, Norwegian restaurants and picture galleries – had been fitted in with goodwill on everyone's part. But in the second round we went out to a mediocre Real Sociedad and it was to be a very up-and-down year.

Early in December the Huns had been beaten 2–1 in the League Cup final and throughout that month Celtic remained comfortable League leaders.

The final honours year at college was condensed into a single term – October to December 1982 – but with a three-term workload to fulfil the requirements of the CNAA (Council for National Academic Awards). Unlike the autonomous universities Glasgow Tech did not award its own degrees, but had them set by the CNAA, who prided themselves on their rigorous academic standards. No one on the Business Studies degree had ever achieved a First, and I therefore decided to go for this class of honours classification (hoping the quality of the degree would make up for the naffness of the institution). With five papers to be sat in the space of two weeks, gaining a First was going to be as difficult as winning the European Cup itself, requiring a good performance in every single paper/round.

I got to the final Final feeling that I must have been averaging just above the 70 per cent mark. Tactically I had been anticipating the examiners' questions with stunning accuracy, and the only problem up until the final Friday Final had been writing fast enough to get the answers down on paper (with the result that I went into it with a niggling injury – a 'louping' writing bump on my right index finger).

Worryingly, Finance II had an afternoon kick-off, which was popular with most of the students since it gave them extra last-minute revision time, but I was as ready as I ever would be by nine p.m. the previous evening, when I simply laid my notes aside and watched television to 'relax' (sitting Finals proved to be as nerve-racking as virginity-losing and driving-test sitting).

Up until this last paper I had managed to avoid all questions which required statistical calculation – we had a choice of four from ten – but the setter of this exam obviously knew my weaknesses and I was faced by the equivalent of a footballing 5-4-1 formation. I was *forced* to bring my calculator – an ageing veteran who had struggled to cope with Higher Maths – into play because one of my 'banker' questions was combined in a *two*-part question with a hideous actuarial table, the completion of which required the application of *unrevised* formulae. These equations remained tantalisingly unclear in my memory, but if I was going to get a First I had to attempt this question for the maximum marks available in Part B, while hoping to pick up a few precious marks in Part A.

I must have sat motionless for a good 20 minutes, while everyone around me in the hall was writing or calculating furiously. My mouth was as dry as my eyes were wet. I looked over at the examinee to my right – a close personal enemy – who sniggered at my obvious mental constipation. 'Fuck you,' I whispered, but loud enough for the invigilator to hear 20 yards away. I got an examination 'booking'. One more and I'd have been off/out.

If I didn't stop 'freezing' soon my First would deteriorate into an Upper, or even Lower, Second. If not a Third. This thought got me moving forward out of my own mental penalty box, but I stupidly decided to get the impossible actuarial table out of the way first (and I actually justified this tactical error by remembering Celtic going 1–0 down to a penalty in the European Cup final of '67). Attempting it left my intellectual confidence shattered, and every question thereafter was written with its disastrous effect on my overall average to the forefront of my mind. What I should have done was left it until last, after having collected as many marks as possible from 'banker' questions with a concentrated effort, before attacking it with devil-may-care abandon. I came out of the examination hall feeling like Dixie Deans must have felt in 1972 when he blasted his penalty against Inter Milan high and wide.

Celtic had a similarly disastrous April, when the League flag began to flutter in the direction of Aberdeen and Dundee United. Watching the 3–2 defeat to United at Parkhead I was *still* brooding on my disappointing 2:1.

Down 2–1 to United in the second half, Celtic proceeded to take advantage of their extra man, courtesy of Richard Gough's dismissal, by pounding Hamish McAlpine's goal with countless shots and crosses. Eventually, in the 73rd minute, Tommy Burns got the equaliser. If the scoreline had remained the same, and the remaining games had gone the same way, Celtic would have won their third title in a row, on goal difference from United. Instead, the subjective experience of playing against ten men began to feel like playing against 12, and United's breakaways were becoming increasingly ominous. With five minutes left Ralph Milne killed an Eammon Bannon cross, and to add insult to injury lobbed it over Pat Bonner as if it was a meaningless consolation goal.

Despite beating the Huns 4–2 at Ibrox on the season's last day, United's bottle held as they beat Dundee, and Celtic lost the title to Jim McLean's men by a single point.

Like Benjamin in *The Graduate*, I was a little worried about my future, but although I had been signing on since January various job offers and academic places were up for grabs by the end of May. I was having a great deal of trouble making up my mind, and without the distraction of a Mrs Robinson or the luxury of an outdoor pool I spent most of my free time trying to get round Alexandra Park's nine-hole public golf course in par figures. With six blind tee shots and greens the size and smoothness of scratched dining tables, I doubt if Jack Nicklaus in his prime could have shot a sub-par round on this course, but I did score a hole-in-one (I *think*). On the par-three fourth, my five-iron soared up and away in the direction of the Parkhead floodlights – which served as directional markers for the blind tee shot – and I strode off after the ball hoping it had reached the brow of the flat fairway with just enough momentum to start rolling down the steep slope that led to the green. From the top of the gradient I surveyed the ball-less green – *Shit!* – which I then noticed was surrounded by dirty-faced urchins. As I approached the green they started to hoop and holler, clapping in congratulation. 'Well done, mister – it curled the lip twice but then it dropped straight in!' Heart in mouth, I approached the hole suspiciously, where my Dunlop ball had supposedly come to rest. When I asked them if it had really gone in on the full, without their mischievous assistance, they ran off shouting, 'Ye'll never know . . . Ye'll never fuckin' know . . . ' If I'd had a rifle in my golf bag I'd have picked the little bastards off one by one . . .

When Charlie Nicholas turned down a £650,000 bid from Manchester United at the end of May, I also crossed off my Manchester-based offers. If Nicholas was willing to stay in Glasgow for another couple of years, maybe I would too. In early June he announced his decision to move to Arsenal. Nicholas was a devastated Jungleite himself when Dalglish pissed off to Liverpool, but it didn't stop him devastating a new generation of Celtic fans when he departed, at the tender age of 21! I decided to follow him to London, rather than continue to sign on every week for under 20 quid in dole money.

Manager Billy McNeill wasn't pleased by Nicholas's decision to take the money and run, but of course it didn't stop McNeill leaving himself at the end of June for more money and a three-year contract with Manchester City.

Before moving to London in August, I used the summer months to read Alasdair Gray's *Lanark* (which took him over 20 years to complete). Watching a *South Bank Show* special devoted to the book and author, I was incredulous. There was Melvyn Bragg having a serious literary discussion about a novel set not just in Glasgow but in Riddrie for God's sake, with Dennistoun, Blackhill and *Carntyne* getting more than passing mentions. But although the publication of *Lanark* proved that it was possible to write a great novel set in Glasgow, page 243 of the 1981 Granada edition confirmed me in my determination to seek fame and fortune in London. As the character Duncan Thaw explains to his friend McAlpin, London is one of those cities – like Paris or New York – which already exists in the imaginations of those who have never even been there, because of its depiction in countless artistic forms. 'What is Glasgow to most of us?' Thaw muses. 'A house, the place we work, a football park or golf course, some pubs and connecting streets. That's all . . . Imaginatively Glasgow exists as a music-hall song and a few bad novels.'

When I packed my bags for London, the last thing I crammed into my bulging suitcase was a copy of Gray's magnum opus (needless to say, I haven't re-read it since).

Nottingham Forest 0
Glasgow Celtic 0

(UEFA Cup, third round first leg, 23 November 1983)

For most of the summer before leaving for London, I was itching to get away from Glasgow, but I was still kicking my heels when Davie Hay (who as a player had departed for Chelsea in 1974 after an acrimonious row over *money*) was appointed the new Celtic manager. With almost no track record in football management, Hay's appointment by the Board of Directors seemed to be based on nothing more than blind trust. In July, too, my father bought a car on a similar basis: a metallic-blue Talbot with an aluminium engine. He had been mightily impressed with the Car of the Week sign stuck on top of it. The whole Bennie clan clambered into it on the garage forecourt, my father and mother in the front, my sister and I in the back. In a scene reminiscent of the *Beverly Hillbillies*, my father handed over hard cash for the car – without even switching on the ignition, never mind taking it for a test drive. In August my father drove me down to London in it. On the way back the aluminium engine melted, and with the money he got for it from a scrapyard dealer he had just enough money to get the train home (or almost – he had to get off at Motherwell).

I may have started off as a provincial hick in the big city, but I matured quickly. I took part-time work down the paper mines of a large multi-national oil company – not Esso – in the Tumbler Promotions Department, where I learned that motorists will drive miles out of their way to complete a set of fluted champagne glasses. With my studies and a girlfriend good-looking enough to be seen in public with – instead of being shoved into shop doorways when approached by people I knew – I thoroughly enjoyed living in London. Most Glaswegians would rather choke on their own vomit than say a good word about the capital, but I found it a much easier city to make friends in than my home town. The problem with the Big G is that 90 per cent of its inhabitants are Glaswegians – with more home-based students than any other city in Britain – whereas less than ten per cent of the people you meet in the Big Smoke are 'Londoners'. With so many transient – and lonely – incomers, most overtures of friendly interest are reciprocated.

I did miss my football team, friends and immediate family, but Saturday afternoons watching West Ham or Tottenham Hotspur went some way to anaesthetising withdrawal symptoms. (Although I lived in Bloomsbury and Finsbury Park, watching Charlie Nicholas submerging his individuality to meet the requirements of the one-arm-raised-for-offside mentality of Arsenal was too painful on a fortnightly basis. It took Champagne Charlie five months to uncork his first goal at Highbury – and even that was a bloody boring penalty.)

At the end of November I travelled up to Nottingham in my second-hand Morris Ital (which although checked over by an AA mechanic was just a Morris Marina in fooling-nobody disguise, British Leyland mutton dressed up to look like designer Italian lamb). On an ice-rink of a frozen pitch, Celtic contained Brian Clough's much-vaunted stars with surprisingly sure-footed ease. At least half of the 32,000 crowd were away supporters and we should have had a crucial away goal to cheer when Paul McStay sclaffed a shot over the bar from close range minutes before the end. In his book *Paradise Lost*[1], ex-director Michael Kelly complains that McStay couldn't 'shoot for toffee', a major drawback for an attacking midfielder that was beginning to become painfully apparent to supporters in season 1983–84. Nevertheless, on the basis of his two goals for the Scottish Schoolboys in the 5–4 win over England at Wembley in 1980 (shown live on ITV's *World of Sport*) and his breakthrough into the full national team in 1983, McStay was developing a reputation for being a *potentially* world-class performer (a reputation that he maintains to this day, despite being in his 30s). In January of 1984, Inter Milan offered over two million pounds for teenage McStay. If this had been accepted – and at the time I prayed that it would – the deal would have been good for Celtic, Inter and McStay (even if Celtic would have benefited most). Serie A is a stage upon which square-passing midfield maestros get enough time and space to look good, and if the transfer had gone through McStay may well have developed into a world-class player (or at least one who isn't now approaching the end of his career with an 'unfulfilled potential' consensus about his ability). Part of McStay's problem was that he was too nice and unnecessarily modest as a human being. If in January of 1990 he had married my sister, instead of becoming an insipid and uninspiring Celtic captain, I would have been delighted. In May of 1992, when he threw his jersey into the Jungle after his 'last' game against Hibernian, the fans bade him an emotional and fond farewell. But the reason the out-of-contract McStay stayed on at Celtic was not because the devotion of the faithful inspired him to change his mind. The fact is that McStay got no offers from any other clubs – and if he did, one of them certainly wasn't two million pounds from Inter Milan.

I didn't travel back to Glasgow for the second leg, because having overcome Sporting Lisbon 5–0 at Parkhead in the previous round (to win 5–2 on aggregate) I assumed that the result was a foregone conclusion. It was, but not in the way anticipated by the 67,000 Celtic supporters who turned up: Forest won 2–1 on the night and on aggregate with a convincing display of counter-attacking, Continental-style football (Celtic's first defeat at Celtic Park in European competition since 1969).

FOOTNOTES

1 *Paradise Lost: The Struggle for Celtic's Soul*, Michael Kelly, Canongate, 1994. Dedicated to 'real Celtic supporters everywhere – in case their children ask', Kelly's account of his time at Celtic Park as a director is not a book I would have bought unless I had to for research

purposes. However, I avoided contributing 79 pence in royalties to the author by buying it from a remainder bin in Bargain Books for three pounds (RRP £7.99). I buy books – even remaindered ones – to have my prejudices confirmed, not undermined, but Kelly's description of the financial takeover battle for the club certainly changed my perspective to a degree. I'm still glad the old Board had to go – if only to prevent the move away from Celtic Park – but the Rebels who took control don't exactly inspire total confidence either.

Aberdeen 2
Celtic 1

(Scottish Cup final, 19 May 1984)

Because this final was set to clash with various personal commitments, I had made no irrevocable plans to attend. But with apocalyptic warnings accumulating by the day about the dire consequences of doing so – with regard to work, professional qualifications, accommodation, and romance – I did what any self-respecting football fan would have done in similar circumstances: I cleared my desk, arranged for a sick line, did a moonlit flit and stuffed old love letters into a Jiffy bag marked 'Return to sender'.

With five minutes to spare I caught the last train to Glasgow from Euston on the Friday night (the chaos I was leaving behind can be inferred from the fact that in normal circumstances I am usually so early for train departures that I arrive breathless on the platform seconds after the previous timetabled service has just pulled out of the station). Having got a block of four seats and a table to myself, the next four minutes were spent anxiously looking at my watch and nervously peering out of the window (as my catastrophising imagination went into mental overdrive). I was so distracted that I forgot to walk the length of the train looking for lone females reading paperback copies of DH Lawrence novels (the state of my nerves doesn't bear thinking about if I'm ever hanging on to the side of the last train out of Paris before the Nazis march in, waiting on my inconceivably late lover like Humphrey Bogart in *Casablanca*).

The final itself was as good as lost in the 39th minute, with Celtic already a goal down when Roy Aitken was sent off for a foul on Mark McGhee. In his autobiography, which has nine pages devoted to defending the fairness of the tackle on McGhee, Aitken states: 'It was a bodycheck, not a vicious or malicious tackle.' What it was was a vicious and malicious bodycheck. 'Hand on heart, all I intended to do was to get the ball.' Good argument, Roy. Next time I rob a bank and shoot someone dead in the process, I won't hesitate to use a variation of it: 'Well, your honour, hand on heart, all I intended to do was to get the money.' McStay almost got Celtic out of jail with a goal five minutes from the end of normal time, but in extra time playing for almost an hour with a man short took its inevitable toll. McGhee scored a 98th-minute winner. Aitken had also helped Rangers lift the League Cup two months previously when he needlessly toppled Ally McCoist in the box, which resulted in the third Rangers goal in a 3–2 victory. Although both finals were refereed by Bob Valentine, a fully paid-up member of the Ibrox Glee Club, neither occasion required iffy decisions to deprive Celtic of deserved silverware (Rangers were the better team on the day and Aberdeen were the better team all season).

Travelling back to London to face the music, with the cheers of the success-spoiled Dons fans still ringing in my ears, I was in spuriously high spirits – the 'affability of despair' as someone once described the feeling. With a window seat to myself in one of the old-fashioned carriages with compartments entered by a sliding door and with two properly upholstered bench seats facing each other, I looked up in ill-disguised annoyance when someone asked me to remove my feet from the seat opposite. I complied pretty damn quick when I saw my travelling companion was a JAP (Jewish American Princess), carrying a copy of, not DH Lawrence, but – even better – *Tropic of Cancer* by Henry Miller! I gave her my most winning smile – which she later described as endearing and non-threatening as Jack Nicholson's grin through the smashed bathroom door in *The Shining* – and by Carstairs I felt that I might be able to persuade her to join me in the British Rail equivalent of the British Airways Mile High Club before we reached Carlisle.

Fat chance. Discussing politics – always a mistake – I was poised to agree with whatever political position she chose to espouse – whether Republican libertarianism or Democratic New Dealism – but when I described myself as a Nationalist and Socialist she became disconcertingly aggressive (the paperback Sven Hassel I had covered up on the seat beside me, complete with swastika and SS flashes, confirmed me in her mind as a *National Socialist*, or modern-day Nazi).

'Six million died in the Holocaust,' she harangued me. 'But I suppose you think that's just a phoney figure plucked from the rancidly pungent air of Treblinka, Dachau, Auschwitz . . . ' When told to wash my mouth out with soap – after calling Menachim Begin a murdering bald terrorist and questioning the moral and legal legitimacy of the state of Israel – I replied that I would 'as long as the bar isn't made out of recycled kike corpses' (I was getting rather confused and angry by this point).

The misapprehension was eventually cleared up by Carnforth, and Irene and I have never lost touch since.

I've never hit a woman or ever really wanted to – although I like to think I am capable of killing a man – but my *ex*-girlfriend in London came close to getting a punch in the mouth when I went round to her flat in De Beauvoir Town (!) in Balls Pond Road (!!) to collect the rest of my Sven Hassel library. She rubbed salt into my open wounds by reminding me that I had ruined my life by 'going to see the bloody Glasgow Celtics *(sic)* who hadn't even bloody well won!'. How could I have got involved with a woman who cared so little about me that she got my first love mixed up with a basketball team that played in Boston?

Glasgow Celtic 0
Vienna Rapid 1

(Cup Winners' Cup, second leg replay, 12 December 1984)

Instead of returning straight to Glasgow, I headed south in an attempt to keep pace with the receding September sunshine. My destination was Paris, where I anticipated subsisting in genteel poverty in a garret – with white enamel wash basin and pitcher (they were essential props in my fantasy) – while writing a Proustian paragraph a day of a novel entitled *Life Sucks – And Then You Die*, which would be published simultaneously in French and English, unbound, in a spring-hinged box file of finest calf's leather, and whose pagination would be 'decided' – not by a Dead Author – but by the reader tossing the loose-leaf pages in the air, à la BS Johnson.

Since all the writers' garrets had been knocked through and converted into hideously expensive artists' lofts, I initially 'took up residence' in a cheap but clean pension, but I had to move out after

I was mugged in the flea market – by a bloody *Glaswegian* punk rocker, or *zonard*, who knocked me out cold with a single haymaking punch. With my wallet already gone I came round to find a gang of pickpocketing Rastafarians attempting to divest me of my passport, travellers' cheques, Hi-Tec training shoes and anal virginity (they eventually got away with the cheques and my *Wee Red Book* after a horizontal struggle).

I got a job as a *plongeur* in a seedy bistro, whose owner was too mean to allow the water heater to be switched on for washing up the stacks of congealed dishes. For scraping solid grease from pots and plates, with bare hands and cold water, I was paid 20 francs for eight hours work, plus all the *bouillon zip* – a soup made from slops, basically – that I could force down my gullet. I paid a Dutch smackhead five francs to sleep in his squat, but had to move out of there when he attempted to reduce the rent to zero in exchange for 'shared bodily warming and reciprocal penis blowing'. I slept one night under the Pont Neuf, before being lifted by 'the Blues', the police squad which rounded up the homeless of the city each night and bundled the *clochards* and other deadbeats into large vans.

I only escaped a night in the cells of the Nanterre dosshouse, the 'Prison for the Hungry', thanks to the intervention of one of the officers, a sergeant, who in 1968 had been a young officer on ground duty for the CRS riot police when St Etienne beat Celtic 2–0 in Paris in the European Cup (he had noticed my green-and-white supporters' scarf, the same team colours as *Les Verts*).

After cashing the replacement travellers' cheques, I made my way home via Belgium, where I saw Celtic lose to Ghent by 1–0. I arrived back in Glasgow at the same time as Mo Johnston, who had just signed from Watford for £400,000 in mid-October. I also sold my partnership share in a Mancunian sweatshop, while stopping off in the city, for just over £400, and today the firm is so successful that it tenders for Marks & Spencer orders.

After disposing of Ghent at Parkhead, Celtic travelled to Austria to play Vienna Rapid in the Hanappi Stadium. I heard the result in the Queen Margaret Students' Union of Glasgow University, and when the announcer on *Sportsnight* stated 'Rapid Vienna 3, . . .' I was honestly hoping that his inflection on the word 'Celtic' a second later would be indicative of an away win by 3–4. When his voice dropped in tone and proceeded to give the Celtic response as *one*, I nearly shattered the pint glass I was holding. In rigid frustration I said out loud that Celtic would have to try overturning a two-goal deficit at

Parkhead without the benefit of my support. The problem was I said it in front of witnesses.

The result was that I missed what was probably the most intense, dramatic, controversial, exciting and farcical game ever played at Celtic Park (since attaining adulthood I'd missed a significant number of home games – through illness, penury, work, travelling and social commitments – but I'd never not gone because of outright disloyalty; my inexcusable absence was a watershed, making future non-attendance that much easier, like a happily married man after a mad fling going on to become a regular adulterer or a crime-of-passion murderer developing into a serial killer, since it's never as difficult after the first one).

On the night Celtic played like the Lisbon Lions unleashed from rattled cages, and after failing to bring them down with elephant-gun tackles the Austrians' final response was to lie down and play dead. 3–0 down (4–3 on aggregate) with ten minutes to go, and with Kienast already dismissed, the Austrian keeper Ehn gave away a penalty for a foul on Tommy Burns. But instead of awarding the kick immediately, Swedish referee Johansson went to his linesman for confirmation. Half the Austrian team surrounded them, a sign for the planned putsch to begin.

Fifth-columnist Huns in the Jungle started throwing coins – and a much discussed bottle. Weinhofer went down as if executed by a Luger bullet to the back of the head (initially the Austrians claimed the bottle had been responsible, but when television evidence disproved this they changed their fabricated story to centre around 'a small, V2-type flying 50 pence piece'). Weinhofer went off swathed in more head bandages than a wounded evacuee from the Russian front. After a 15-minute delay, Peter Grant blasted his penalty wide.

Independent medical observers confirmed that Weinhofer's head was in perfect shape – if somewhat big – but they were never called by UEFA's disciplinary committee (of its two dozen members at the appeal stage only three heard the case, all of them appointed and given new identities by the Odessa at the end of the war). Incredibly Celtic were ordered to replay the game, over 100 miles away from Glasgow. Nazi gold at the bottom of Lake Geneva continues to accrue some bizarre repayment interest.

Over a month later at Old Trafford, Glasgow 'Gemeinschaft' Celtic had to take on Vienna 'Gesellschaft' Rapid one more time. I travelled down to Manchester with Alex, in his Mini Metro, and both of us were fired up with self-righteous optimism, convinced that the conniving Austrians were about to lose the footballing equivalent of WWIII. The early December weather was stunningly crisp and clear and we stopped off for gin-and-tonic refreshment and ploughman's lunch sustenance in a charming Borders hotel. Morale was sky high as we neared Manchester, even as an ominous fog descended, and the M62 was a slow-moving convoy of motorised Celtic cavalry, with horns blaring, flags flying and scarves twirling. All along the hard shoulder, Celtic supporters were relieving their bladders, then shaking their dicks dry with military precision. My chest felt tight with emotion, pride and anticipation. I'd never felt so confident about getting a result, which is all the more surprising when one notes that Celtic had the formidable 1–3 mountain to climb all over again. I think I must have been ODing on adrenalin, thereby destroying all my critical faculties, because I actually reconsidered the architectural design of the Arndale Centre and decided that it was 'quite nice for a cathedral to consumerism'.

Arriving early to take our seats behind the goal in what was usually the end reserved for away supporters, Manchester United's ground was an impressive sporting sight. With 51,500 Celtic fans in full battle cry, the emotion generated was electrifying. For the first 16 minutes the charged atmosphere positively hummed and crackled, and when Aitken hit the post I leapt to my feat in premature celebration. Before I was back sitting on my seat, Rapid had broken upfield and scored through Pacult. The goal flattened the atmosphere, immediately and permanently, and with it Celtic's hopes of riding to victory on a wave of Wagnerian emotion. At the anti-climactic end two supporters ran on to the field and assaulted Feurer (the keeper) and Pacult. Having watched in silent horror, we left Old Trafford expecting the club to be banned from Europe indefinitely (in the event, Celtic 'merely' had to play their next European home game behind closed doors, which meant that we lost to that other bunch of Continental cheats, Atletico Madrid).

At the start of the retreat from Old Trafford, I was of the opinion that it should be every shell-shocked man for himself, but Alex heroically agreed to give a lift to three stranded drunken yobs as we were getting into the Metro (before I could interrupt him and lie about our heading for London). Thankfully they *eventually* fell asleep on the back seat and on the long drive back home Alex himself was in danger of nodding off at the wheel as he came down from his own adrenalin high. On a couple of occasions the car drifted over dangerously towards oncoming traffic, but I was too emotionally exhausted to care.

Celtic 2
Dundee United 1

(Scottish Cup final, 18 May 1985)

The walk to Hampden was a mere five minutes from the bedsit where I was living in Govanhill (or Queen's Park, as the Rachmanesque landlord insisted on describing the flat in his small ads). The flat had a high turnover of residents since this type of accommodation tends to serve as a half-way house. Those on the way up, like students and graduates starting new jobs, are usually no problem to share a bathroom with. It's the people on the way down that you've got to worry about, since the ex-cons, psychiatric outpatients, suicidal divorcees, teenage runaways and terminally old are often approaching the homeless gutter at 10ms^2 and will take you with them given half a chance. The most permanent residents were: Mikey, a half-wit who had found undemanding employment somewhere in the bowels of the Strathclyde Passenger Transport Executive compiling timetables for bus convoys; Cat Woman, who subscribed to the *Lady* magazine; Michael, who was something very low down in the IRA; Flora, a permanently resting actress; and Harry, an unemployed schizophrenic (who would wake me at two in the morning to complain about my playing folk tunes on the water pipes).

At night I wrote novels, which flowed to their conclusions on a river of whisky – the genres covered ranging from science fiction, through crime thrillers, to literary epics. I also wrote short stories, poems, plays and film scripts. Most ended up at the bottom of my sock drawer, unfinished (or laid aside as 'works-in-progress'), but what they all had in common, what tied their disparate themes and styles together, what formed their common *leitmotif* was the fact that, without any encouraging exception, they remained unpublished.

Without whisky my life merely had width and area. With whisky, about half a bottle a night, I had a fulcrum for my imagination to turn on, whereby I could experience three-dimensionality and depth.

Alcohol allowed my mind to slip its moorings and soar higher and higher into the cerebral stratosphere, until I could see all the twinkling stars in the firmament of my imagination – at least for a few glorious, conscious moments. Before all the lights went out.

By three o'clock my hangover was just about gone – Saturday and Sunday hangovers taking that bit longer to shake off than their weekday counterparts – and I joined the mass ranks on the sloped terraces of the national stadium. When United took the lead just after half-time, I felt like drowning my despair in a full bottle of what Aldous Huxley called 'a protoplasmic poison which in small doses may depress the system in a psychologically valuable way' (ie whisky). But when Davie Provan scored the equaliser in the 75th minute with a stunning, swerving free kick, my internal spirits lifted and fermented. Frank McGarvey's late, late winner, when he threw himself at a superb Roy Aitken cross, made me drunk with happiness – which didn't stop me getting drunk on Scotch as the celebrations continued long into the night.

Wales 1
Scotland 1

(World Cup qualifier, 10 September 1985)

Prior to this live transmission from Cardiff, I'd only ever cried once while watching television (during the movie *Sweet Charity*, made maudlin by whisky, when Shirley Maclaine's eponymous character had just been ditched by her fiancé, when he discovered that she was a quasi-prostitute). Before this date, too, the only reported death of a celebrity which had moved me to tears was that of Karen Carpenter (who possessed the finest voice of any female singer of her generation).

When Martin Tyler eventually announced Jock Stein's death, after the Scotland manager had been carried up the tunnel moments before the final whistle, I felt the empty void of real grief in my chest, as if a much loved and respected uncle – 'Uncle John' – had just died. In writing about it now, the memory is made even more depressingly poignant by the recent death of Davie Cooper – Thursday, 23 March 1995 – whom on the balmy night in September at Ninian Park Stein threw on as a late substitute in order to try and salvage the equaliser that would take Scotland to Mexico. It was a last, typically effective throw-of-the-dice by Stein, as Cooper not only started to turn the game for Scotland but converted a pressure penalty with nine minutes to go (the strain of watching which may well have induced, or at least contributed to, Stein's fatal heart attack). Tears only came – in a flood – when a fan interviewed outside the ground observed that he'd rather have seen Scotland not qualify for the World Cup than to have lost Stein in such terrible circumstances.

In his early days at Parkhead I had regarded Stein as nothing less than a god, but as his abilities declined from the mid-'70s onwards it became obvious that he was a fallible human being after all. Not a god, then, but definitely a hero.

Along with thousands of others I lined the route of the funeral procession to Linn Crematorium, where my old school chaplain, Jimmy Martin (ex of Motherwell FC), gave a moving and thoughtful eulogy. Dead at 62, a great man gone. As my father would be, five years later, aged 65, and whose funeral cortege I would be part of as it made its unnoticed way to the same crematorium . . .

Celtic 1
Heart of Midlothian 1

(Premier League, 22 February 1986)

If I was a hypochondriac – which I am (mildly) – I would be convinced that I contracted a recurring bladder infection by sharing a bottle of vodka with the unwanted back-seat hitchhikers from Old Trafford (the symptoms flared up almost immediately after the return from Manchester). Whatever the source of the infection, it was initially and repeatedly misdiagnosed by my doddering GP, and then undertreated. Eventually, a week before this game I was prescribed powerful Amoxil penicillin, but without any warnings about possible allergic reactions or unpleasant side-effects. While taking the course of gobstopper capsules, my – how to put this politely? – below-the-belt mucous membranes erupted in red and agonising fury; so much so that I had to stop the medication for a day. On the Friday I finished the remaining capsules, but when I woke up on the morning of the game I was covered from head to foot in red weals, spots and lumps. On the plus side, at least I could now piss – however painfully – in a steady stream instead of a geriatric dribble.

I had spent the night at my parents – in case I went into anaphylactic shock by restarting the penicillin – and despite the non-fatal allergic reaction I set off for Celtic Park at about two o'clock on the Saturday. Although every step – on the outside of my soles – from Carntyne to Parkhead was an itchy anal torture, there was no way I was going to miss this chance for Celtic to gain ground on league leaders Hearts.

Baby Albert, Fat Saul and the Syringe were in their appointed places in the Jungle, but I was treated like a leper and told to go and stand amongst the Jam Tart supporters (which I couldn't have done even if I had wanted to, because the previous year a fence screen had been erected on the east terracing to keep rival fans apart, in the wake of the Heysel disaster).

'What the fuck are you talking about?' I whined. 'It's not infectious, for Chrissake. It's an allergic reaction to penicillin, that's all.'

'Whitever . . . But ye've turned intae a fuckin' Hun!'

And I had, too, because when I got back to the bedsit my face was bright, carotene orange. I felt like the star of the movie about the white supremacist bigot who wakes up one morning to find that he's turned black overnight. Or vice versa rather.

St Mirren 0
Celtic 5

(Premier League, 3 May 1986)

Hearts had been top of the table since the turn of the year, but in the run-in they began to exhibit the edginess that one might expect from a team who hadn't won a league title since 1960. On the last day of the season, they only needed a point away to Dundee to secure the flag (to lose it they not only had to lose to Dundee, but Celtic had to beat St Mirren by a scoreline which improved Celtic's goal difference vis-a-vis Hearts' by four clear goals).

Although my 'sunburned' face and nettle-rashed body had returned to normal soon after the Hearts match in February, other bizarre allergic reactions took their place. The most remarkable, initially, was the histamine-type substance which 'leaked' from the forefinger knuckles of each hand, like spilled red ink. Over a period of a couple of weeks, all my knuckles proceeded to become red and inflamed, then the forefingers of each hand, then the index fingers, followed by all the other fingers one after another (with the firework display of both hands in total synchronisation!). By the time Celtic beat Dundee 2–1 at home at the beginning of April my palms and soles were exploding in urticarial agony, and an all-over tingling sensation of the skin meant I had to go 'on the panel'.

As well as destroying the infection in my bladder, the penicillin had also wiped out all the benign bacteria in my gut, allowing *candida albicans* yeast to run riot. In some discomfort I made it to Paisley, where I confidently expected St Mirren to be on the end of a severe tanking. I saw Brian McClair's headed opener in only six minutes, but I missed the three Celtic goals which followed in a six-minute spell just before the break because of uncontrollable diarrhoea. For the first time ever at a football ground I had to use a toilet cubicle, and although I expected to be confronted with disgusting graffiti at eye level (sitting) I didn't expect it to be written in excrement. As Mo Johnston was cracking in two goals in quick succession, I was crouched over the seatless and blocked toilet 'pissing' stool which felt like a mixture of hot vinegar and crushed razor blades. When Paul McStay scored a fourth I was still stuck in the stall, micturating through a urethra that felt as if it was being subjected to the apocryphal cure for the clap (ie having a mini-telescopic umbrella inserted, having the release button pressed, and then having the expanded spokes of the instrument slowly withdrawn).

My only lucky break was the complete absence of any other supporters in the toilet at the time – because of the incredible conclusion to the first half – but as I'd always suspected football-stadia stalls were not equipped with nice soft rolls of Andrex (or even the cheap cardboard boxes of shiny medicated fly paper). I'm ashamed to say I would have traded any kind of bog roll for four St Mirren goals scored in the four minutes before the break (which would have deprived Celtic of the title because they only scored once more in the second half, while Hearts were going down 2–0 to two late goals from Albert Kidd at Dens Park). I'm also ashamed to say what I used for an alternative – namely, a sock (but it was clean on that day).

When news of Kidd's second goal filtered through the transistor-radio static, joy was unconfined on the Love Street terraces. Pleased but in pain I just wanted to get back to the bedsit, where I only got to sleep with a near overdose of antihistamines (which didn't help the symptoms but at least made me drowsy). Next morning the Sunday tabloids carried a poignant picture of a solitary Hearts fan, sitting stunned and disbelieving on a Dens Park terrace. It gave me a sardonic laugh and the inspiration to get through another debilitated day.

West Germany 2
Scotland 1

(World Cup finals, 8 June 1986)

Before the Amoxil attack I had been planning, and saving, to go to Mexico, but the possibility of contracting Montezuma's Revenge on top of the alimentary-canal problems I already had made the trip utterly impractical. Gordon Strachan's acutely angled goal was the one highlight of the tournament, all through which the Scotland team played in a strip which made them look like beach bums – what with white shorts with a ridiculous blue hoop. Scotland also played like beach bums and they were so bloody awful that they didn't even manage to not qualify for the next round on goal difference.

Hibernian 2
Rangers 1

(Premier League, 9 August 1986)

As a boy worrying about death, I used to imagine all kinds of infernal and eternal tortures, all of which I thought would be infinitely preferable to not existing at all, forever and forever. One particularly persistent image was that of myself on a roasting spit, being slowly turned and basted by one of Auld Nick's lip-smacking under-devils. Despite an eternity of skin-crackling agony stretching out before me, I always refused to submit and say 'Keys' – which would have stopped the pain but at the expense of my not continuing to exist. As long as I remained sentient, I thought I would rather 'thole' any degree of physical discomfort than accept the dubious relief of death. No pain. No pleasure. No nothing.

By July of 1986 I was beginning to reassess where the line between chronic physical pain and continuing physical existence should be drawn. With constant all-over itching, periods of tear-inducing agony (normally in the bathroom), recurring rashes and flaking skin, I was referred to a dermatologist in Glasgow, whose allergy skin tests were either negative or inconclusive. In a shabby NHS consulting room, the doctor suggested that my 'atypical somatising disorder' was being exacerbated by *not* working and that if I got a nine-to-five job again I'd be less aware of the symptoms. Knowing of my interest in books – 'Bookish but bitter', it said in my medical notes – the consultant suggested that I follow the example of Zola, 'who killed pain with work'.

'A rock?' I deliberately misheard.

'*Work*,' he repeated, with Calvinistic contempt.

I then told him about an incident I had read in Norman Mailer's autobiography, where the 'White Negro' (?) author had struck up a conversation with a fellow drinker in a New York bar. This particular bar bore was undergoing clinical investigation at the city's renowned Mount Sinai Hospital in order to try and discover why his extremities were turning fiery orange. The outpatient actually peeled off his shoes and socks to show Mailer his mottled soles. A few days later Mailer learned that the man had thrown himself off the Brooklyn Bridge (after all the test results proved to be normal). I repeated this to emphasise to the consultant the point I was, if not at, gradually approaching.

'Aha!' he cried, waving his Mont Blanc at me accusingly. 'When did you read about that? No, don't tell me – it was before these mysterious post-Amoxil reactions, wasn't it?'

I looked at him in lachrymose misery, not saying anything.

'I think we'd better refer you to a psychologist!'

'It was after, for God's sake. Otherwise I wouldn't have remembered it, would I?'

'Oh well . . . Make another appointment at the desk for three months time.'

Father Flyte, a young priest who occasionally accompanied Baby Albert & Co to games at Celtic Park, arranged for me to stay at a retreat in Northern Italy, a monastery, where in return for chores frazzled laity were offered some respite from the trials and tribulations of the modern world. Towards the end of my stay I had a serious discussion with the Order's Superior General, a convivial Irishman, about the possibility of my becoming a novitiate brother, but we both agreed that because of my unconquerable atheism the only ministry that I could have, in all conscience, taken up would have been with the Church of England (believing in God is like supporting Rangers – you can't *make* yourself do it, no matter how hard you try). The vows of Poverty, Chastity and Obedience, however, would have presented no insurmountable problems, although Missionary Work for Lost Huns probably would have. Nevertheless I rather fancied the idea of myself as either a devout monk or zealous priest, zooming around my peasant parish on a motor scooter, totally pissed but immaculately dressed in soutane and black biretta, excoriating my charges for the venal sins engendered in equal measure by the false gods of Capitalism and Communism (a fantasy centred around an Alpine, Pyrennean or Mediterranean village which collapsed when I tried to transpose it to a run-down inner city parish like that of Father Flyte's). I actually prayed for a sign – preferably an overnight cure – and if I had woken up as the Stigmatic Atheist of Carntyne, the future St David of Atypical Somatising Disorders, I may well have been able to make the required leap of blind faith (although as a future religious name I favoured 'Brother Billy', as an ecumenical acknowledgment of my Protestant heritage).

On the Monday after the start of the Premier League, I was desperate for news of the opening fixtures. Earlier in the summer, Rangers had appointed Graeme Souness as player-manager, and although no Catholics were amongst his first signings the new players at Ibrox shocked Celtic supporters to their complacent cores, because of the quality and cost of, initially, Terry Butcher, Chris Woods and Colin West. In Ivrea, an Olivetti company town in Piedmont's Valle d'Aosta, I met an English family at the railway station while they waited on an exorbitantly priced copy of the *Observer* to be off-loaded from the Milan train. I arranged to meet them later for an alfresco aperitif, after we had all completed a day's hard hillwalking on the lower slopes of the Alps.

A few hours later I saw them getting out of their Volvo estate, hundreds of feet below me, as I took a cigarette break – to get my breath back – and surveyed the stunning Alpine vista laid out in front of me.

'What was the score with Rangers?' I bellowed down, my harsh Glaswegian vowels echoing around the valley.

'Hi-bernian two, Ran-gers one . . . Souness sent off!'

I was so happy that I forgot to ask the Celtic score (which was a 1–0 home win against Dundee). I picked up my hill-walking companion and guide, Nadia, and swung her round in a celebratory circle. Wishing I had been wearing a cassock from the monastery, which I could then have hitched up in the manner of Julie Andrews in *The Sound of Music*, I ran and skipped down the grassy hill towards the carpark like a member of the Von Trapp family in full gambol. The Miracle of Easter Road had happened, thanks to the intercession of St Michael (Delaney, the match referee). Hun hubris had been suitably humbled, with Souness's Tower of Babel collapsing around him before it had even got off the ground.

As I read the 'Old Firm' match reports, with the broadsheet pages spread out on the bonnet of the Volvo, I noticed that my nettle-rash-mottled hands were returning to normal, even as I watched in amazement. At the time I thought it was a genuinely miraculous cure, but it was simply a scientifically explicable reaction to my surging adrenalin level.

A healthy diet, lots of Alpine air and sunshine, and plenty of exercise had nevertheless relieved my chronic symptoms significantly. A grossly sentimental *Life of the Saints*, written by some long-dead nun, also inspired me to bear my weariness of bodily anguish with greater fortitude.

On my final night in Italy, I stayed in Nadia's apartment. On the balcony the night air was a mixture of honeysuckle, dog roses and some ozone-hostile detergent from the laundry downstairs. Lights danced in the Dora Baltea river, while overhead the Alps loomed darkly. The full moon slipped behind pregnant clouds. The cicadas stopped chirping. A few raindrops quickly became a fully fledged thunderstorm. Back inside I flicked on the television, with the sound down. An Italian housewife was pouting provocatively at the camera, completely naked except for her moustache. Being a Sunday, the only alternative viewing was coverage of that day's 0–0 draws in Serie A. When the rain stopped, the oppressive September heat had lifted. I smoked a delicious Marlboro back out on the balcony. How could Souness have chosen to give up the *dolce vita* of Northern Italy (with Sampdoria in Genoa) for the dubious pleasures of managing Glasgow Rangers through a brutal Scottish winter? Was he mad? Or just madly ambitious?

I took one last look at 'Ivrea by Night' before going to bed, where I went over Monday's itinerary in my head: Ivrea, change at Chivasso, Milan, Manchester . . . Glasgow – where there were no cicadas to cicada.

Celtic 1
Rangers 2

(Skol League Cup final, 26 October 1986)

Back seeing the consultant, a few days before this game, he asked if I was working. When I said I had a job in public relations, he promptly suggested that such highly stressful employment was probably exacerbating my symptoms (having obviously forgotten his previous glib observation about unfilled days giving me time to dwell on my 'ASD').[1] I was still fuming with anger and frustration when I went along to Hampden, emotions which were not helped any by Roy Aitken giving away yet another penalty – for a shirt-tugging foul on Terry Butcher – and from which Rangers scored their winner through Davie Cooper. Near the end Mo Johnston was sent off for giving Rangers full-back Stuart Munro a 'Glasgow kiss' and as Johnston made his way off the pitch he crossed himself. The Huns in the stadium went absolutely tonto. Because of this incident I thought 'Blessed Mo' had just taken the first step on the complicated road to becoming a canonised Celtic saint, but it was a double bluff worthy of a Nazi secret agent shooting Gestapo prisoners of the French Resistance, because after signing for Nantes in 1987 Johnston came back to Glasgow in 1989 to play for *Rangers*, reneging for more money at the last minute on his promise to rejoin Celtic. Outstanding player that Johnston undoubtedly was, he was also a thick-as-two-planks Judas.

This cup final defeat, combined with Souness's resurgent Rangers catching Celtic in the league and staying in front, cost Davie Hay his managerial job. Celtic's response to Souness was to re-recruit the prodigal Billy McNeill from Aston Villa, an appointment which worked superbly in the short-term for the club's centenary season but which was not nearly bold enough to counteract the Hun hegemony of the early '90s.

FOOTNOTES

1 Dermatologists are not exactly the élite of the medical profession, outranking only
  obstetricians in Hippocratic kudos, and it took a neurosurgeon to identify and cure my
  symptoms – which, to be fair, he only recognised because his sister-in-law had been one of
  the only seven people in Britain in any one year who suffer from the particular condition (and
  which can be triggered by overexposure to antibiotics).

Scotland 2
Hungary 0

(Friendly International, 16 September 1987)

Sponsored by Whyte & McKay, the only reason I went along to this
meaningless match was because I won two VIP tickets in a letter-
writing competition run by the *Evening Times*. In answer to Chick
Young's question about why I'd 'always be a member of the Tartan
Army' – from which I'd gone AWOL years before – my excruciatingly
naff reply was duly published.

The pre-match hospitality – dinner and drinks in Whyte &
Mckay's plush corporate headquarters in St Vincent Street – was a
bit of a social strain for most of the ticket winners, even although
we were all coralled off at a separate table, well away from the SFA
apparatchiks and company executives. Most of the nervous diners
at our table had committed sartorial suicide before leaving home –
with lethal combinations of acrylic, polyester and raylon – and I was
relieved that I'd decided, at the last minute, to wear a shirt and tie.
I did regret bringing my sister Lynn as my guest in order to let her
experience some genuine fat-cat truffle-snorting, because none of the
other winners had given their spare tickets to wives or girlfriends,
preferring instead to invite what appeared to be destitute dossers
whom they'd fallen over on the way to the dinner – in other words,
best mates. With unrestricted whisky on tap at our table, the PR dolly
bird assigned to look after us was looking increasingly worried about
her future career in the industry.

When she disappeared towards the front entrance I thought she'd
gone to get reinforcements from the security desk – we had by
then overcome our initial nervousness and were experimenting with
the aerodynamic properties of the monogrammed 'W & M' table
napkins – but she came back with Chic Young in tow. C-list celeb

Chic did the round of our table, schmoozing and glad-handing as he went. Personally, I thought he had about as much charismatic appeal as a used sanitary towel, but his braying bonhomie and trumpery tarradiddles had the desired effect of quietening us down.

I would have skipped attending the game itself if I could have, but the complimentary bottles of whisky remained locked away until after the final whistle. A luxury, air-conditioned coach whisked us all to Hampden, but not before one of our number managed to be 'car sick'. I think Ally McCoist got Scotland's goals, but I can't recall exactly. I was extremely drunk.

Celtic 2
Dundee United 1

(Scottish Cup final, 14 May 1988)

With the league flag already flying over Parkhead, hopes were understandably high before this match that Celtic could go on to secure the double in their centenary season, a fairy tale ending which only a year earlier would have seemed as likely as Rangers signing a card-carrying Catholic altar boy on 'S' forms. In May of 1987 Davie Hay had been sacked as manager, and although Billy McNeill had been appointed in his place McNeill himself had just been dismissed from Aston Villa, after leading the 1982 European Cup winners into the English Second Division. And just as McNeill was arriving back at Celtic Park through the front door, four of the club's best players were preparing to leave by a back entrance: Brian McClair (Manchester United), Mo Johnston (Nantes), Alan McInally (Aston Villa!) and Murdo MacLeod (Borussia Dortmund). Celtic's only big-name signing was Frank McAvennie, for a club record fee of £850,000 from West Ham. Rangers, meanwhile, were recycling massive amounts of Masonic protection and drugs money by buying up every Protestant psychopath that came on the market, like Richard Gough, whose Aryan bad looks and South African accent were procured for a mere £1.1 million. (When I first saw banner newspaper headlines heralding 'FALCO FOR IBROX' I almost burst into tears, thinking that the Huns were about to start buying Catholics in the form of Brazilian World Cup superstars, but the Falco in question was Mark, a £280,000 dud from non-sambaing Watford.)

To see the final I had to travel back through to Glasgow from Edinburgh, where I had moved earlier in the year. Despite having a successful football team to support, yet another Glaswegian winter to get through proved to be that much more difficult than all the ones that had gone before. The job in public relations – which is a phrase redolent of CV censorship – was so badly paid that I had to supplement my income with market research and opinion poll interviewing in the evenings and at weekends (missing more than a few home games in the process). Cold-call interviewing on doorsteps, even although you're not trying to sell anything (which makes people suspicious immediately), is depressingly hard and boring work, with each social class of interviewee presenting their own specific kind of problems.

Although the DEs in areas of urban deprivation tended to be as thick as mince, their cholesterol-clogged hearts were in the right place and you usually got invited in for a cup of weak tea made with two heaped teaspoons of pure, white and deadly sugar.

In a typical DE household, respondents would answer absolutely anything they were asked – including made-up questions about frequency of conjugal relations and exact capital savings – but only after I listened to inarticulate complaints about blocked cisterns, broken loo seats, late Giros, rising damp, out-of-control fungal growths (on bedroom ceilings and in vaginal tracts), screaming weans who came in from middens covered in rodent bites, junkies across the landing whose front door was made of steel thicker than the hull of the QE2, the injustices of the housing points system (which was commonly believed to favour unmarried single mothers with AIDS), boarded-up flats that were used as dead-letter drops for Housing Benefit scams, lifts that were always out of order (or if they weren't were always full of people urinating, injecting or copulating), how life would be unbearable unless the video was fixed (which couldn't be done under warranty since it invariably fell off the back of a hi-jacked lorry), intransigent social workers and health visitors who refused to recommend increased dosages of Temazepam (or 'jellies') to the 'fuckin Paki doketur doon ra health centur who disnae even speak English prope-er, like'. The questionnaires were normally completed with a staggering proportion of 'Don't knows' and I eventually filled in the answers for most DE households sitting in the car, in the end making up names and addresses as well as answers, since if I designated them as 'N/Ts' (no telephones) my supervisor couldn't back-check on their existence without sending out verification forms, which DEs never, ever returned.

Willing and articulate interviewees were no problem to get in affluent AB districts, because most suburbanites are delighted to be asked to participate in an opinion poll (but not so keen on market research). However, even if I was lucky enough to be invited across the threshold of 'Chez Hun' or 'Cad'oro' (with the Beware of the Doges sign on the gate), I was never offered a cup of filter coffee, never mind a mug of herbal tea. These interviews took an inordinate amount of time to complete, since the middle-aged, middle-brow middle classes pondered over every reply like conscientious police witnesses.

As already mentioned the worst part of any quota was the C1C2 element, hiding behind their net curtains and dusting their hideous lava lamps.

For once, the Cup final weather was glorious, and I was joined in the sun-bathed Celtic End by Baby Albert & Co, Father Flyte and most of the 'Papal Bull' pub team that I occasionally turned out for: Slap Head, Tricity, Hovis, Battleship Potemkin, Tizer, Gonk, Wee Willie and Big Dickie. (I never had a nickname, even although I tried in vain to promote 'the Professor', and I think this lack must have some kind of social and personal significance; even today in the early-morning newsagents where I pick up the papers for work, I am the only customer whom the proprietor isn't on first name terms with – and that includes the homeless dossers who come in to buy *single* cigarettes.)

Just after half-time United took the lead through Kevin Gallacher, who embarrassingly outpaced Roy Aitken to a through ball which he volleyed confidently past Allen McKnight, whose inept clearance moments earlier had gone straight to Eammon Bannon's bald bonce. Tricity and Hovis – the pub team's central defenders – were screaming blue murder at Aitken, who had uncharacteristically failed to 'bodycheck' Gallacher in the race for the ball, but Aitken had already been booked – pointlessly – and any deliberate obstruction at this stage would have resulted in his sending-off.

Celtic came back with predictable determination and United were soon under sustained pressure. When Frank McAvennie scored with 15 minutes to go, heading home an Anton Rogan cross, I *knew* United would crack completely before the end, because of historic inevitability and the 65,000 Celtic fans roaring their team on to victory. When Celtic got a corner with less than a minute to go, someone behind me actually said, 'This is it, lads.' And so it was, as McAvennie hammered his shot past a sprawling Billy Thomson from close in.

The perfect end to an unbelievable centenary season, although Aitken could have gone a long way to redeeming himself in my eyes if he had refused to shake hands with Prime Minister Margaret Thatcher before she presented him with the Cup. (When she first appeared in the VIP box, the Secretary of State for Scotland Malcolm Rifkind must have squirmed with embarrassment, because Hans Krankl of Rapid Vienna would have got a warmer welcome from the crowd.)

McAvennie's performance in the final had been typically impressive, but within a year he was sold back to West Ham. On the park 'Macca' was everything a Celtic fan could have wished for in a striker – intelligent, unselfish, hard-working, reliable, honest and courageous. Off it he was almost the complete opposite. But with his transfer went any chance of retaining the Premier League, although even without him Celtic managed to reach another Scottish Cup final . . .

Celtic 1
Rangers 0

(Scottish Cup final, 20 May 1989)

I have absolutely no memory of *not* being at this game, and I would have sworn in a court of law that I was there, but after telephoning one of the people I thought I went with I was assured that I was most definitely not there. This may well be an example of what Douglas Coupland in *Generation X* terms 'Legislated Nostalgia', whereby people are so desperate to remember something that they acquire false memories.

If not there in person – which begs the question, where the hell was I? – I must have watched the final live on television, because I do remember Joe Miller's goal, when he latched on to a woeful pass-back from Rangers' Gary Stevens and hammered the ball past Chris Woods with a low shot. I was going to write that I was especially pleased for Miller because earlier in the season he became the only Celtic substitute that I've ever seen substituted (because of poor form and not injury), but according to his entry in *An Alphabet of the Celts* this bizarre claim to infamy didn't take place until the League Cup semi-final against Aberdeen in September of '89 (which I do remember being at, because Celtic lost and the Dons went on to beat the Huns 2–1 in the final).

Having total recall of a false memory may be undermining my omniscient narration, but as the history books will confirm Celtic were to use this victory over their arch-rivals as a launch pad for the longest barren spell of footballing failure since the late '50s and early '60s . . . Which is why my non-attendance still sticks in the craw of my memory.

TROPHYLESS, RUDDERLESS AND ABSOLUTELY BLOODY HOPELESS
1989–1994

Glasgow Celtic 5
Partizan Belgrade 4

(Cup Winners' Cup, first round second leg, 27 September 1989)

With Celtic having scored a mythical thing called an away goal in Europe, which many young fans had only heard stories about from their misty-eyed fathers, my sister and I joined 59,998 others crammed into Celtic Park, confident that Mike Galloway's goal in Yugoslavia would prove invaluable in overcoming a 2–1 first-leg deficit.

Because of the 'away-goals-count-double-in-the-event-of-a-tie' ruling, second-leg European matches like this one can provide more drama and excitement than any of Shakespeare's plays, Hitchcock's movies or Hemingway's novels (since the ending is not merely unclear but unknowable). Up until the 81st minute the sequence of goals was as follows, with the aggregate scores in brackets: 0–1 (1–3); 1–1 (2–3); 2–1 (3–3); 2–2 (3–4); 3–2 (4–4); 3–3 (4–5); 4–3 (5–5).

The first three Celtic goals had all been scored by Dariusz 'Jacki' Dziekanowski, a Polish international bought during the summer after Mo Johnston had just volte-faced his mercenary way into Ibrox. The move from Poland to Scotland, however, revealed an appetite for disco decadence and horizontal dancing that made Johnston look positively wallflowerish by comparison. Although Andy Walker had put Celtic 4–3 ahead on the night, at 5–5 on aggregate Celtic were still behind on away goals.

With nine minutes to go, Dziekanowski got his fourth and Celtic's fifth, putting us ahead for the first time in the tie. The apoplectic celebrations in the Celtic End had a – frankly – hysterical edge to them.

Any other team would have got ten men behind the ball for the remaining few minutes, but Celtic continued to counter-attack, with the suicidal bravery of the Hitler Youth defending the Führerbunker with empty machine-guns. Arguably, back-to-the-wall defending would have been useless anyway, because all through the game the Celtic back four had been about as effective as the Maginot Line – and about as mobile.

Partizan's most influential player had been the midfielder Milco Durovski, who hadn't taken kindly to being jeered for his unusual appearance by the Jungle in the opening period. With the minutes ticking away with excruciating slowness, Durovski was still prancing around in his distinctive black tights, à la Rudolf Nureyev playing Prince Siegfried in *Swan Lake*. In Celtic's midfield Galloway and Roy Aitken were far from wizardly enough to put a spell on him – although Aitken should have laddered one of his tights by breaking a leg. Still, we did have Dziekanowski, who looked perfectly capable of adding to his tally right until the end, but he was to be cast in the heroically tragic role of the Swan Princess – scoring *four* goals and ending up on the *losing* side.

With less than a minute to go, Durovski released the ball to an overlapping full-back. The bowels of the Celtic defenders must have turned to water, because they stood rooted to the spot, watching the move develop with mounting horror. The East German referee, Kurt Peschel, actually glanced at his watch before the cross ball was swung over. Scepovic went to meet it with his funny-shaped head.

When I opened my eyes – after screwing them shut for the first time ever while watching a football match – I knew Partizan had scored. The black-and-white striped shirts of the Partizan players were surrounding Scepovic, and the Yugoslav bench were cavorting on the running track, including manager Ivan Golac. 5–4 to Celtic on the night. 6–6 on aggregate. Partizan through on away goals.

The final whistle pierced an eerie silence a few moments later. The booing which followed had a bathetic bleating quality to it, as if the residents of the Janefield Street Cemetery were giving voice to their misery. Imagine, if you will, Edvard Munch's *The Scream* brought to life, given vocal cords and multiplied by 60,000.

Personally, I couldn't have felt worse if I'd just reached the head of the queue for the last helicopter out of Saigon, moments after it had lifted off the roof of the American Embassy. This game had been a roller-coaster of a ride which left me in a state of parrot sickness. Lynn was as white as a bleached sheet, as well as trembling uncontrollably in what appeared to be medical shock. I actually considered giving her a hug – for the first time in my life – but decided instead to push her roughly in the back, to get her moving towards the nearest exit, which we filed through in shuffling automatic pilot with the other traumatised zombies, like Fritz Lang's underground workers clocking off work in *Metropolis*.

'That was unreal,' she gasped.

'Surreal,' I mumbled.

Walking through the car park, I saw the Syringe shouting spit over Baby Albert, who was standing stock still with his eyes squeezed shut.

In a dialectic that must have been repeated endlessly throughout the city long into the night, Baby Albert had tried to mitigate his visceral suffering by mentally rationalising the incredible sequence of events we had just witnessed. He sought some solace in the view that, for neutrals, this game must have been the apotheosis of European cup competition. The Syringe's outraged response was that it was simply 'another fucking first round exit, part of a fucking yearly pilgrimage to Parkhead to see sacrificial fucking lambs in ceremonial green-and-white hoops being fucking slaughtered by the fucking high priests of fucking Continental football'.

I walked Lynn back to our parents' house, with not a word spoken between us. A measure of our depressed distraction was the fact that we failed to walk the extra 600 yards on main roads to avoid a notorious short-cut across deserted and unlit waste ground, the footpath of which led under a disused railway bridge, and on top of which Hun hoodlums usually lay in wait for stray Celtic fans. I noticed about six of them as we approached, sitting on exposed girders swinging their Doc Marten boots and bicycle chains. Director John Boorman could have substituted any one of them for the in-bred mountain boy in *Deliverance*. They had obviously heard the score from Parkhead and merely grinned like evil trolls as we passed underneath. A few yards further on I picked up a half brick and knocked the one in the middle off his perch like a coconut from its cup at a fairground sideshow.

'I sick,' said Dziekanowski during the post-match post-mortem. He must have felt that the back four of FSO Cars, with whom he started his career, would have made a more professional stab at keeping Vajacic, Dordevic, Durovski and Scepovic off the scoresheet than the Celtic defence of Peter Grant, Anton Rogan, Paul Elliott and Derek Whyte.

Since the trauma of this night, Celtic have gone into subsequent ties against Continental opposition with raging Europhobic neuroses embarrassingly evident. Whereas the 1984 disappointment of going out to Rapid Vienna can be dismissed as unlucky, because of events outside the team's control, losing to Partizan Belgrade in such self-destructive and pathetic fashion has opened up a Pandora's Box of psychological self-doubt. If traumatic events can cripple individuals, the same must be true of institutions like football clubs. Freud often related the story of little Armaud, who as a toddler peed through one of the gaps in some chicken wire. A chicken which tried to peck his little man-root left the subject of Freud's investigations mentally scarred for life. In Celtic's case history, the Partizan Belgrade chicken not only succeeded in snapping at the exposed penile worm – it held on with its beak until a distraught father killed the hen with a meat cleaver, an act of paternal protection from which the *castrated* offspring has not yet recovered or been able to forgive.

The day after the match, I got the early-morning red-eye special out of Buchanan Street Bus Station for Edinburgh. In the light of the result, Glasgow had taken on an even greyer hue than normal and I was desperate to get back to the aesthetic delights of the capital (Edinburgh I was in love with, Glasgow I just masturbated over). Like Belgrade – at the time – Edinburgh is a great European capital city, a claim to fame that Glasgow cannot boast (and not just because the Big G is not a *capital* city).

Instead of force-reading myself through the match report in the *Daily Record*, I tried to settle down on the back seat with Evelyn Waugh's *Brideshead Revisited*. The fact that Glasgow was mentioned on the very first page woke me up with an unpleasant jolt of culture shock. Having read it before, however, I knew that Waugh's brilliant novel thundered against the Age of the Common Man, as personified by the character Hooper. The initial reference to the Big G – which is full of McHoopers – was not meant to be complimentary, with the book's opening set in the suburb of 'Pollock' to provide maximum dramatic contrast with the Arcadian splendour of the Marchmain estate.

In the earphones of my Walkman, Abba were damning the Big G with very faint praise, in their Number One record *Super Trouper*, the lyrics of which begin: 'I was sick and tired of everything/ When I called you last night from Glasgow.' Since such subtly sardonic commentary is not normally associated with the saturnine Swedes, it is all the more effective.

I may have been transferring anger that should have been directed at Glasgow *Celtic*, but in the aftermath of the Partizan Belgrade game my home town had never seemed so parochial and provincial. To be fair, Glasgow itself was no longer an industrial inferno located somewhere between the Dante-esque circles of Hull and Hell, but its attempts to transform itself into a 'dear green place' where upwardly mobile young professionals could live lives of designer diuturnity in wally-dug-tiled closes protected by security intercoms were largely the triumph of image over reality.

In the early and mid-'80s the city fathers spent half-a-million pounds on the 'Glasgow's Miles Better' campaign, the most tangible result being the vacuously eerie smile of Mr Happy – a yellow balloon with thalidomidic arms and legs – who beamed down on the unemployed populace from every billboard, gable end and council building like a cartoon Big Brother (ironically, the 'personality cult' of Mr Happy reached its five-year-plan peak in 1984). No one in Edinburgh begrudged Glasgow the Garden Festival City 'honour' in 1988, but when the Big G became European City of Culture in 1990 Edina's self-satisfied complacency was shattered for good (not that it prevented Glasgow from snatching the even more incredible title of City of Architecture and Design from Edinburgh in the 1995 selection process).

In between beating Inter Milan in 1967 and losing to Partizan Belgrade in 1989, Glasgow's cultural *leitmotif* had changed from razor kings to Burger Kings. In the same period the city regenerated itself by ripping out its Victorian heart in order to transplant a motorway pacemaker, giving it the distinction of the highest mileage of urban motorway per head of the population in Europe, but with the lowest car ownership. As the coach picked up speed on the M8, through Tollcross, I warily admired the tarted-up tenements and tower blocks, before remembering that the Council's new policy of preservation and modernisation – but with a budget significantly constrained by PR spending – was depressingly reminiscent of a Hollywood movie company's back lot, with sham exteriors hiding support struts and non-existent interiors. If you were a tenant of Glasgow District Council and you wanted your breezeblocked rabbit hutch housing made fit for human habitation – along with plastic pilasters and pediments, concrete castellations and glass gazebos – you were unlikely to get labourers from the Direct Works Department setting up camp outside your front door unless you were lucky enough to live in a tenement block or multi-storey which overlooked the motorway or a railtrack carrying London trains. What would have been the point in stone-cleaning and reroofing tenements which weren't visible from main communication arteries and along which foreign dignitaries never travelled in their first-class compartments or chauffeur-driven limousines?

As the coach shuddered through Easterhouse, I thought about the Syringe, who lived near the top of one of the damp-infested tower blocks. From his living-room window you could see the motorway unravelling itself in the direction of the West End, a view made even more dramatic at night with the floodlit Gothic of the University Tower and the neon-bathed Neo-Classicalism of the Trinity College

Tower – a vista memorably described as being lifted straight out of *Jude the Obscure* (but only if you ignored the tower blocks near to St George's Cross). But high up in the concrete stalagmites of Easterhouse – designed by in-house Council architects, engineers of the soul and lowercase le corbusiers – the Sky worshippers preferred to gape at the mindless programming on the Lifestyle Channel, as they sipped from cans of Special Brew and nibbled on benzodiazepines.

By the time the coach pulled into Harthill Service Station – where no one ever got on or off – Glasgow's oppressive effect on my psyche was beginning to lift. I further managed to improve my spirits by re-evaluating the PR hype that I had left behind, because in the run-up to the Year of Culture the hyperbole had to be heard to be disbelieved.

John Mauceri, Musical Director of Scottish Opera, was actually quoted as saying that Glasgow in the '80s had had the same intellectual and artistic feel as Paris in the 1920s. Oh really, Jean? *Excuse moi*, while I spray a mouthful of Chateau Irn Bru '88 over my nouvelle cuisine mince 'n' tatties. That's better . . . So James Kelman is Hemingway; Alasdair Gray, Joyce; Steven Campbell, Picasso; Edwin Morgan, TS Eliot; and Molly Weir, Gertrude Stein. I think not, Monsieur Mauceri!

Coming off the motorway at the Newbridge Roundabout, the coach lurched right on to the dual carriageway for Edinburgh.

Ever since the publication of *Lanark* in 1981, Glasgow has been a fashionable subject for artistic exploitation, whether in literary fiction, agitprop theatre, modern art or commercial television – almost all of which propagate romanticised and sentimental myths about the working class. In the creative middle-class (Marxist?) mind 'the workers' are forever borrowing cups of sugar, leaving their front doors unlocked, committing heroic acts of bravery on the shop floor, getting undernourished limbs mangled in threshing machines, dying *en masse* in pit disasters (normally in Ayrshire), living on bread and dripping in order to clothe tubercular weans, dying of untreated pneumonia for want of half-a-crown for the doctor, studying Shakespeare and Engels in the public library to broaden their minds, joining up to fight Fascism in Spain or Nicaragua, going on strike in support of their black brothers in South Africa, recounting rude but 'ideologically sound and politically correct' jokes, until in a rousing finale the oppressed proletariat all link arms and kick-step down Sauchiehall Street singing the final chorus of the *Internationale*. In reality, however, Jimmy the Obscures do not dance in the streets, drink in the saloons and neck in the parlours – they commit criminal assault in the streets, get paralytically scoobied in the pubs and indulge in incestual rape in the bedrooms.

Walking up to Princes Street to get a double-decker bus home, my heart soared at the sight of the Castle, the Gardens and the Seat (Arthur's). Prince Charles may have some bizarre ideas about transforming himself into a sanitary tampon and disappearing up his amorata's vaginal drainpipe, but his championing of Edinburgh as Britain's most beautiful city is more than aesthetically justified.

Then I remembered the aggregate scoreline and started to slide down the bus-stop pole . . .

Celtic 0
Aberdeen 0

(Scottish Cup final, 12 May 1990, aet)

'An ever increasing sense of neglected merit . . .'
'I want to insist upon the fateful power of trivial incidents.'
(George Gissing, *New Grub Street*)

In the spring of 1990 the frustration alluded to in the first of Gissing's quotes was beginning to drive me up off-licence walls once more. Having read voraciously and scribbled furiously for many years, my autodidactic literary style was finally approaching an acceptable standard. Not that my postman would have confirmed this, since he returned self-addressed and stamped A4 envelopes on an almost daily basis. I had pinned both of the above quotes on the pinboard over my writing desk, but I was fast losing faith in the latter, to the point where I would have positively welcomed all my rejected MSS going up in smoke like poor Harold Biffen's. (In retrospect, I had simply developed a talent for language – like a lot of people – but without the necessary editorial and structural discipline required, like a footballer who could do impressive keepie-uppie tricks in training but who saw the game pass him by in competitive matches.)

At 29 I felt like a prolific goalscorer for a Second Division team who invariably failed to find the net in 'shop window' Cup ties against Premier League opposition and who was becoming convinced that the prospect of full-time football was receding into the historical distance. The fact that most writers do not reach their peak until they are between 35 and 45 was not much of a consolation, since most have served the equivalent of a footballing apprenticeship with small publishers or magazines in their mid-to-late' 20s. Nevertheless, 'trivial incidents' do occasionally lead to ageing players in lower divisions getting transferred to bigger clubs.

Life, like football, throws up hideously unexpected own goals and gloriously out-of-the-blue last-minute winners, none of which can be seen coming. In early April I was flicking through a copy of the *List* – Central Scotland's equivalent of *Time Out* – when I saw an obsequious interview with Su 'Poor Cow' Pollard spread over two pages, in which she claimed her husband was 'a former homosexual' (?). When I saw the prize for best readers' letter in the next issue was a bottle of Jose Cuervo tequila, I immediately wrote in asking if he was now 'cured'? I padded the letter out with a few other terrifically witty observations, including a sarcastic reference to Mainstream's publication of Graeme Souness's *A Manager's Diary* – namely, 'He may use the F word as much as Kelman, but he's hardly in the same literary league, is he?' (Ironically, if not for this letter I wouldn't have a publishing contract with Mainstream today, which just shows that cause-and-effect schema branch out in an almost infinite variety of directions.) When published I would have collected my hooch from the *List*'s Edinburgh offices without further ado, but the italicised editorial comment at the end of the letter got me thinking. It began: '*Great stuff. Do you want your own column?* . . . ' I decided that I did and sent off a two-thousand word epic to try and persuade them. At the very least I thought I might be able to wangle some book-review work, as a first step to building up a 'portfolio' of literary journalism. But when I showed my father the published letters and told him of my foot-in-the-door plans he was rather sceptical, probably because he'd just about given up trying to get his own stories and scripts sold or produced (especially after BBC Scotland had lost the MS they were 'considering').

On the Thursday before the Cup final, the literary editor of the *List* – now assistant sports editor of the *Scotsman* – left a note at my flat inviting me to do some writing for the magazine. When I got back in the late evening I was very pleased, and I knew my father would be delighted, but I decided to keep the good news until the Saturday when I would see him in person . . .

A telephone that nerve-jarringly awakens one from deep sleep before six o'clock in the morning is either going to be, upon answering, an extremely irritating wrong number or an extremely bad piece of family news. At 5.40 a.m. I somnabulistically groped my way out of the bedroom, banging a shin against an invisible chair in the process. In the hall I picked up the receiver by the light which leaked in through the fanlight, trying to formulate a stinging rebuke with which to chastise an inattentive STD dialler. The possibility of bad news did not enter my sleepy head, since all my immediate family were in reasonably good health (and to my knowledge safely tucked up in bed). Hence my heart stayed in my chest, not in my mouth.

The moment I had dreaded for years, played out countless times in my imagination, had finally arrived. But there was to be no dramatic dash to get there in time; no tearful, emotion-choked farewell in a cancer ward, with dry emaciated fingers clutching desperately at unproffered hands. At least I was to be spared the ordeal of entering a ward or bedroom to say goodbye to my dying father, with *both* of us conscious of the fact that *he* was about to cease to exist.

He had died in his sleep.

I tried to recall the last time I had seen my father, and struggled to remember the exact time, place or circumstance. Dropping me off outside Queen Street railway station, probably . . .

I remembered returning his wave with absent-minded indifference, but I didn't watch as he turned left into George Square in his spluttering jalopy. By Thatcherite standards I suppose he was a failure (and regarded himself as such); by the standards of a loving son he was a success (but probably did not regard himself as such). A nice, slightly deaf, recently retired old man, with a dangerously occluded left anterior descending artery. A massive heart attack just waiting to happen.

I opened the shutters and squinted against the bright May sunlight. On Leith Walk the good citizens of Edinburgh were going about their business as if nothing out of the ordinary had happened (and God knows what I'd been doing for the previous three hours). I packed my best suit and a white shirt in a travel bag. I searched in mounting frustration for a black tie in the wardrobe, until I realised that I'd never been to a funeral as an adult before and therefore didn't possess one. I made a mental note to buy one in the Tie Rack in Waverley Market on the way to the train station, since it never occurred to me that I could have used my father's. After locking the front door of the flat, I hurriedly reopened it. I stuffed my green-and-white striped football scarf into the travel bag and checked my wallet for the match ticket. If I needed them I certainly wasn't coming all the way back to Edinburgh for them.

To make up for my tardy arrival in Glasgow, which my sister immediately criticised me for (she was still staying at home), in the afternoon I attended to all the pressing legal formalities and urgent funeral arrangements. (Thankfully by the time I did arrive home my father's body had been removed.) At London Road police station I collected the examining doctor's cause-of-death certificate, which I read unseeingly half a dozen times while parked outside the hideous new façade of the main stand at Celtic Park. One of my cousins accompanied me to Martha Street in order to register the death with the authorities and to obtain the necessary insurance and burial chitties. The utilitarian waiting-room was crowded (the Friday rush?), full of teary-eyed Glaswegians exhibiting shock and grief worthy of Brazilian soap opera stars. I read the back pages of the *Evening Times*, but I wasn't really able to concentrate on the reported team news. After selecting an extortionately expensive coffin from the Co-operative Funeral Service's 'tasteful' range and writing the obituary notice for Monday's paper I reluctantly returned home in my father's five-year-old Volkswagen.

According to Lynn, our father had shown no signs, or complained of any symptoms, which might have heralded imminent cardio-vascular infraction. However, he had been 'up to high doh' with local unemployed youths playing football in the street, and since my parents were the only residents courageous enough to report them to the police for smashing car windows and street lights, they were subjected to a campaign of nuisance as a consequence.

As I stood at the kitchen sink filling the kettle for the tea-and-sympathy brigade that were trooping in and out, I looked out of the window and saw them kicking a heavy leather football around in desultory fashion, right outside the gate where the car was parked. As I stood there, racked by indecision, I fought an internal battle between feelings of cowardice and fury, as well as having to decide between the conflicting needs of prudence and retribution.

'Hey, you – that's oor ba' . . . '

'Listen, pizza-face. My father died last night of a fucking heart attack caused by the stress of keeping an eye on you lot. Now, fucking well clear off.'

I looked round at their blank, uncomprehending stares. As I

walked away, the big fat lout with symmetrical acne mumbled something, which elicited nervous sniggers from his mates.

'What did you say?'

With his peer-group standing at stake he repeated it with defensive aggressiveness. 'Yer faither wiz a crabbit auld bastard, onyways, and A'm glad he's deid.'

After grabbing his jug ears for purchase, I foreheaded his snotter-encaked nose. Blood splattered absolutely everywhere as he fell back. On the ground I sat astride his chest, grabbed a handful of greasy red curls and started to hit his head against the road. Again and again. But not again. Even in such highly charged circumstances my liberal, humanist conscience remained a tenacious monkey on my back.

Back inside the house I was violently sick down the toilet pan. At the time I wished I'd killed him. But if I had there would have been repercussions and I would have regretted it, if only for my mother's sake . . .

The next day I decided not to go to the final – partly for fear of pizza face's hoodlum big brothers coming round to the house seeking to escalate the violence (incredibly no one in my family knew anything about the previous day's confrontation) – and I had nothing to do except sit around drinking endless cups of tea. The television was switched on at three o'clock, but with the sound down as a mark of respect. When my sister and her boyfriend settled down on the sofa to watch it, too, I turned the volume back up. I was somewhat surprised that I still cared who won, but it was hardly an example of the male adult's unique ability to compartmentalise emotions, because Lynn obviously wanted Celtic to beat Aberdeen as well.

After a goalless two hours the game went to a penalty shoot-out, the first ever in a Scottish Cup final. By this stage I was so engrossed in the on-pitch drama that I half-expected my father to wander in from the kitchen or garden to enquire with a mischievous twinkle in his eye as to whether Celtic had lost yet.

Worryingly Celtic had to start the penalties, in front of the Aberdeen fans, and it was no real surprise when Dariusz Wdowcyck missed the target completely. Mass telekinetic concentration by the Celtic legions managed to lift Brian Grant's fourth penalty for Aberdeen over the bar. Thereafter all the kicks were successfully converted and at 8–8 it looked as if the respective goalkeepers were going to be called into shooting action – which would have been hilarious viewing for neutrals, considering the unpredictable way Pat Bonner and Theo Snelders usually connected with their own dead-ball goal-kicks – but Celtic still had their secret self-detonating weapon in reserve. When Anton Rogan slowly stepped out of the centre circle, he looked about as relaxed as a walking time bomb wired up with plastic explosives and a battery pack. If I'd had the remote-control detonator in my hand I'd have auto-de-fed him without hesitation. As he stepped up to the spot my heart sank. In the previous two 'Old Firm' games the Northern Ireland left-back had given away two needless penalties for rush-of-blood-to-the-head handling offences.

Hyperventilating, I had to consciously concentrate on breathing in and out, lest I induce a heart attack in myself. After all, these things were hereditary.

When Snelders parried the weak shot, I was out of my seat before Rogan was on his knees. Still on my feet I watched with fatalistic resignation as Brian Irvine made it 9–8 for Aberdeen . . .

Later on the Saturday night I drove to the Co-op's chapel of rest in Morrison Street, a solitary building in a desert of empty car parks. With a melancholy sense of detachment, I saw my father's body laid out in his open coffin, dressed in a blue silk funeral shroud like a Renaissance pope. As I was leaving I noticed that all the Catholic rest-rooms were named after saints, whereas as a Protestant my father was allocated a room named after one of the Western Isles – Tiree to be exact. Driving back through the city centre I envied the pockets of morose Celtic fans that I passed, since they had only lost a Cup final and not a father . . .

To be honest, I was dreading the funeral service at Linn Crematorium on the Tuesday – in case the turn-out was embarrassingly low (as it would undoubtedly have been for mine) – but the slow drive up the loose gravel road in the black mourners' limousine to the chapel ended in a quite moving scene: row upon row upon row of parked Gas Board vans from the Uddingston depot, their blue-and-white livery glinting in the sunshine (all in response to a quick phone call I made to the Personnel Department to inform them that only a widow's pension would be required from then on). The number of private cars was gratifyingly large, too.

After the funeral meal back at the house – which the police had had to patrol past in case it was burgled – I made my excuses and left. Back in Edinburgh I collected my review copies from the *List* offices in the High Street and walked back to the flat feeling intellectually electrified but emotionally frazzled.

My father had always worried about my passing over career jobs with prospects to pursue my writing ambitions, but he never

once criticised me for it. If he had lived to see my small but
significant breakthrough into paid print, it would have made him
'chuffed to bits'.

It was enough to make you want to weep . . . I mean, 9–8!

Scotland 0
Costa Rica 1

(World Cup finals, 11 June 1990)

Just when you thought Scotland's humiliating record in World Cup
opening fixtures couldn't get any worse, the disappointing outcomes
against Zaire, Peru, New Zealand and Denmark were made to look
positively respectable. Scotland contrived to lose to a country whose
translated name of 'Rich Coast' disguised an economy based on a
penal colony and whose national currency was the banana. Despite
losing half their squad to outbreaks of malaria, beriberi, dysentery,
yellow fever and green-banana poisoning prior to departing for Italia
'90 in a banana boat, Costa Rica opened the scoring against Scotland
in 49 minutes, when Juan Cassayo beat Jim Leighton from seven
yards. Thereafter their goalkeeper Luis Conejo – a banana-packer
from Puntarenas – had the temerity to play well, an eventuality
national coach Andy Roxanana could hardly have been expected to
take into account when preparing his flow-chart diagrams and video-
tape analyses. Scotland played in yet another hideous 'away' strip,
consisting of dark blue shorts and a jersey with hoops like a colour
TV whose horizontal hold was wonky. We beat the suicidal Swedes
2–1 by reverting to our traditional strip and discarding creative pass-
painting-by-numbers in favour of kicking lumps out of the opposition
and blootering the ball up the park – with none of this playing football
out of defence crap. Moving up from Genoa to Turin, we played
a mediocre Brazilian side, with a sweeper system – as alien to the
Scottish mentality as non-alcoholic lager – but still succeeded in losing
1–0. Brazil and Costa Rica qualified from Group C.

Only a month after failing to save any of Aberdeen's ten penalties
in the Scottish Cup final against Aberdeen, Celtic's Pat Bonner put the
Republic of Ireland into the quarter-finals by saving a penalty from
Rumania's Daniel Tomofte in another penalty shoot-out.

Glasgow Celtic 4
Atletico Madrid 3

(European Cup final, sometime in the future)

If the Partizan Belgrade drama has caused Celtic to come down with stage fright in every European tie thereafter – the worst example being a 5–1 defeat in Switzerland to Xamax Neuchatel – then the loss of the Scottish Cup final 9–8 to Aberdeen has undermined the team's confidence in domestic football to a similarly disastrous degree. Up until their disappointing performance in the League Cup final of 1994, the nearest Celtic came to adding silverware to the trophy room was in season 1990/91, when the Huns beat us 2–1 in the League Cup final. Since 1989 my attendance record has been one of accelerating decline, punctuated by upward blips, since Celtic have become not only habitual losers but, much worse, habitually *boring* losers. With the successive appointments of Liam Brady, Lou Macari and Tommy Burns, I have initially joined the returning faithful – before being driven away by further inept and apathetic performances.

Shelling out ill-afforded money week-in week-out to see crap players who couldn't give a shit was not something I was prepared to do indiscriminately, with the consequence that nostalgic reminiscence and unfettered fantasy began to take up an ever-increasing amount of my mental resources. I can now lose myself in virtually real daydreams at any time, and in any situation, from sitting a Master's exam in English Literature to sitting at a civil service desk mechanically stamping upside-down Land and Charge Certificates. The ideal conditions for imaginary games, however, require a personal stereo, sunny weather and somewhere to walk.

Taking on Atletico Madrid in the Parc des Princes is a particular favourite, although my chanted-for appearance in this constantly rerun European Cup final is normally restricted to the last 30 minutes, with Celtic 3–0 down after a trio of dubious penalties and reduced to nine men. My initial relegation to the substitutes' bench is necessitated by career-threatening cartilage injuries and a barely attached retina. After scoring four goals in increasingly incredible fashion, I'm only prevented from scoring a spectacular fifth by a psychotic Spanish fan, who succeeds in stopping me by thrusting a star-headed screwdriver into my right kidney (from behind). In intensive care in the American Hospital I'm given the last rites, while outside in the landscaped grounds tens of thousands of subdued Celtic fans kneel in prayer with lighted candles. Twenty-four hours later I regain consciousness to discover that the College of Cardinals in Rome has elected me as the next Holy Pontiff. Adopting the religious name of Pope Walfrid I, I excommunicate all left-footers who have committed the mortal sin of signing for the Sons of William. Down 3–0 to Rangers in the following year's final in Rome's Stadio Olympico – despite having moved the seat of the Holy See to Restalrig – Pope Walfrid leaps from the VIP box (he's still a registered player and 'honorary' substitute), pulls off his white vestments to reveal a kit immaculately ironed by nuns and polished Predator boots, and joins the spit-splattered Bhoys on the park, where he helps the nine men of Celtic to fight back for a miraculous 4–3 victory. Whereupon the Hun heathens in the Lazio end see the light and start genuflecting – bowing and rising with outstretched arms while chanting, 'We're not worthy'. As I give them my blessing one heretic Hun attacks me with a star-headed screwdriver . . .

I also play fantasy matches in the privacy of whichever flat I happen to be living in at the time, but since moving to Edinburgh every flat I've stayed in has been directly opposite other tenements, with the consequence that my manic leaps, athletic turns and exuberant celebrations have often been witnessed by neighbours looking out of their windows (although I suppose I should make it clear that I normally employ a soft children's playball for these indoor matches, restricting goals scored by opposing teams to shots struck with my weaker left foot). Family groups and giggling girls have been known to gather to watch from overlooking windows, but they always disperse when I crook a finger and indicate for them to come over for a game – a somewhat risky response to being observed by solitary males.

In reality, having to play the Huns in a European Cup final would be a nailbiting nightmare. The Huns bitterly resent us for having won the most prestigious club trophy in the world, and the best way to prevent them from winning it themselves is to replace them as Scotland's sole representative in the European Champions' League, preferably before they equal our record nine-in-a-row league titles (they've currently chalked up an ominous seven). As Scottish champions, Celtic supporters would not have to endure another heart-stopping season like 1992/93, watching on TV as the Huns made what appeared to be an inexorable but incomprehensible march towards the final in Munich. When the eventual winners Marseille beat AC Milan 1–0, I thought I could relax until the next season's tournament began, and even when the French club were warned that their victory might be retrospectively cancelled because of bribery allegations, I remained nonchalantly unconcerned – expecting beaten finalists Milan to be awarded the Cup instead. When UEFA intimated the possibility of a replayed final, with corrupt Marseilles' place being taken by Rangers (who were the highest placed runners-up in either of the two European Champions' League sections) and Radio Rangers (ie Radio Clyde) reported the possibility, I snapped the string of my rosary and sent the beads bouncing all over my mother's tiled kitchen floor. My dread of a Hun victory on a foreign field that will forever be part of Govan is right up there with the fear of going bald, contracting testicular cancer and being subjected to non-consensual buggery.

Such pro-Proddy bias even affects pub cup competitions. After the 'Papal Bull' (a spit-and-sawdust saloon bar) beat the 'Pink Pound' (a West End wine bar) in a quarter-final in 1990, we had to play the semi-final against the 'Happy Hun' (a velour-and-chrome lounge bar), whom we had *eliminated* in an earlier round but who got back in because of a 'technicality' on appeal.

One endless source of mental entertainment – alone or with others – is constructing all-time fantasy teams. Excluding those who played in European Cup finals, my current Star Celtic XI is as follows: Pat Bonner; Danny McGrain, Pat Stanton, Paul Elliott, Tommy Boyd; Davie Provan, John Collins, Kenny Dalglish, Tommy Burns; Mo Johnston and Dixie Deans. This is a dream team that would soundly beat the Lisbon Lions and which at today's prices would cost over £25 million to assemble. If you added a substitutes' bench of Frank McAvennie, Lou Macari, Charlie Nicholas, Murdo MacLeod and Tom McAdam the European Cup could be won three times in a row without losing a game, home or away.

If the virtual reality software ever lives up to the hype – unlike the far-from-seamless Reebok commercial featuring Manchester United greats playing in the same team – endless fun could be had manipulating this team on a computer screen, especially if they were lined up to play the Hoop Disgracing XI of: Ian Andrew; Lee Martin, Willie Garner, Davie Moyes, Brian Whittaker; Danny Crainie, Tony Shepherd, Mike Galloway, Martin Hayes; Tony Cascarino and Wayne Biggins.

McGrain and Elliott were particular personal favourites, but only the Englishman has managed to carve out a media career for himself as a match analyst, on Channel 4's *Football Italia*. Even Scottish producers are prejudiced against McGrain for his – admittedly! –

excruciatingly broad Glasgow accent, which includes a lisp, and which is even more pronounced than taciturn Kenny Dalglish's. To non-Scottish ears McGrain may be barely intelligible, but that does not mean he is incapable of comment with intelligent content. The young Daniel Fergus (now MBE) was probably unlucky in that he did not have to be 'bilingual' as a youngster, whereas like many working-class schoolkids I had to speak one way in the playground and another at home (transgressions in vocabulary and pronunciation being punished by thick ears in both places). Having to switch constantly between 'parliamo' Glaswegian vernacular and the Queen's English while growing up has left me with a Glaswegian *accent* that I wouldn't lose even if I lived in Australia for 40 years, but combined with 'proper' phonetic pronunciation. In other words, I speak with a distinctly Glaswegian monotone but not in the city's provincial patois. When in social or business contact with the chattering classes this means that I'm immediately pigeonholed as a 'Weegie', but when I'm approached – aggressively – by drunken Glasgovians I can normally pass myself off as Glasgow-born but London/New York/Johannesburg-bred (which has defused potentially dangerous confrontations more than once). Conversely, on the Victoria tube line in London I only have to growl 'Whit's goin' on here, Jimmy?' to scatter late-night muggers and rapists heading for Brixton. (That's not true – I simply get robbed or sexually molested instead of the intended victim. More the Diverter than the Enforcer.)

South Londoner Elliott is the verbal antithesis of McGrain, exhibiting a high degree of articulation. He does, however, talk absolute gibberish, with the spoken syntax of an excited but aphasic Hal 2000 computer.

One ambition that I've never harboured is that of being a sports presenter on television, especially after having seen the horror show of Ian Archer's pieces to camera on *Scotsport*, in the days when the STV programme was held together, woodenly but securely, by Arthur Montford. Archer was an award-winning print journalist with the *Glasgow Herald*, who could be relied upon to write super, spur-of-the-moment match reports or longer analytical 'think pieces' full of wit, wisdom and compassion. Each week on *Scotsport*, however, he delivered the equivalent of a live column addressed directly to the viewers. The content was uniformly excellent, but it was Archer's presentation that held viewers enthralled. When the red light went on or the floor manager cued him in, Archer started to sweat like the Albert Brooks' anchor man in *Broadcast News*. His perfectly pleasant voice began to tremble and quiver, whereafter his breathing became laboured and out of sync with his lungs. With his breath control lost in panicky self-consciousness, he struggled like a drowning man to reach the lifebelt of sentence endings. Trembling with nervousness he normally got to the end of his script in hyperventilating distress and looking as if he needed an oxygen mask. On my knees a foot from the screen I used to will him home to his conclusion, while my sister rolled in sympathetic agony on the couch. His weekly appearances made for uncomfortable but riveting viewing. I really suffered with him, and since watching him I've come down with similar but not so severe symptoms on three separate occasions when presented with prose to read from a *cold, cued* start in front of large, expectant audiences (I've just got to remember not to start off a sentence on a deeply *exhaled* breath). If all heroes are flawed, Ian Archer is certainly – gasp – one.

Dundee 1
Motherwell 3

(Premier League, 17 December 1993)

If my freelance writing career from 1990 onwards had taken off in inverse proportion to Celtic's plummeting fortunes, I'd currently have a mantelpiece overflowing with prizes and awards from literary sponsors and arts patrons like the Saltire Society, the Scottish Arts Council, Booker plc, NCR, Whitbread, McVitie's, William Hill, James Tait Black, Pulitzer and Nobel.

Since a couple of letters had resulted in regular book-reviewing work for the *List* – letters which I continued to write in order to wind up the waffle-stomping, yuppie-puppie-breeding PC readership – I decided to continue with the strategy. One strand involved collecting £5 and £10 prizes for best published letters in various newspapers and magazines, while the other required a barrage of letters sent to *Scotland on Sunday* to bring myself to their editorial attention. I was ridiculed by family, friends and foe alike for becoming an 'inveterate letter writer', but when a telephone message was passed on asking me to call the editor of the (now-defunct) *SoS* magazine, I literally rubbed my hands together in anticipation of being offered either chief features writer, roving reporter or regular columnist. When Alexandra Henderson arrived at my flat to 'conduct the interview', prior to the photo-shoot (for my by-line picture?), I was wryly amused to find out that she was only visiting as part of a feature she was writing on letter-writing lunatics, bores and obsessives. I submitted with good grace, giving her some interesting copy and an exclusive about my first ever published letter – in the *Victor* comic when I was ten. I won a camera for relating the slightly exaggerated tale of my mother's near arrest on a shoplifting charge, after my toddler sister had been caught surreptitiously slipping sweeties and Heinz baby foods straight into my mother's shopping bag in the local Co-op supermarket. The local paper sent a reporter and photographer round to follow up on this 'human interest' story, but they failed to use the angle of my protestations of snivelling apology or photographed thick ear.

Eventually my *SoS* letters paid off and I started to sell contributions to the quirky 'Watching Brief' column. It was welcome money, with an occasional by-line to boot. The paperback review column followed and I was also selling odd features, articles and fillers elsewhere (from English broadsheets, through trade magazines to top-shelf publications).

After an enjoyable interlude my transfer request from Books to Sports – which I had no recollection of submitting – was accepted, on the proviso that I paid myself into a Hibernian-Celtic match and wrote up a dry-run report acceptable to the new sports editor. I promised Kevin McKenna faithfully to complete it in no more than an hour, which I did in Vittoria's diner straight after the boring 1–1 draw. Over an extended dessert I spent another hour rewriting it in more literate and amusing fashion. An additional and final hour, lubricated by a bottle of house red, saw me re-rewriting it to make it look as if it had been written quickly but skilfully in under an hour.

The first two games I covered were stressful affairs, with a total of nine goals and two sendings-off to be compressed into a combined total word count of less than 800. As well as factual accuracy, *SoS* required style, wit and originality from its match reporters, despite extremely tight deadlines. A skilled sub-editor 'saved' my first chaotic effort, but the second read rather well, all things considered.

In the last league game before Christmas I reported on Dundee–Motherwell, and at 1–2 a nagging headache turned into a thumping migraine (of the debilitating kind that normally prevents me from making it out of bed, even if only as far as the kitchen for medication, never mind the local chemist). As Dundee pressed hard for an equaliser, I was in no fit state to rewrite my outlined concluding paragraph (based on a Motherwell victory). Through one squinting eye – my non-dominant left – and a forest of ten trembling fingers I saw Tommy Coyne net a third for Motherwell from the penalty spot, which thankfully didn't change the sense of my last paragraph. When the final whistle eventually blew I felt as if my right eye was being stabbed from the inside with a serrated knife, while a firework factory was exploding inside my skull. Drenched in sweat, seeing double and fighting false vomiting alarms, I managed to refrain from throwing up until I had phoned in my report. Then a parabola of vomit spewed out of my mouth even before I had time to replace the handset in its cradle. Most of the regurgitated Marks & Spencer's lunch was captured in their complimentary plastic bag (the very thin and flimsy kind after they stopped charging five pence), except for the overflow of stomach contents which exited spine-tinglingly through my nostrils.

Luckily no one witnessed my distress, since the stand and 'press row' of seats were now deserted, whereas only moments before hundreds of irate Dundee fans had been right in front of me, with Jim Spence of BBC Radio Scotland sitting on my left and Wallace Moore of the *Sunday Mail* to my right (they had both gone to attend the post-match press conference). I rubbed the latter's plastic seat free of vomit dribbles that had leaked out of the four small air holes at the bottom of the bag, knotted the carrier and then put it inside a gratifyingly strong John Menzies bag (tying it up with a double knot). I then strolled nonchalantly through the players' lounge smiling serenely and nodding knowingly at the directors, players' wives and blazered officials, all the time carrying my stomach's undigested contents at arm's length, held by two delicate fingertips. In the plush-carpeted foyer I felt my gorge rising once more, necessitating a quickening of pace. Outside in the street I immediately doubled-up over the gutter and retched violently, a performance I repeated all the way down Tannadice Street like a hopelessly sick drunk, much to the disgust of passing *Sunday Post* readers. Getting back to the railway station was like trying to find my way out of a maze while blindfolded and overdosing on emetics. Ironically, this was the first report that the sports editor complimented me on – if only with reference to the cleverly impromptu ending. I simply smiled wanly at the memory.

After this difficult start I began to enjoy match reporting, even if my usual destinations of a Saturday afternoon were far-flung outposts of Scottish football like Dundee, Kirkcaldy, Kilmarnock, Stirling or Perth. Reporting on Hibernian at Easter Road was a plum game to get, since it was within walking distance (even if the press box is a telephonic throwback to Alexander Graham Bell's first laboratory). I have covered one Celtic game, a vitally important pre-season friendly at Clyde's Broadwood stadium in Cumbernauld – the Scottish equivalent of the Citrus Bowl in Orlando – and contrary to some malicious sports desk rumours the Parkhead Bhoys were *not* listed on the team sheet as a 'Celtic XI'.

Sports reporting is not normally associated with creative writing, with most tabloid hacks simply having to cobble clichés together and press agency representatives merely having to give blow-by-blow accounts to the nearest minute – the equivalent of door-to-door salesmen with suitcases stocked with limited samples. The old 'fans with typewriters' tend to be crabbit cynics, who only get excited when relating their name-dropping anecdotes at tedious length, and in response to which the PA stringers and cub reporters from local rags pay sickening homage. There are exceptions of course, many of whom are crammed into the rabbit-hutch at Raith Rovers' Stark's Park – which has the worst sight-lines but best atmosphere of any press box in Scotland. (When it's raining the standing fans in front of the box put up golfing umbrellas, the windows mist over and goalscorers have to be identified by a process of group osmosis.)

Most of the *SoS* team are 'cultural commentators with word-processors', part of the new breed of university graduates who tackle their prose at head height, rather than bruising the English language with hackneyed sliding fouls from behind. Spiers, McCarra, McGarry, Morton and McKay are high-brow writers with popular touches whose reports are always worth reading even if you don't support either of the teams involved. Ron McKay is a special hero, whom I've never actually met but who has been incarcerated in the pokey to protect his journalistic sources, who normally dresses in black, and who will square up to tabloid gorillas to secure scarce telephone points (even if they are ostensibly reserved for English-based 'Scottish' editions).

If this book has been written by a self-confessed member of the *soccerati*, as part of the continuing intellectualisation of football and aimed at an ABC1 readership, it is bound to offend the 'cloth-capped' traditionalists who would prefer to see football restricted to its historical ghetto of newspaper back pages. But there is no valid reason why football should not have its own literary canon, like golf, cricket and fly-fishing. As working-class offspring like myself went through state-funded higher education, they learned how to think laterally and how to express themselves literately. And since our love of football is often the only connection left with our withering working-class roots, it is not surprising that we choose to write about the now ubiquitous icon of British popular culture (which has been opened up to the mass middle-class and female market by improved stadia infrastructure, a crack down on hooliganism and sophisticated media marketing).

On 30 May 1994, BBC2 devoted an evening's viewing to *Goal TV*, which consisted of archive video clips interspersed with talking heads. Mike Aitken – an amusing and normally perceptive graduate of the old school of sports reporting – railed against 'the pretensions of the metropolitan thirtysomethings who watch and write about [football]' (*Scotsman*, 1 June 1994). He went on to claim that football 'doesn't have an aesthetic' and that 'the game's greatest strength is its simplicity'. Football does, of course, have a sense of beauty when played by great players under ideal conditions, and Aitken was guilty of indulging in a knee-jerk reaction to the term 'aesthetic', forgetting that before the aesthetic movement lapsed into pretentiousness in the early 20th century, its love of the beautiful was an intellectually rigorous and defensible position to adopt. Even today football is not called 'The Beautiful Game' for nothing. As for his second claim about football being basically a simple game, this ignores the fact that soccer is as wonderfully complex as chess when you look beyond the uncomplicated basic rules. Like chess, no two games are ever alike, with infinite variations and possibilities to be played out before a conclusion is reached. And like chess also, football is a powerful metaphor, embracing different styles, strategies, personalities and interpretations. In addition football has an important moral dimension, as well as being an accessible popular art form for the masses.

Literate intellectuals can still be passionate followers of football, and their ability to analyse the cultural phenomena of the game does not necessarily detract from the irrational commitment to their own team. Capturing the zeitgeist of *fin-de-siècle* football is no longer in the hands of the hacks but in the brains of the bourgeoisie. Except for sociologists from Leicester University's Centre for Football Research, of course, who ought to be taken out and bound naked to lampposts in Govan, after having had their bodies painted in green-and-white hoops.

Raith Rovers 2
Celtic 2

(Coca-Cola Cup final, 27 November 1994, aet)

Reaching this final under new manager Tommy Burns – who had been appointed in July – rekindled the hubristic hope that the becalmed oil tanker that Celtic had become was being turned around and was beginning to move purposefully forward once again. By March of 1994 the board of directors had taken the club to the brink of financial sinking without trace, after years of in-fighting, back-stabbing and double-dealing, when the Bank of Scotland threatened to put Celtic into receivership after the unauthorised purchase of Willie Falconer for a mere £350,000 exceeded the overdraft limit. The skulduggery and incompetence of the board was horribly reminiscent of the directors satirised in Bruce Beresford's *The Club* (in which the arrival of an expensive Tasmanian player at an Aussie Rules football team who haven't won anything for years causes hilarious boardroom ructions). The Celtic board, however, preferred to draw inspiration from Kevin Costner's sentimental and mawkish *Field of Dreams* (in which a deluded dreamer decides to build a baseball diamond in the middle of nowhere on the basis of advice given by *ghosts*), and even used the film's title at the top of press releases dealing with the proposed move to the fantasy super-stadium at Cambuslang, an area notable only for its Hoover factory. Moving from Celtic Park – which is built over disused mine workings – to the Cambuslang site – which according to some reports was a toxic timebomb of methane fumes capable of making Hiroshima seem like the Clarkston Disaster – was never going to happen, but its impossibility did not stop the board spending hundreds of thousands of pounds on feasibility studies, architectural blueprints and scale models (which chairman Kevin Kelly liked to mull over in Hitlerian fashion). Beresford's scriptwriter would have balked at the scenario, but at one point the directors almost had to submit to a series of lie-detector tests, in order to try and find the informer – 'Shallow Thorax' – who was leaking damaging stories to the press and rebel shareholders.

Celtic were only saved from the ignomy of bankruptcy by Fergus McCann, a Scots-Canadian millionaire who had led the rebel shareholders. Securing financial control and becoming chairman, he immediately cancelled Cambuslang and initiated the redevelopment of Celtic Park.

Because Celtic were forced to decamp to Hampden for their home games, Ibrox was chosen as a neutral venue for the final against First Division Raith Rovers, who in their 111-year history had only ever succeeded in winning promotion and the Kirkcaldy Cottage Hospital Cup.

Entering the portals of Hun Heaven I was far from confident about qualifying for the UEFA Cup by beating Jimmy Nicholl's underdogs – even after beating Aberdeen in the semi-final Celtic were continuing on a league run which was to become the worst in their 106-year history – and I took my seat with a slippery snake of anxiety gnawing at my intestines.

The raw teenagers and brittle rejects of Raith took the lead through Stevie Crawford in 18 minutes, and although Celtic deservedly equalised with a headed goal by Andy Walker before half-time, my sense of impending doom only lifted in the 84th minute when Charlie Nicholas poked the ball home after Walker had hit the post. Although we had been the better team, it was impossible to relax completely for fear of the Celtic Goalkeeping Curse striking before the end – which it duly did with two minutes left. Jason Dair hit a hopeful shot from 20 yards which a quadriplegic could have smothered. Instead, Gordon Marshall let it pop up invitingly from his hands. Ex-Hun Gordon Dalziel stooped to head home the rebound. Dancing ensued in the aisles of the Govan stand, which continued all through extra-time when skipper Paul McStay's inspirational leadership failed to generate one shot on goal.

In the penalty shoot-out, Raith scored with their first five penalties, as did Celtic through Falconer, John Collins, Walker, Paul Byrne and Mike Galloway (just). Progressing to the sudden-death kicks, Jason Rowbotham scored Raith's sixth. The intestinal snake in my guts was writhing like crazy when I saw McStay, a player whose last penalty had been taken against Aberdeen in the Scottish Cup final of 1990, making his way out of the centre circle. A footballing millionaire on £5,000 per week and he couldn't beat Scott Thomson from 12 yards, his telegraphed sidefooter being easily parried.

Victory to the Rovers, by 6–5 on penalties. Dancing in the mythical streets of Raith continued all night – or in Jackie O's nightclub to be exact. The owner had made the sponsorship deal of the decade earlier in the season by paying £50,000 to have the disco's name emblazoned on the club's jerseys.

If I had not watched the European Cup final in 1967, I might well have been bopping the Sunday night of Celtic's defeat away in Jackie O's myself, because I have had a soft spot for the Kirkcaldy men ever since my Dunfermline-supporting cousin dragged me along to a Pars-Rovers derby when we were both still of primary school age. Visiting my grandmother in Glenrothes, I escaped one Saturday afternoon to watch the Rovers being soundly beaten. Naturally, I supported them during the match, and all through the '80s I drove up to Kirkcaldy at least once per season to see how they were getting on. I never saw them win once. But their supporters never expected them to win, which must have made their Coca-Cola Cup victory all the sweeter (while I was choking on Diet bloody Pepsi).

EPILOGUE:
CHAMP-IONEES!

Airdrie 0
Celtic 1

(Tennents Scottish Cup final, 27 May 1995)

Not 'Champ-ionees' exactly – after finishing fourth in the league behind Rangers, Motherwell and Hibs – but Cup-winners, 20 years to the month after I sat with my father in the South Stand of Hampden watching Celtic beat the 'Diamonds' 3–1. Pierre van Hooijdonk's superb headed goal in the ninth minute at the refurbished national stadium ended the six-year trophy famine, got us into Europe and necessitated the writing of this addendumed epilogue. A happy ending in the final reel, then, but as in most movies I saw it coming.

When I watched Celtic beating Meadowbank Thistle 3–0 in February – the first time Celtic had managed to score more than two goals all season – I suspected our name was set to be engraved on the Scottish Cup. Confidence was also boosted by the fact that the previous month's much-mocked share issue had raised over £10 million, with 10,000 fans contributing between £620 and £62,000 each. Although the smallest shareholders were merely indulging in an emotional investment, with no prospect of long-term financial gain or voting muscle, my failure to join them in the over-subscription was not due to cynicism or niggardliness. I simply didn't have a spare £620 to part with, and I wasn't prepared to go to the irresponsible lengths of some would-be investors who had no hesitation in liquidating insurance policies, family heirlooms or funeral plans (not that I had any to convert). To raise the minimum capital investment required, some deluded individuals even sold their cars, missed mortgage repayments or took out knee-cap security loans – all for the privilege of going on a 'priority list' for season tickets and getting a ten per cent discount in the Brother Walfrid restaurant (but only on meals not drinks). At the time the new board were honest enough in their prospectus about the lack of tangible benefits or returns for small investors, but only a fraction of the £8 million promised for new players had been released by the time of the Cup final (£1.2 million on van Hooijdonk). It's only to be hoped that Kevin Kelly's proverbial Biscuit Tin hasn't been replaced by Fergus McCann's Fridge-Freezer.

Even without the injection of new blood to pep up an anaemic squad, Celtic beat Kilmarnock to reach the semi-finals. And despite missing a penalty in the first game against Hibs at Ibrox on a Friday night, I returned to Edinburgh disappointed but not despondent (Celtic had played superbly during the 0–0 draw). The next afternoon First Division Airdrie beat red-hot favourites Hearts 1–0 in the other semi-final, and walking along Princes Street on the Saturday evening after having seen *Amateur* at the Filmhouse I passed a group of bevvied Hearts' fans, surrounding one of their more distraught number who was lying on his back and repeatedly wailing: 'Fuckin' Airdrie, man . . . Fuckin' *Airdrie* . . . ' Trying to stop my smirk spreading, I read the Jambolic entrails of this touching vignette as a good omen, especially after Hibs were beaten 3–1 in the replay.

A ticket for the final itself proved tantalisingly impossible to get, and on the Friday before the match my sister was too late to get to an appointment with a scalper who had two spare tickets, because she had to be interviewed – for her own job – in the ever-more pruned groves of academe, where doctorate-lecturers have to blossom in short-term contractual bursts, with tenured roots being ruthlessly weeded out amongst fledgling academics. Baby Albert & Co could once have been relied upon to procure me a ticket, but they have all been subjected to an unemployment diaspora in recent years, with ever-less frequent postcards arriving from Manchester, Brighton, Berlin and Melbourne. Even Father Flyte has had to move to Latin America of late, where I've no doubt his 'liberation theology' has found an even more receptive flock. One of the 'Papal Bull' regulars offered to get me a ticket 'in the same row as Rod Stewart', but when I asked him how he could acquire it I was appalled at his proud explanation, which involved a nocturnal drive, skeleton keys, a ski mask, six oranges and a bath towel (the latter two instruments of persuasion having been gleaned from a copy of Jim Thompson's *The Grifters* that I'd given to him; I also introduced him to the works of Elmore Leonard, and I hate to think of the underlined descriptions which have now been incorporated into the *modus operandi* of the petty-criminal fraternity in the East End of the Big G). He was a bit hurt when I point-blank refused to accept his offer, but at least my conscience is clear (and as George Steiner has pointed out – with specific reference to Goethe-reading Nazis – an appreciation of great literature doesn't necessarily make its readers better people).

Broadcast live in England for the first time, this tedious game must have confirmed Sassenach prejudices about the unglamorous nature of Scottish Cup finals. (Indeed, it was only screened by Sky because the English FA Cup final was not played in tandem with the SFA equivalent, Everton having beaten Manchester United a week previously.) Hooijdonk's glorious goal was the *one* memorable moment, and after it was scored neither team seriously threatened the opposition goal. I watched the uncultured blootering battle at my girlfriend's flat in Edinburgh – for the luxury of colour coverage on BBC1 Scotland – with raging gingivitis requiring my can of lager to be sucked through a straw (with my inflamed and agonising gums padded with chunks of Mother's Pride bread soaked in Corsodyl mouthwash). After the early goal there was no danger of my again spluttering soggy dough all over her white living-room carpet. When she got back from town after a shopping expedition to expand her Imelda-Marcosian collection of shoes, she was less than understanding about the walked-in stains. Her only main character flaw is the fact that she was brought up as an East Fife supporter and therefore cannot understand why I get so excited/enraged when watching my – proper – team attempting to win things.

Celtic turned out in their *fourth* strip of the season – the Scottish Cup final edition – an aesthetic eyesore which combined three thick hoops and seven thin ones, but the financial exploitation of the fans was much more offensive than the actual design.

When referee Les Mottram – an ex-Airdrie player! – blew the final whistle after an inordinate amount of injury time, I slumped back on the sofa in utter relief rather than pure joy (a reaction that most of the players seemed to share). The six-year nightmare of being boring losers was finally over, even if we'd only woken up from it to find ourselves in the role of boring winners. But we'd played some good football against Raith Rovers and lost, and psychological hurdles need to be overcome even if in the most ungainly fashion.

After the initial relief, the post-match, on-park celebrations made for emotive viewing, with more than a few players succumbing to tears. I felt especially proud and pleased for left-back Tosh McKinlay, whose excellent cross set up the goal. Never having won anything before – with Dundee or Hearts – he had promised before the final to dedicate his first winner's medal to his late baby son, who had died less than a year before. Besuited Tony Mowbray, who missed the match through suspension, joined in the celebrations with gusto, despite having lost his young bride to cancer at the beginning of the year. Man-of-the-match Peter Grant played with a seriously damaged knee, putting years of disciplinary madness behind him with a display of controlled aggression and surprising skill. Even Paul McStay's reaction to lifting the Cup was one of obvious and infectious delight. Manager Tommy Burns was jumping about and punching the air like a fanatical fan (which he is). Burns had had a traumatic and stressful first year in charge and the intense pressure he was under took its inevitable, and obvious, toll. The cruellest press treatment was run by a Scottish edition of an English paper, which had videos of him being interviewed by the media analysed by a tame pop psychologist, who highlighted the nervous tics and unconscious physical mannerisms, like ear-tugging, which supposedly supported the diagnosis of a persecution complex and near nervous breakdown (an example of appallingly gratuitous but irresistibly gripping tabloid journalism). The manager's unrestrained delight was a pleasure to witness, as was the lap of honour which concentrated on the wheelchair-bound supporters.

After a couple of pints in my local – the 'Puke "n" Vomit' – I settled down on my own in serene contentment – happiness even – to watch *2001: A Space Odyssey* on Channel 4 (during which, and well after midnight, Father Flyte called from his hacienda to find out the score).

Hopefully, like the catalytic Black Monolith and Jock Stein, Tommy Burns' management will now have a similar dramatic effect. During Stein's first year as manager he won the Scottish Cup of 1965, while in his second he won the league and led Celtic to a European Cup Winners' Cup semi-final against Liverpool, followed in his third by the European Cup triumph of 1967. If Burns follows the same timetable, May of 1996 will see us play Everton in a Cup Winners' Cup semi as well as preventing the Huns from making it eight-in-a row. Then in 1997, 30 years after the Lisbon victory, Celtic will compete in their third European Cup final (ideally in the Parc des Princes against AC Milan). If I hadn't fallen off my bike as a boy, or if my parents could have afforded contact lenses, I could *conceivably* have been a Celtic player, even at a very hard push leading the 1997 finalists out as captain in my role of battle-hardened and experienced sweeper.

Beating Airdrie in this year's final has hardly sent warning shock waves reverberating around the football giants of Europe, but having witnessed the emotional scenes which followed, it seems appropriate to quote Milton once again:

> Some natural tears they dropped, but wiped them soon;
> The world was all before them, where to choose
> Their place of rest, and Providence their guide:
> They hand in hand with wandering steps and slow
> Through Eden took their solitary way.

(Paradise Lost, XII)

If Celtic make it to the European Cup final in 1997, I shall *definitely* be there in person, even if I have to watch the game on TV in a local bar. Not being a Celtic player has been a disappointment – or an unfulfilled pipe dream – but not being a Celtic supporter is now inconceivable:

> They also serve who only stand and [watch].
>
> *On His Blindness*

I have assembled my team of words on the subject closest to my heart as best I can and, like a football manager, I'm just about to send them out on to the (sales) pitch:

> Since first this subject for heroic song
> Pleased me long choosing, and beginning late.
>
> (*Paradise Lost*, LX)

Like a manager, too, I'm prejudiced in their favour (outwardly at least, even if I despair of them at times inwardly), and I hope my team selection and tactical arrangement of words do well. How to judge? Well, a high-scoring defeat from the Reviewers XI of 10–1 would be better than an anonymous 0–0 draw. As for sales? Well, an average Celtic home game of over 20,000 would probably allow me to go full-time as a writer, whereas the attendance of 473 for Meadowbank Thistle's final home game under their old romantic name (which I attended), before becoming Livingston FC, would probably relegate this book and my writing ambitions to the literal and metaphorical remainder bins of inglorious commercial failure. But if you're a Celtic fan and you've enjoyed it, that's the main thing. And if you're not but have still got pleasure from it, that's almost as good. However, if you're a Hun and you've got this far, you're supporting the wrong team, mate.

Whatever the reaction to the book, its publication will have served at least one purpose. Again in the words of Big John:

> Books are not absolutely dead things, but do
> contain a potency of life in them to be as active as
> that soul was whose progeny they are; nay they
> do preserve as in a vial the purest efficacy and
> extraction of that living intellect that bred them.
>
> (*Areopagitica*)

In conclusion, whether the book bombs or balloons, or whether Celtic go on to achieve further European glory or first-time domestic relegation, I'll bear in mind one thing I've learned from being a Celtic fan and from writing this memorial memoir:

> A mind not to be changed by place or time.
> The mind is its own place, and in itself
> Can make a heav'n of hell, a hell of heav'n.
>
> (*Paradise Lost*, I)

It may be a grand old team to play for, but it's also a grand old team to write about.

MAIN BIBLIOGRAPHY

Tom Campbell and Pat Woods, *The Glory and the Dream: The History of Celtic FC 1887–1986* (Mainstream, Edinburgh, 1986)

David Docherty, *The Celtic Football Companion: A Factual History 1946–1986* (John Donald, Edinburgh, 1986)

Eugene MacBride, Martin O'Connor and George Sheridan, *An Alphabet of the Celts: A Complete Who's Who of Celtic FC* (ACL and Polar Publishing, Leicester, 1994)